McElmeel Booknotes

McElmeel Booknotes
Literature Across the Curriculum

Sharron L. McElmeel

Illustrated by Deborah L. McElmeel

1993
Teacher Ideas Press
A Division of
Libraries Unlimited, Inc.
Englewood, Colorado

TEACHER IDEAS PRESS
A Division of
Libraries Unlimited, Inc.
P.O. Box 6633
Englewood, CO 80155-6633

Library of Congress Cataloging-in-Publication Data

McElmeel, Sharron L.
    McElmeel booknotes : literature across the curriculum / Sharron L.
  McElmeel ; illustrated by Deborah L. McElmeel.
      xiii, 217 p. 22x28 cm.
      Includes bibliographical references and index.
      ISBN 0-87287-951-8
      1. Language arts.   2. Literature--Study and teaching.
  3. Interdisciplinary approach in education.   4. Activity programs in
  education.   I. Title.
  LB1576.M3976   1993
  372.6'044--dc20
                                                    92-35886
                                                      CIP

For   E. J. M.

Michael

Deborah

Thomas

Matthew

Steven

Suzanne

Contents

Acknowledgments

Grateful acknowledgment goes to those who read *My Bag of Book Tricks* and encouraged this book. Thanks especially to my friends and colleagues Marilyn Benda, Carolyn Horton, Evelyn Neenan, Mary Northup, and Jan Woods—they listen and encourage. I am also grateful for the continued professional support from the staff of the Grant Wood Area Education Agency, Mount Mercy College, in Cedar Rapids, Iowa, and my colleagues in the Cedar Rapids Community Schools—especially those at Harrison Elementary. They are important because they have helped the seeds of reading and writing to propagate, grow, and spread and have allowed me to see a new set of children's faces glow with the knowledge that they have discovered a new author or a new connection with a favorite book. They make the sharing of ideas a rewarding experience and give every day a new dimension.

But inspiration and support are not enough. To write about books and children one must have access to both—and the time to write. For all of these things I thank my family, especially Jack, who allows me the luxury of being a writer. Special thanks, once again, to the reference department and the children's services division of the Cedar Rapids Public Library and to Jennifer Jennings and Nancy Jennings of O. G. Waffle's Bookhouse in Marion, Iowa—true friends of literacy.

It is important that the suggestions for responses in this book be used in a manner consistent with the teacher's personal philosophy and methodology and with both the teacher's and students' joint goals. Only basic ideas and suggestions are given for helping children tie together meaningful experiences and books. Educators who use the basic ideas must flesh out the details as only they can, details that will fuse the ideas to their curriculum goals. They also will be the ones who must bring the warmth, expression of enjoyment, and excitement to the involvement with books as readers share the books and ideas with others.

Read, share, and enjoy.

Part

I

Literature Connections

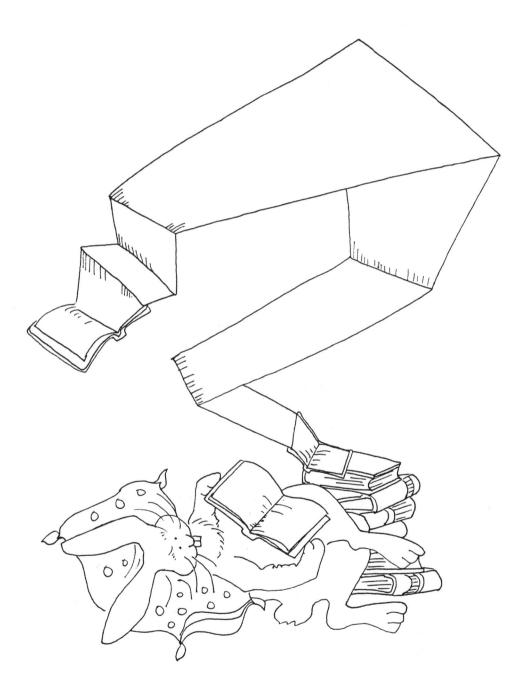

1

Creating a Language-Rich Environment

School libraries should contain an abundance of what may be called collateral reading, relating to every part of the curriculum.

—G. T. Little, 1896

BRINGING LITERATURE INTO THE CLASSROOM

If the value of literature has not been demonstrated, administrators and teachers alike will view the time spent sharing books and reading aloud in a classroom as time being taken from "more valuable learning time." During one graduate-level college class I was teaching for educators on motivating children to read, I had a few educators who felt that reading was something to be done after all the *real* curriculum work was completed, and that the "teaching of reading" would or should be enough to inspire young people to read. In presenting many ideas for motivating young people to read a variety of books, I shared a list of 10 points that help inspire young learners to read.

Ten Ways to Get a Student to Read, and Read, and Read

1. Make sure your students see you read, and read, and read.

2. Read to your students *every* day.

3. Make reading for pleasure a part of your daily routine.

4. Read to your students *every* day.

5. Keep an often-changing display of books in your classroom.

6. Read to your students *every* day.

7. Keep book reports to a minimum.

8. Read to your students *every* day.

9. Advertise books throughout your school.

10. Read to your students *every* day.

The assignment given to the class was to use one of the motivational ideas that had been discussed and to report back to the class during the next session. One class member, who was a middle school teacher, reported back that she had used "five of the ten ways to get students to read, and read, and read." She had read aloud to her class every day for five days and then found that her students would not let her stop on the following days. The library media specialist, unaware of the teacher's new project, came to the classroom to inquire what the teacher was doing in her classroom to inspire her students to visit the library with such enthusiasm. The students came knowing what they wanted—they wanted the book their teacher was reading aloud. But because there were not enough copies to go around, the library media specialist had begun recommending related books—books by the same author and other books on related topics by other authors.

In the same manner, when I share a book in the library by reading it aloud, many children want to check out the book. The book is seldom on the shelf the remainder of the year. I read excerpts from novels to intermediate students and picture books to primary-age children, but I also read excerpts from novels or story collections to primary-age children and picture books to intermediate readers. According to James Zarrillo, assistant professor of teacher education at California State University, Long Beach, "The question is no longer if their classrooms should be literature-based, but how to develop the best literature-based program possible."[1]

Using Picture Books in the Intermediate/Middle School Classroom

Though often used in the primary classroom, the picture book is an overlooked resource in the intermediate and middle school classroom, despite the efforts of many who promote the use of picture books at all grade levels. Picture books are perfect for continuing to develop vocabulary, motivating the study of a specific focus, or providing a motivation for finding connections. And many times picture books have layers of meaning that are available only to more mature and sophisticated readers. For example, the message about some children having two homes, one with mother and one with father, in Barbara Abercrombie's *Charlie Anderson* (McElderry, 1990) will be lost on the young child, who will most likely enjoy the story on the very simplest story level. More mature readers will be able to identify parallels between Charlie Anderson and a child who alternates weekends or weekdays between the mother's home and the father's home. The book will readily stimulate a meaningful discussion of the disadvantages and advantages of having two families.

As early as 1984 articles were appearing in professional journals expounding the advantages of using picture books with older readers as well as with primary-age readers. Carol O. Hurst shares ideas for stimulating critical thinking and for sharing picture books in many curriculum areas. Her article "Picture That! Using Picture Books in the Fourth Through Eighth Grades" appeared in the March 1984 issue of *Early Years* (vol. 14, no. 7:31-34). The following year Susan Baum's article "How to Use Picture Books to Challenge the Gifted" appeared in the April 1985 issue of *Early Years/K-8* (vol. 15, no. 8:48-50). In the April 1987 issue of *Learning*, Susan Ohanian promotes the use of alphabet books as "engaging models to inspire critical thinking and wordplay." In her article "Across the Curriculum from A to Z," she suggests using alphabet books to correlate with many curricular objectives. Each of the articles mentioned above promotes the use of picture books to stimulate thinking and suggests ways that the books may be incorporated into every aspect of the curriculum, from science to music to writing. In 1991 *Book Links: Connecting Books, Libraries, and Classrooms*[2] was first published and now shares with readers books and collaborative titles that support general themes of study six times a year. In a recent issue, *Book Links* featured African-American stories, versions of "Beauty and the Beast," and a section dealing with books about mail

---

[1]James Zarrillo. "Teachers' Interpretations of Literature-Based Reading." *The Reading Teacher* 43 (October 1989): 22-28.

[2]*Book Links* is a bimonthly magazine published by Booklist Publications, an imprint of the American Library Association, 50 E. Huron Street, Chicago, IL 60611.

and writing letters. Each topic discussed includes a bibliography of picture books and lengthier texts. *Book Links* includes many classroom connections for using picture books, as well as novels, in all areas of the curriculum.

A Variety of Books in the Classroom

Those who work with children must also continue to promote the use of novels and books of information in the classroom. Books of both types must be read aloud to groups of children. Children of all grade levels must be immersed in a variety of literature. The standard for time spent reading aloud has been, for several years, once a day. Now that most teachers read aloud to their children at least once a day, the movement is toward setting a minimum of three times a day for reading aloud.

Two of the three read-aloud sessions can be scattered throughout the day and used whenever there is an appropriate opportunity. Readings might be selected from novels, books of poetry, informational books, or picture books. Opportunities to read these two selections each day will have to be sought out and consciously scheduled so that the sessions occur. The teacher must always be on the lookout for an opportunity that will lend itself to sharing a read-aloud. One day a reading of chapter 4 of Clifford Hicks's *Alvin's Secret Code* (Holt, 1963) might begin a mathematical focus on codes and ciphers. Later that day a poem from Caroline Feller Bauer's *Snowy Day: Stories and Poems* (Lippincott, 1986) might share the joy of the first snowfall. The next day a reading of *Leo the Late Bloomer* by Robert Kraus (HarperCollins, 1971) could bolster the confidence of some students who are struggling a few steps behind the others in the class. After a discussion of "cause and effect," one may wish to read Jack Prelutsky's poem "I Went to Wisconsin."

The third reading session for the day should focus on a selection that is read in its entirety over a period of days. This is the traditional read-aloud session that is most often scheduled at the same time each day. Often the selection chosen is a novel that is a favorite for the specific age group being read to. Careful selection of the novels to be read will allow students to be introduced to new authors and characters. Once a favorite author or book character has been read in the classroom, the educator's role is to encourage children to either read other books by that author or extend their reading to other books. Booktalks highlighting other books related either by author, character, or theme will further promote more reading. After one novel is completed, the next classroom read-aloud should be selected to introduce students to other authors who and topics that will continue to expand the students' horizons. Students of all ages can benefit from hearing a story read chapter by chapter. Reading novels aloud is appropriate for seniors in high school as well as for kindergartners. Two excellent resources to start parents and teachers making appropriate selections to read aloud is Jim Trelease's *The New Read-Aloud Handbook* (Viking, 1989) and Margaret Mary Kimmel and Elizabeth Segel's *For Reading Out Loud! A Guide to Sharing Books with Children* (Delacorte, 1983). Each book includes lists of many titles that are appropriate for reading aloud to every age group from infants to teenagers. Many picture books are suggested, but novels are the mainstay of the suggestions. Just as picture books are appropriate for students of different ages, novels are also appropriate for reading aloud to students of various ages.

Novels in the Primary Classroom

Picture books are usually viewed as appropriate as read-alouds for primary-age students; however, novels are also appropriate choices for reading aloud. Even kindergartners should be introduced to the longer narratives that present a story they can visualize while they listen, an ongoing story that brings a sense of anticipation to storytime. A book that can be finished over a period of five days might be appropriate beginning at the start of the school year. Later, longer novels will be appropriate. Teachers who are just beginning to read aloud in the primary grades may wish to start with several books that provide a continuing story. For example, the complete adventures of Peter

Rabbit may be read in Beatrix Potter's *The Tale of Peter Rabbit, The Tale of Benjamin Bunny, The Tale of the Flopsy Bunnies*, and *The Tale of Mr. Tod* (all Warne, reissued 1987). Read consecutively, these tales will bridge the gap from reading a single book at one sitting and reading a longer story over a period of days.

Carol Carrick has a continuing series about Christopher and his dog. Children will get a sense of the continuation of the total story when Carrick's books are read in order: *Sleep Out* (Clarion, 1973); *Lost in the Storm* (Clarion, 1974); *The Foundling* (Clarion, 1977); *The Washout* (Clarion, 1978); and *Ben and the Porcupine* (Clarion, 1981). Each book might be considered a "chapter" in a longer story that tells of Christopher and his dog Bodger. When Bodger is killed, Christopher must deal with his grief and learn to accept a new puppy. The final stories are episodes about Christopher and Ben, Christopher's new dog.

Evaline Ness's illustrated junior novel *Sam, Bangs and Moonshine* (Holt, 1971) is a popular early read-aloud. The book is only 34 pages long and can be read in a one- or two-day reading session. *Sam, Bangs and Moonshine* is also a Caldecott winner (1972) and will provide a link to more heavily illustrated titles that have been or will be shared in the classroom. Munro Leaf's 64-page *The Story of Ferdinand the Bull* (Viking, 1936) and Beverly Cleary's *Ramona the Pest* (Morrow, 1968) are also popular choices for first read-alouds in the kindergarten classrooms.

The New Read-Aloud Handbook and *For Reading Out Loud!* are filled with a multitude of suggestions for reading aloud. *My Bag of Book Tricks* by Sharron L. McElmeel (Libraries Unlimited, 1989) provides thematic booklists for using picture books, books of fiction, and information literature in curricular units of study. Beverly Kobrin has a guide for choosing informational books to share with children, *Eyeopeners! How to Choose and Use Children's Books About Real People, Places, and Things* (Viking, 1988). These books will help educators select longer selections for reading aloud.

Responding to Books and Reading Aloud

It is important in literature activities that readers are given an opportunity to experience the story elements in some concrete form. Children must be given the opportunity to discuss and work with a story in ways that provide meaning for them. Students may gain meaning by re-creating the story characters and scenes through their own paintings, models, drama, or puppetry. Through such activities they will gain a better understanding of the literature. Experiencing a book in a concrete manner will extend the experience and make it a memorable one. Reading aloud to children, however, is the single most effective activity to help children learn to read and to enjoy reading. The literature will also provide opportunities for building writing skills through innovating the text, extending the story, and encouraging the development of episodic chapters, sequels, or prologues. Reading aloud to children introduces children to new and interesting words and sounds and helps them extend their imaginations. Good oral reading also helps children develop a taste for the best in literature and extend their thinking skills.

Children will respond to the reading aloud of a specific title in various ways. If the title has been read aloud or enjoyed as a common reading, the readers will be able to join together to dramatize an event from the book, to share their favorite episodes, to explore and discuss characterization and plot development, and to build an innovation on the story grammar. The most effective response is to want to read more books. Enjoying a good book motivates students to read other books by the same author or a group of books tied together thematically.

Focusing on a specific book or author will provide a structure for the organization of activities and a time to read in a way that achieves curriculum or program goals. As connections are made between books and authors, other connections will emerge. A sense of achievement develops as all of the library's bookshelves become a potential reading source and a source for books with connecting themes. As repeated connections are found, readers will be challenged to think in new terms to identify universal themes and topics. As children and their teachers explore the shelves of the library and learn more about literature that is available, more and more books will find their way into the classroom.

WHOLE LANGUAGE—AN INTEGRATED PROGRAM

Andrea Butler of Rigby Education, Australia, while speaking at the International Reading Association's annual conference in Toronto, Canada, in May 1988 said, "If we are going to create classrooms that are whole language, we must involve children in a variety of experiences that reflect a variety of purposes of how language is served up outside the world of school." Avelyn Davidson, speaking at the same conference, expressed the idea that a central component of a whole language classroom includes a way of observing and working with children and reading aloud to and with children—a way that is built on a language-rich, success-oriented, noncompetitive environment where students make choices about their learning. The classroom will include a variety of materials and place an emphasis on process and attitude rather than on product; and the method will focus on a less formal evaluation process.

During the discussion, Anna Cresswell of Ginn and Company, Canada, added: "Whole language is not a program, it is not a big book, it is not how you rearrange the desks in your classroom, it's not whether or not you have parent volunteers. It is a mind set, an attitude about how children learn ... it is truly integrated language arts."

An effective reading program brings the language arts (including reading) into all areas of the curriculum.[3] Effective reading programs incorporate and integrate the rest of the curriculum because content area materials are critical elements in establishing a literate environment. In a

---

[3]D. E. Alvermann. "Learning from Text." In *Research Within Reach: Secondary School Reading (A Research Guided Response to Concerns of Reading Educators)*, edited by D. E. Alvermann, David W. Moore, and M. W. Conley. Newark, DE: International Reading Association, 1987, 38-51. M. Early and D. Sawyer. *Reading to Learn in Grades 5 to 8.* San Diego, CA: Harcourt Brace Jovanovich, 1984.

literate environment children spend their time creating and responding to authentic texts for real and legitimate purposes. Reading and other language arts are viewed as important because they are crucial for communication, not an end in themselves. The curriculum is a major part of what is to be communicated.

Educators who integrate language arts skills throughout the curriculum help their students develop their comprehension of the total curriculum in four basic ways. First, children are taught the background knowledge, specialized vocabulary, symbols, and graphics found in various content areas—science, social studies, mathematics, etc. Second, note taking, outlining, and other study skills are taught to help improve the students' comprehension of content texts. Third, teachers help children understand the various text structures they will encounter as they read various content area materials: cause and effect, sequence, comparison and contrast, and problem and solution. Fourth, both teachers and children focus on the issue of transfer directly by comparing and contrasting different types of reading materials and discussing which skills and strategies are appropriate for which kinds of reading.

Writing in the Letters to the Editor section of the Winter 1990 issue of *The New Advocate*, noted poet Myra Cohn Livingston stated that it is her belief that "it is neither instant product nor arduous process that wins out. The best teachers, those who will impart a sense of the love of reading and writing, will find this balance."

When elements of the language arts curriculum are integrated with content area material, the total package of information is presented to children as related elements of a single unit, rather than as isolated areas of learning. All of these elements become part of a total classroom experience. Underlying all of the language arts and content area curriculum objectives is the thinking process. In reading, children engage in a series of thinking activities as they assess the author's meaning in a written passage. While engaging in the writing process, students focus on organizing their thoughts. As children build an information base, they involve themselves in activities to explore concepts (themes) taken from the curriculum base. Regardless of the topic being explored, the skills taught in the langauge arts component of instruction are viewed as tools necessary for locating information, making new discoveries, and establishing connections between old and new learning.

Why Integrate?

Why integrate? Simply stated, integration of curriculum promotes thinking and learning—and it is also fun and exciting for students. Integration also compacts curriculum goals and objectives, making more efficient use of teaching time. A more appropriate question is, Why *not* integrate? During the 1990-91 school year, I informally questioned dozens of educators who felt they were embracing major elements of the whole language/integrated language philosophy. Without exception they expressed the belief that their students were enjoying learning more. The children were reading more, asking more questions, and generally acting more interested in their studies. Many teachers commented that although they felt the approach was successful, it was not a cure-all any more than other methods. Some students were not progressing as fast as other students in the class. But several teachers were quick to point out that no other method they had used to teach the basic skills totally eliminated a variance in student progress. Students on the low end of the achievement scale were not suffering the effects of being in the "low" group; most viewed themselves as capable, productive learners, and as readers. One first-grade teacher told of a new student who, when the class settled down for their daily uninterrupted sustained reading time, informed her that he could not read. Almost in unison three or four students informed him that everyone can read: "We'll help you." They did, and within a week the young man announced that he could read now. In a few more weeks he was reading and writing with the best of those in the class—but *most* important was his change in attitude.

Implementation of the Integration Plan

Those who wish to move their classrooms and teaching methodology further toward a fully integrated, literature-based classroom will find that there is a continuum along which they can move. Some will take the integration plan step-by-step, and others will be able to move in longer strides; some will move slowly along the continuum, others more rapidly. The work of such people as Ken Goodman,[4] Lucy Calkins,[5] Donald Graves,[6] Jane Hansen,[7] H. A. McCracken and M. J. McCracken,[8] Frank Smith,[9] and many others is furthering the idea of looking at the whole of any process rather than at the small bits and pieces, especially when we don't know what the bits and pieces build. The work of these people tends to indicate that the most successful educators are moving toward a goal at the end of the continuum—toward a total integration of curriculum built on student interests and needs. The difficult part of any integration plan is not establishing literature ideas, but firmly identifying the needs of individual students and the needs of groups, and clearly understanding the school's and district's curriculum objectives within each grade level. It is the knowledge of students' needs and the grasp of curriculum objectives that will allow the teacher to become a facilitator and move the students through appropriate activities to enhance their ability to understand concepts and processes rather than to merely cover content or predeveloped units. Those who develop predesigned integrated units for grade levels, either for widespread commercial distribution or for a specific district, often miss the most basic element of an integrated curriculum. To provide a fully integrated curriculum, students must be involved in the plan; if the topics and activities are predetermined, there is little room for students' genuine investigation and planning for their own learning. In most cases, a predesigned integrated "unit" is just additional content that finds its ways into the curriculum and serves to fill the day rather than being a legitimate scheme for the integration of student learning. Preplanned step-by-step integration plans merely offer more of the thematic units popular dozens of years ago. The units tend to be built on what educators *think* youngsters will be interested in rather than on the topics youngsters *are* interested in. Bear units seem to be in ample supply. But where are the frog and crawly snake units? If the objective is to learn to count, does it matter if students count bears, snakes, or something else they care about? If the objective is to learn to use an index, could the skill be practiced using a book with information about extinct animals as well as a book of poetry? And could we add an index to a book published by a student?

A well-stocked shelf of book ideas will help bring books into integration plans built *within* each classroom. Teachers can pull the ideas from the shelf and adapt the ideas to their own needs and the needs of their students. In this book, the response suggestions in the chapters that focus on specific connections and the response suggestions given in the more general bookshelf section are indeed only suggestions. They are merely seeds from which to cultivate activities that students are interested in and that fulfill the goals of the children and the instructor. Seeds must be nourished and cared for until they develop into well-thought-out instructional plans. Those plans are the beginning of an integrated approach and of learning within individual classrooms.

---

[4]Ken Goodman. *Reading: A Conversation with Kenneth Goodman.* Glenview, IL: Scott, Foresman, 1976.

[5]Lucy Calkins. *The Art of Teaching Writing.* Portsmouth, NH: Heinemann, 1986.

[6]Donald Graves. *Writing: Teachers and Children at Work.* Exeter, NH: Heinemann, 1983.

[7]Jane Hansen. *When Writers Read.* Portsmouth, NH: Heinemann, 1987.

[8]H. A. McCracken and M. J. McCracken. *Stories, Songs, and Poetry to Teach Reading and Writing.* Chicago, IL: American Library Association, 1986.

[9]Frank Smith. *Understanding Reading* (3d ed.). New York: CBS College Publishing, 1982.

Three Formats for Integration

If children are to become real readers, they should meet good books not only at reading time but also as they study social studies, science, the arts — all the subject areas. The integration of books of literature (including informational literature) will bring a new focus to how learning is approached. Integration of curriculum can be categorized into three basic formats: within each of the language arts, among the language arts, and across the curriculum. Curriculum objectives should be the driving motivator in the development of any classroom activity or integration structure.

Integration Within Each of the Language Arts

The first format, within each of the language arts, provides for the blending of writing with writing, reading with reading, listening with listening, and speaking with speaking. It is very rare that activities, except for reading with reading, can be kept within the specific language art. Invariably, reading is a part of activities that go beyond one-dimensional listening, speaking, or writing activities — becoming activities that would be more accurately classified as being "among the language arts" (see pages 14-17). However, the blending of reading with reading is a common pattern of integration. One example of reading being integrated with reading utilizes a critical reading list. Critical reading often involves reading three or four versions of the same story or books and then comparing and contrasting them. Reading several versions of a story allows for more practice in reading a familiar story and provides opportunities for the readers to examine and play with the story grammar. The following is an example of a basic critical reading list that uses versions of a similar tale.

The Three Billy Goats Gruff

Asbjørnsen, P. C., and Jørgen E. Moe. *The Three Billy Goats Gruff*. Illustrated by Marcia Brown. Harcourt, 1957. (Available as a filmstrip/cassette from Weston Woods®.)

Chase, Richard. "Sody Sallyraytus." *Grandfather Tales*. Houghton, 1948.

Galdone, Paul. *The Three Billy Goats Gruff*. Illustrated by Paul Galdone. Clarion, 1973.

Stevens, Janet. *The Three Billy Goats Gruff*. Illustrated by Janet Stevens. Harcourt, 1987.

Three of the titles in the list involve variant versions of the same basic story, involving the same characters doing essentially the same things. It is the details of the retelling, dialogue, clothing, etc., that differ. Chase's version, however, presents an Appalachian tale that has a similar story grammar but tells the story of a squirrel, a family of four humans, and a bear that attempts to keep the others from returning from the story with the sody sallyraytus (baking soda) Ma needs to make baking powder biscuits. Instead of being knocked off the bridge, the bear is tricked by the squirrel into falling out of a tree; when he falls, he splits open and the characters he had swallowed are freed. So elements of "Red Riding Hood" and other "swallow" stories are brought into play as well as the basic "Three Billy Goats Gruff" story line.

A step beyond reading versions of the same story would be to read stories that include similar motifs, as told in stories from different countries or areas. Rumpelstiltskin is a popular example. There are several versions of this classic tale from the Grimm Brothers.

Rumpelstiltskin

Galdone, Paul. *Rumpelstiltskin*. Illustrated by Paul Galdone. Clarion, 1985.

Grimm, Jacob, and Wilhelm Grimm. *Rumpelstiltskin*. Illustrated by William Stobbs. Walck, 1971.

Grimm, Jacob, and Wilhelm Grimm. "Rumpelstiltzkin." In *Arbuthnot Anthology of Children's Literature*. 3d ed. Scott, Foresman, 1971.

Grimm Brothers. *Rumpelstiltskin*. Illustrated by Diane Diamond. Holiday, 1983.

Zelinsky, Paul O. *Rumpelstiltskin*. Illustrated by Paul O. Zelinsky. Dutton, 1986. (Available as a filmstrip/cassette and in video format from American School Publishers.)

A close look at the techniques of each illustrator will yield interesting comparisons. Zelinsky's luminous golden spools of thread contrast with the Galdone's dull gold. The Rumpelstiltskin character provides yet another point for comparison. Note the use of lightness and darkness in the illustrations of each of the versions. Also of significance is the coda (verse) used to close out the story. Some endings are decidedly more gruesome than others, where Rumpelstiltskin simply disappears.

Other countries have slightly different versions of the Rumpelstiltskin tale, with different characters and different titles. Reading the variant forms will provide an opportunity to focus on the story grammar (basic outline of story plot). The story grammar will be similar in each of the Rumpelstiltskin versions, but the characters in the versions play roles slightly different from those of their counterparts. Although the story grammar is basically the same, the details are different. My favorite variants include the Cornish version illustrated by Margot Zemach and Evaline Ness's English version.

Tales with Rumpelstiltskin Motifs

Jacobs, Joseph, editor. "Tom Tit Tot." In *English Folk and Fairy Tales*. Putnam, n.d.

Ness, Evaline. *Tom Tit Tot*. Illustrated by Evaline Ness. Scribner, 1965.

"Tom Tit Tot." In *Arbuthnot Anthology of Children's Literature*. 3d ed. Scott, Foresman, 1973.

Zemach, Harve. *Duffy and the Devil*. Illustrated by Margot Zemach. Farrar, 1973.

An emphasis on the role each character plays will provide a focus for a discussion about the story grammar (plot) of each story.

Other critical reading activities can lead from one story to the next. Rafé Martin has retold a jataka tale from India, *Foolish Rabbit's Big Mistake*, illustrated by Ed Young (Putnam, 1985). From that tale one can move to a discussion of the origin of the jataka tales and the reading of another jataka tale, *The Monkey and the Crocodile* by Paul Galdone (Clarion, 1969). Then, using Paul Galdone as a focus author, one can move into Galdone's version of *Henny Penny* (Clarion, 1968). Wide reading of versions of "Henny Penny" or "Chicken Little" will eventually lead to a modern-day retelling, *Chicken Little* by Steven Kellogg (Morrow, 1985).[10] The focus could continue with an emphasis on Paul Galdone and lead from his edition of *The Gingerbread Boy* (Clarion, 1975) to reading other versions of similar "runaway" tales.

Runaway Tales, Including "The Gingerbread Boy"

Bennett, Rowena. "The Gingerbread Man." In *Sing a Song of Popcorn: Every Child's Book of Poems*. Edited by Beatrice Schenk de Regniers, et al. Scholastic, 1988. (Poem)

Brown, Marcia. *The Bun*. Illustrated by Marcia Brown. Harcourt, 1972.

Cauley, Lorinda Bryan, reteller. *The Pancake Boy*. Illustrated by Lorinda Bryan Cauley. Putnam, 1988.

Galdone, Paul. *The Gingerbread Boy*. Illustrated by Paul Galdone. Clarion, 1975. (Available as a filmstrip/cassette from Listening Library®.)

The Gingerbread Boy. Illustrated by Scott Cook. Knopf, 1987.

Jacobs, Joseph. "Johnny Cake." In *Tomie dePaola's Favorite Nursery Tales*. Edited and illustrated by Tomie dePaola. Putnam, 1986.

Lobel, Anita. *The Pancake*. Illustrated by Anita Lobel. Greenwillow, 1978.

Rockwell, Anne. "The Gingerbread Man." In *The Three Bears & 15 Other Stories*. Illustrated by Anne Rockwell. Crowell, 1975; Harper Trophy, 1984.

---

[10]Activities to correlate with Steven Kellogg's *Chicken Little* and comparison notes for the "Henny Penny" and "Chicken Little" tales are included in the chapter featuring Steven Kellogg in *An Author a Month (for Pennies)* (Englewood, CO: Libraries Unlimited, 1988), 137-38.

Sawyer, Ruth. *Journey Cake, Ho!* Illustrated by Robert McCloskey. Viking, 1953. (Available as a filmstrip/cassette from Weston Woods.)

Schmidt, Karen. *The Gingerbread Man*. Illustrated by Karen Schmidt. Scholastic, 1985.

This list includes versions of "The Gingerbread Boy" and variant retellings from other countries or origins. A comparison of the story grammar, especially the story characters, can bring about a better understanding of the elements necessary to qualify the tale as a variant form. This can lead easily into integration activities across the language arts and across the curriculum as well.

Other examples of activities for integrating reading with reading include reading poems that express a feeling or tell a story similar to those told in prose. Examples of such activities follow.

- Read poems by the poet William Blake (1757-1827) and correlate those poems and the symbols within the poems with those used by Nancy Willard in *A Visit to William Blake's Inn: Poems for Innocent and Experienced Travelers*, illustrated by Alice Provensen and Martin Provensen (Harcourt, 1981). In Blake's and Willard's poetry are symbolic angels, dragons, and the moon and stars. New vocabulary can be learned as Willard refers to a "sullen" rat in "Blake Leads a Walk on the Milky Way" and uses the word again in the title for her fanciful *The Nightgown of the Sullen Moon*, illustrated by David McPhail (Harcourt, 1983; Voyager, 1983).

- Correlate the reading of traditional versions of "Cinderella" with Shirley Climo's *The Egyptian Cinderella*, illustrated by Ruth Heller (Crowell, 1988), and then connect the prose stories with Myra Cohn Livingston's humorous poem "Look Cinderella" in *A Song I Sang to You* (Harcourt, 1984) and Judith Viorst's "...And Then the Prince Knelt Down and Tried to Put the Glass Slipper on Cinderella's Foot" in *If I Were in Charge of the World and Other Worries* (Atheneum, 1981).

- Read Tomie dePaola's *The Art Lesson* (Putnam, 1989), an autobiographical story that tells of dePaola's childhood interest in art and his evolution as an illustrator of children's books. He tells of hiding under the covers of his bed and drawing pictures on his sheets. He relates the same experience in poetic form in a poem that begins, "It was my secret place...." The poem can be found in *Once Upon a Time... Celebrating the Magic of Children's Books in Honor of the Twentieth Anniversary of Reading Is Fundamental* (Putnam, 1986) and in *Tomie dePaola's Book of Poems* (Putnam, 1988). (*The Art Lesson* is also available in a big book format from Trumpet Books.)

- Read versions of "The Gingerbread Man" and Rowena Bennett's poem cited in the booklist on page 12.

The process of integrating reading with more reading is the most obvious integration pattern within the language arts. And although activities that combine writing with writing are less obvious, there *are* opportunities. For example, writing literary letters about an author or illustrator or a book's characters can be responded to in writing by another child. However, because the children must read the letter to respond to it, the activity is technically one involving two of the language arts—in this case, reading and writing. The same is true when a story scripted by one group provides the stimulus for the same or another group to write another version of the same story or another favorite scene, or when a readers theatre production promotes the development of a puppet play.

Integration Among the Language Arts

Critical reading activities lead easily into writing additional versions or new endings of favorite stories. To model the writing process, the teacher sometimes will use the exercise as an opportunity to write the new version as a class activity using the overhead or chalkboard. At other times individual students might create the new stories. A comparison of variant tales (see list on page 12) leads into the development and writing of a literary version of a similar tale. Characters and setting must be chosen and the plot developed along the lines of the story grammar (basic plot outline) in "The Gingerbread Boy" or other runaway tales. For example, if the story setting is to be Christmastime in a northern and snowy area, the story will take a definite turn. After the main characters are chosen, the story writing can begin. The result might be a story that begins as follows.

The Sugar Cookie Girl

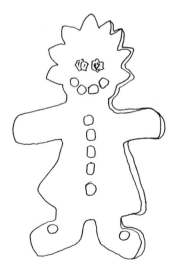

Snow twirled and whirled outside the cottage door. Warm logs in the fireplace inside kept the little old man and the little old woman warm. Logs crackled in the fireplace as they trimmed their Christmas tree with strings of cranberries, popcorn, and frosted sugar cookies and added a silvery star to the treetop. They wished they had a little girl to share their happiness. The little old woman scraped the bottom of the flour canister to get enough flour to make just one more sugar cookie. This time she gently mixed the flour with eggs, milk, sugar, and orange peel. She stirred the dough and kneaded it until the dough was soft and smooth. She patted the dough and shaped it into a round jolly sugar cookie girl. Raisins formed the little girl's eyes and nose. Red cinnamon candies made a smiling mouth and buttons down her cookie tummy. The little old woman put the cookie on a baking pan and put the pan into the oven so the cookie could bake. Before long the jolly round sugar cookie girl was brown and warm and full of energy. The old woman took the pan out of the oven and set it by the tree so the little girl could enjoy the twinkling lights.

The story develops as one lone sugar cookie decides she doesn't want to be hung on the tree, so she jumps up and takes off, out the door, and through the glittering white snow. It is probably obvious that she will not meet ditchdiggers, but perhaps she will meet snow shovelers. And she will have to meet her end in some other fashion than by crossing the stream on the back of a fox, because the stream will probably be frozen solid. Some might be inclined to require each student to create his or her own version of the gingerbread boy, but this would invariably result in some very artificial writing. Generally, writing activities based on other stories or patterns are best used as group activities that allow the teacher to demonstrate and model the process of writing for students. Eventually, the students will incorporate the form of the story (and others demonstrated over a period of time) into their own writing. Model the writing activity often and completely. During the sessions in which the writing is modeled, the skills, forms, and patterns modeled will become part of the writing of those ready to assimilate the instruction conveyed.

Connections among the language arts are not merely connections that bring together only reading and writing, although those connections are part of the total integration process. Each time reading leads to writing and the writing process is modeled, direct instruction in specific writing skills can be included. For example, if a class collaborates on a letter to a favorite author, structuring the letter, including paragraph indentations, can be demonstrated. As the letter is written it may be reread and revised using standard proofreading marks. Other types of writing can provide opportunities to focus on other specific skills inherent in the total language arts curriculum. When modeling the composition of a twist on folktales, the group will be exposed to the thought patterns used by the teacher and to the creative thinking other students use to innovate a story. Writing sentences for wordless books will expose students to the structure of sequence in storytelling and, as with the suggestion given below for *Ed Emberley's ABC*, the model could also focus on beginning consonants or the concept of alliteration, depending on the goals and objectives appropriate for the specific group of students. Scripting stories will provide students an opportunity to focus on dialogue and the critical elements of the narration. Once scripted, the story provides an opportunity to develop expression and oral interpretation. Reading prose selections can lead to the reading and writing of other forms of literature, such as poetry and information books. To further illustrate this concept, nine examples of connections and other activities to help teachers integrate among the language arts are summarized below.

- Focus on twists in folktales by reading Fred Gwynne's *Pondlarker* (Simon, 1990). Read other princess and frog stories and then share *Pondlarker*. At the last minute, the frog changes his mind and chooses to remain a frog. Discuss the change in the character from haughty to humble. Then compare the frog's change in character to the change in character in *Once a Mouse: A Fable Cut in Wood* by Marcia Brown (Scribner, 1961). In Brown's book the mouse is at first humble but during the course of the story becomes very haughty.

- Write sentences to correspond with the four-panel double-page spreads for each letter in *Ed Emberley's ABC* (Little, Brown, 1977). This will help students organize thoughts, develop sequential statements, and focus on beginning consonants. Start the writers off by developing some group examples: "The brown bear dressed in a scratchy-looking burlap-like jacket and sitting in a bamboo chair is watching a bug building a **B** using blueberries from a brown basket on the table. On the back of the chair sits a bluebird with an orange breast wearing a blue ball cap with a bill. On the other side of the chair is a butterfly. The bear is wearing bifocal glasses and has several buttons down the front of his jacket and a boutonniere in the lapel." Other sentences can be written about the other four-panel segments.

- When reading poetry and attempting to write poems, read a selection from *Anastasia Krupnik* by Lois Lowry (Houghton, 1979), pages 8-13. That selection has Anastasia struggling to write a poem for her class poetry day, only to have her efforts rebuffed by the teacher, whose idea of poetry is anything that rhymes. Anastasia's poem does not rhyme, but its poetic rhythm will not escape those who hear her poem. Reading about Anastasia's experiences with poetry might serve as an introduction to the great variety of poems being written by poets today.

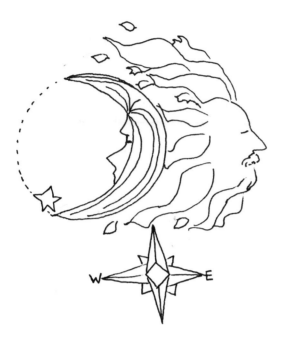

- Use Nancy Willard's *East of the Sun & West of the Moon* (Harcourt, 1989) to prepare a dramatic presentation of that story or a scripted version of another favorite tale. To become familiar enough with a story to be able to script it will take much reading. The actual scripting of the story will be a writing activity, but the dramatic interpretation will bring in oral language arts. And those who are the audience for the dramatic presentation will be involved as listening participants.

- Compare and contrast Verna Aardema's *Why Mosquitoes Buzz in People's Ears* (Dial, 1975) with Benjamin Elkins's *Why the Sun Was Late* (Parents, 1966). Aardema's story is one that comes alive when dramatized. Another tale by Aardema, which is actually illustrated as a play even though the text is not scripted, is *Who's in Rabbit's House?* illustrated by Leo Dillon and Diane Dillon (Dial, 1977). Both of Aardema's tales will provide opportunities for dramatization and script writing.

- Use for readers theatre activities the angels' conversations focusing on the angels coming to eat the cake in Nancy Willard's *High Rise Glorious Skittle Skat Roarious Sky Pie Angel Food Cake*, illustrated by Richard Jesse Watson (Harcourt, 1990), and investigate the difference between an angel food cake and other types of cakes.

- Introduce cursive writing by sharing Beverly Cleary's *Muggie Maggie* (Morrow, 1990) and role-playing the scene where Maggie refuses to learn cursive and eventually changes her mind after being tricked by a clever teacher.

- Introduce the purpose and use of quotations by using any of Aliki's books in which she uses bubble speech. If the words in the bubble are written as conventional text, the sentences should be enclosed in quotation marks. Model the writing of one page of text in a style incorporating quotation marks. Any book with bubble speech can be used for this exercise.

- Use *The Empty Pot* by Demi (Holt, 1990) in a story theater experience to help strengthen participants' memorization skills and provide a drama experience. The unlimited number of characters assist in allowing a large group to participate in the drama activity. Because of its theme of honesty, the book could also be used in a personal development unit. The basic story involves young children who are given a seed by the emperor—a seed each child is to plant and nurture. However, because the emperor has boiled the seeds before giving them to the children, germination will be impossible. All the children, except for one little boy, find substitute plants to replace their seed. That lonely boy arrives in front of the emperor on the appointed day with an empty pot. The emperor has been looking for an honest child, and this experiment has helped him find that child. The element of plants and germination make the story appropriate to use during a science unit involving seeds and plants—a direct lead-in to integrating *across* the curriculum.

Integration Across the Curriculum

The language arts skills provide the tools for exploring information within the curriculum of many content areas. When trade books are brought into content area curricular studies, students are able to gain new perspectives and make generalizations about an event or person. Students are able to clarify and summarize their findings through writing activities. Access to a variety of viewpoints will stimulate critical thinking. Whereas most textbooks are written in an expository style with controlled sentence length and vocabulary and a minimum of elaboration, trade books often present information through a strong narrative with few stylistic restraints. The use of the present tense in trade books brings a sense of vitality to the narrative.

Many opportunities exist for bringing literature (including information literature) into other curricular areas. Following are 11 suggestions that will help teachers integrate language arts skills and other curricular goals and objectives across the curriculum.

- When the topic of Abraham Lincoln is the focus in the social studies curriculum, make available many biographies of Lincoln and share them throughout the unit. One good choice is Russell Freedman's *Lincoln: A Photobiography* (Clarion, 1987). A timeline of Lincoln's life could help students put into perspective the period during which Lincoln lived and how long it has been since his assassination.

- Introduce the study of Egypt and the Nile River with Tomie dePaola's *Bill and Pete* (Putnam, 1978) and *Bill and Pete Go Down the Nile* (Putnam, 1987). Then set out to discover the "facts" about Egypt and the Nile that dePaola incorporated into his fictional story.

- During discussions of the United States expansion into Texas read a personal account of the battle at the Alamo by sharing John Jakes's *Susanna of the Alamo* (Harcourt, 1986).

- Create interest in immigration experiences by reading books such as *The Road from Home: The Story of an Armenian Girl* by David Kherdian (Greenwillow, 1979; Puffin, 1987) and *Sam Ellis's Island* by Beatrice Siegel (Four Winds, 1985).

- Begin a study of the continuing strife for civil rights for all U.S. citizens by reading *Rosa Parks* by Eloise Greenfield (Crowell, 1973) and *Rosa Parks: My Story* by Rosa Parks and Jim Haskins (Dial, 1992).

- Use the knowledge gathered during a social studies focus about a specific location to create a version of a folktale that reflects the geographical region, customs, and beliefs of that area. A variant form of "The Gingerbread Boy" could be written as part of a study of Japan. The variant form might be titled "The Runaway Rice Cake," and the characters the rice cake meets might include the *jizo* (patron of travelers) and the *oni* (wicked ogres) — characters often found in Japanese literature. A discussion of the reason rice and water are often part of Japanese folk literature could result from the study of informational literature about Japan.

- Read Gerald McDermott's *Arrow to the Sun* (Viking, 1974) as an introduction to a study of the Pueblo Indians of the southwestern United States. Diane Hoyt-Goldsmith's *Pueblo Storyteller*, illustrated by Lawrence Migdale (Holiday, 1991), is an obvious book to include in the study.

- Share examples from literature as students create linoleum blocks in art class. Marcia Brown's *Dick Whittington and His Cat* (Scribner, 1950) provides one example, and much of the work of Ashley Bryan gives additional examples. Gail E. Haley has also used this technique to illustrate some of her books, which she discusses in the Weston Woods filmstrip/cassette *Gail E. Haley: Wood and Linoleum Illustration*.

- Read books about food groups as part of a study of food groups. For example, readings about the dairy group may include Lucia Anderson's *Mammals and Their Milk* (Dodd, 1985); Gail Gibbons's *The Milk Makers* (Macmillan, 1985); James Cross Giblin's *Milk: The Fight for Purity* (Crowell, 1986); Donald Carrick's *Milk* (Greenwillow, 1985); and Aliki's *Milk from Cow to Carton* (HarperCollins, 1992). A similar list of appropriate books can be generated for the other food groups by using the catalog in your library or library media center.
  Note: Aliki's book was originally published in 1974 with the title *Green Grass and White Milk*.

- Introduce the concept of division with Pat Hutchins's *The Doorbell Rang* (Greenwillow, 1986). The book is also available in a big book format from Scholastic.

• Use Robert Quackenbush's *Pop! Goes the Weasel and Yankee Doodle* (Lippincott, 1976) to bring a revolutionary song into the study of music and social studies. Quackenbush's notes in the book about the origins of the songs bring an added dimension to the study of the revolutionary period.

A high school mathematics teacher began reading aloud at the beginning of each class period. He read about famous mathematicians—their careers, their ideas, their discoveries, and their inventions. He was delighted when one day he realized he was no longer dealing with tardy students. The students were clamoring to be in their seats at the beginning of class. He feels that his students' interest in mathematics and mathematics-related careers has definitely increased. He also no longer feels that he needs to have an "excuse" to read aloud to his high school classes; he does it because it has unmeasurable but demonstrable benefits. If other teachers took his lead, they would reach for books to introduce songs in music class, and to introduce famous artists or provide examples of art techniques in art class. Math lessons would begin with a story from a book. Some of the reading would be instructive and informative, and some would simply arouse students' interest in the subject. For example, computer skills would be introduced with a reading of the first chapter of Louis Sachar's *Wayside School Is Falling Down* (Morrow, 1989). A study of black holes would begin with Franklyn M. Branley's *Journey into a Black Hole*, illustrated by Marc Simont (Crowell, 1986; Trophy, 1988). A lively discussion of the arms race might be generated by a reading of Dr. Seuss's *The Butter Battle Book* (Random, 1984).

Picture books as well as chapters from books can be used successfully to introduce ideas and specific focuses. Picture books are short enough to allow the books to be read in conjunction with almost any activity. They can bring an immediate focus to a topic and can provide a way to demonstrate a technique or skill that can later be applied to longer selections. They can help provide a bridge to many other books and activities.

Throughout this book ideas will be given to utilize literature across the curriculum—ideas that can be adapted for use at several grade levels. But it is essential that educators who use the ideas correlate them with their own classroom or district objectives. By so doing they will be taking a first step toward building a totally integrated literate and literature-rich learning environment.

GETTING STARTED

Over a period of years I have found that organizing teaching files is a very personal matter. It seems that each of us has a slightly different method of organizing resources, but some sort of organizing scheme is essential to effective teaching. Organization permits quick and easy access to materials as they are needed. Organization is especially important in literature-based classrooms because it facilitates integrating the literature into other areas of the curriculum.

My own organizational structure for literature-based materials includes two types of files. One set of files is related to author and illustrator information. For example, when I think I will want to use the information about Pat Hutchins from *An Author a Month (for Nickels)* (Teacher Ideas Press, 1990), I photocopy the two poster pages, mount them onto a letter-size manila file folder, and place the author's name on the tab. I add some color or a border, laminate the entire folder, and place it in my author files. As I gather other material about the author and illustrator, I add it to the folder. When I am featuring Pat Hutchins as an author/illustrator in conjunction with an individual book title or in conjunction with a full author focus, I pull the folder to use the information with my students or place the folder on an author bulletin board. If I only want to check a bit of information about the author, I refer to the folder and relay the information to the class as we discuss her books or literature related to her books.

My other set of files is arranged by book title. These files serve the main purpose of providing a list of numbered activities (often including prereading activities, response suggestions, and culminating activities) for specific book titles. See the literature response sheet in figure 1.1—this sheet was generated using the basic suggestions given for *Fortunately* on page 20. (The pattern sheet referred to in 4 of the literature response sheet is a reproducible page in appendix A, page 181.) The

Literature Response Sheet

Book title: _Fortunately_

Author: _Remy Charlip_

Illustrator: _Remy Charlip_

Publisher: _Macmillan_   Date: _1964_

Book call no.: _ECHA_

Location: ☐ personal library ☐ _____library

Lesson Plan Options

Objective: To provide a model and motivation for writing an innovation on a text.

Steps:

1. Read the book aloud. Share the humorous illustrations.

2. Read the book again encouraging listeners to participate in the reading, particularly the parts beginning "unfortunately."

3. Brainstorm a few situations that would follow the pattern Fortunately ... Unfortunately ...

4. Use transparencies of the pattern sheet to model the sentence structure for three or four ideas. Discuss the cause/effect relationship. The action that results in the "unfortunately" statement dictates the topic of the next "fortunately" statement. Note also that the very beginning problem is resolved in the final "fortunately" statement.

5. Complete a class story with at least seven sentences.

6. Ask pairs of students to copy one of the sentences onto two sheets of paper: "Fortunately" on one page and "Unfortunately" on the next page. Illustrate the pages.

7. Add a title page, table of contents, list of illustrations, dedication, or other book elements. Bind the pages together and display as a published class book.

8. Read the class book.

Fig. 1.1. Literature response sheet.

completed literature response sheet is either affixed to the outside of the folder for the specific book or the sheet is reproduced on colored paper and inserted into the folder. (A reproducible literature response sheet is in appendix A, page 174.) I keep my literature response sheets consistent in color so that they can be easily identified in the folders. I always make sure that full bibliographic information and the location of each book are recorded in the folder. Even though it takes a few extra minutes, over the years I have found this information to be valuable for locating a book, especially if I wish to use it at a later time.

On the basic literature response sheet I often include variations to be used with learners according to their age and prior experience. For example, if the plan calls for a compare/contrast activity and the group has not had much previous experience, the lead-in activities will need to be more detailed. If, however, the group has participated in similar exercises, their experiential level will allow some of the preliminary steps to be omitted. Thus, on the literature response sheet each step of any suggested activity is numbered as a separate item. As other ideas occur they may be given the next sequential number and added to the response sheet. Then when I am ready to plan a particular day's lesson for a specific class I am able to indicate the book folder and the particular items (steps and variations) from the literature response sheet that I wish to use. Specific lesson plans can be generated using this response sheet and the numbered items on it. The first entry in the actual lesson plan book for *Fortunately* by Remy Charlip might look like this:

> Language arts — Writing Workshop
> Activity: Class-written story
> See book folder: Fortunately by Remy Charlip
> Steps for this lesson: # 1, 2, 3, 4, 5
> Put story sheets aside for Tuesday

For Tuesday the following might be written into the lesson plan book.

> Language arts - Reading Workshop
> Activity: Demonstrating comprehension by
> illustrating sentences
> See book folder: Fortunately by Remy Charlip
> Steps for this lesson: Review and #6
> Reread aloud the sentences created
> previously. Read from transparency sheets
> projected on the overhead. Pass out sheets
> of paper to designated pairs. Explain #6.
> Put story sheets aside for Tuesday.

Once these plans are written, the book folder is put in a designated place on the teacher's desk. A copy of the book is located and placed with the folder. When the lesson plan is to be implemented, the materials necessary are close at hand and the step-by-step plan is written in sufficient detail to allow the plan to be successful. The book folder organizational plan is particularly helpful when a substitute teacher is in the classroom. The materials are all in one place and the plans are sufficiently detailed to allow the teacher to know where the day's activities are leading. In addition, the book folders may be used as contingency plans in the event the original plans can not be carried out. You can include contingency plans by referring to a specific book folder in your files.

The organizational charts in appendix A, pages 175 and 176, can serve as models in outlining the activities for a specific book or in organizing an overview of a content area focus. The literature-based chart is self-explanatory. The "File#" space is intended to accommodate those who wish to assign numbers to specific curriculum objectives and file folders holding materials specific to various objectives. The focus overview chart is intended to allow long-range planning. Notations for the objectives and activities should simply state the objective or activity and the reference files and manual pages that will give the complete information regarding objectives and activities. In the resource section a separate bibliography or specific titles might be cited. The evaluation activity should be included in the appropriate space. Many variations of these chart forms can be developed and utilized. Once the charts are completed, they should never be viewed as static. As students offer their own interpretations of events, these should be recorded on the literature response sheet as an additional suggestion for a possible activity.

WEAVING IT ALL TOGETHER

Developing an integrated curriculum is like weaving. The curriculum strands are the warp threads—of different colors, textures, and strengths. The language arts—the tools of communicating—are the weft threads. The weft threads are woven in and out, over and under, and around the warp to create the tapestry of learning. The tools of communication, the weft, hold everything together, creating something beautiful and useful. Each class of students causes the design on the weaving to be ever changing. The following chapters offer suggestions for weaving the weft threads in and around the warp, but the design of the tapestry must be the design of those implementing the suggestions in their own classrooms and for their own lifelong learning.

Chapter

2

Reading on the Write Side

There is no simple way [to write] and the
discipline is essential. I never leave the room
during my workday even if all I do is sit there.
　　—Theodor S. Geisel (Dr. Seuss), 1985

THE WRITING WORKSHOP

The writings of Lee Gunderson and Jon Shapiro;[1] Andrea Butler and Jan Turbill;[2] Jane Hansen, Thomas Newkirk, and Donald Graves;[3] Jo-Anne Parry and David Hornsby;[4] and Thomas Newkirk and Nancy Atwell[5] set the tone for any discussion of the writing process and the writing workshop concept. Gunderson and Shapiro begin by discussing the development of writing in a first-grade classroom. The other writers cited bring an overall view to the writing process.

From their philosophies and experiences an organizational plan can be built—a plan that promotes writing and uses all types of literature as models of writing. The writing workshop includes time for students to keep a journal, time for teachers to provide writing instruction, and time for students to use their writing skills to polish a selected piece of writing. The polishing process includes time for choosing pieces of writing as well as for rereading, revising, rewriting, editing, and publishing them. The sharing time gives students an opportunity to read and respond informally to the writings of others.

---

[1]Lee Gunderson and Jon Shapiro. "Whole Language Instruction: Writing in 1st Grade." *The Reading Teacher* 41, no. 4 (January 1988): 430-37.

[2]Andrea Butler and Jan Turbill. *Towards a Reading-Writing Classroom*. Portsmouth, NH: Heinemann, 1987.

[3]Jane Hansen, Thomas Newkirk, and Donald Graves, eds. *Breaking Ground: Teachers Relate Reading and Writing in the Elementary School*. Portsmouth, NH: Heinemann, 1985.

[4]Jo-Anne Parry and David Hornsby. *Write On: A Conference Approach to Writing*. Portsmouth, NH: Heinemann, 1985.

[5]Thomas Newkirk and Nancy Atwell. *Understanding Writing*. Portsmouth, NH: Heinemann, 1987.

The Writing Workshop
   Journal time
   Planning time
   Modeling-writing process
   Instruction conferences
   Polishing time
      Select a piece
      Reread and elaborate
      Rewrite and polish
      Edit and revise
      Publish
   Sharing time

In the beginning the writing workshop in any classroom will probably be more structured than it will be later in the year when students better understand the options and the procedure for planning their own day's writing activities. During the early days when the writing workshop concept is being implemented in your classroom you will want to start by sharing something you have written. It may be a story about something that happened to you but it could also be a letter to a friend or an excerpt from your own journal. (I always use the word *journal* or *learning log* to describe any school writing that will be read by others. I avoid using the word *diary*, since I believe that a diary is too personal to share with anyone—even a trusted adult or a very close friend.) Once you have read aloud your piece of writing you might want to project it on the overhead so that students can actually see the form your writing has taken. Reread the piece of writing. Then explain the concept of journal time, a component of the writing workshop.

Journal time is a time synonymous with uninterrupted, sustained reading time. It is a time when students can choose what they wish to write and are given time to write. The time, just as the uninterrupted reading time, is a scheduled part of the day, occurring, when possible, at a specific time each day. Knowing the time is scheduled, students can begin to plan for their writing time. During the time between journal sessions students are able to identify topics or to mentally plan the writing they will do during their next session. Students can plan their writing because they know when they will write. Each day individual students decide to either start a new piece of writing, continue with a piece of writing started the day before, or return to a draft created earlier. Barbara Steiner and Kathleen C. Phillips thoroughly address the topic of journal keeping in their book *Journal Keeping with Young People* (Teacher Ideas Press, 1991). They discuss the rationale behind journal keeping, the techniques and definitions, and various types of journals and their uses.

In most writing workshops the journal time is a time for student's to react to stories and to activities in the classroom, parody a story they have heard, write about a topic on which they are considered an expert, or simply write about anything they wish. Often, journal entries are stimulated by the reading of books and group writing activities. Books can provide students with models of good writing and often will provide an original text pattern (story grammar) on which the class can build innovations. These patterns and stories are often internalized and show up in the journal writing of students who are given the freedom to react and discover their own view of life in their journal.

Often I encounter teachers who feel that the students in their classrooms are too young to be asked to journal, but they are not. At one time I might have thought that kindergartners were too young to write regularly. An innovative kindergarten teacher (now retired), Lillian Frantz, showed me and many others that children of that age *can* write. The key, it seems, is to give them the opportunity. She did not assign topics. She did not ask them to copy her writing from the board. She simply asked them to write, accepted what they had written, and helped them grow as writers as they were ready to progress. She did not demand that they use "book spelling" for all of their writing. She allowed them to draw pictures first if that helped. She modeled writing for them using one-on-one conferences and whole group instruction. She read to them often, giving them a continuing experience with the writing of others. She got incredible results with seemingly little effort. Their writing was stimulated in many ways. For example, one March when Dr. Seuss was still living the kindergarten class decided to send an audiotape of them singing "Happy Birthday" to him. The song was recorded and sent to Dr. Seuss. A couple of weeks later he sent back a card thanking them for the song. The card showed the Cat in the Hat prominently on the front. So that the children could all see the card (and read the words) better I made a transparency of the card and invited them into the library media center to see what Dr. Seuss had sent to them. Later in the day, Kevin wrote about seeing the card. See figure 2.1.

Fig. 2.1.

When Kevin read what he had written he said, "We are looking at a Dr. Seuss Card." His drawing shows the projected image of the card, the teacher (me) with all five fingers on each hand, and the back of the boys' and girls' heads as they are reading the card with me.

Kevin's writing shows a good awareness of consonant sounds and periods—even though he does not yet understand the function of the punctuation mark.

Another youngster was inspired by some science activities to conduct an experiment of his own. He had previously been interested in the length of objects and eventually had become interested in how much things weighed. This particular day he was interested in how much water in a container would make it sink. In his drawing he replicated the bulletin board and ledge above the countertop where he was conducting his experiment. Later he wrote about it: "I did a science experiment with water. The water in the container overflowed. And Sal came along and got it down and it just went down." Even though this piece of writing came earlier in the specific school year, Jacob was more knowledgeable about the use of periods and was able to use vowels more often and more appropriately (see figure 2.2).

As a teacher notices that a specific student has a piece of writing that is especially well done she or he might suggest that the piece be polished and published. The first step in publishing might simply be the student reading the selected piece of writing to a friend or to a small group. As time progresses the reading of a piece of writing could be followed by rewriting it with "book spelling" so that someone else could read the piece. As this evolves different students will be at different stages of the writing process at any one time. At each stage individuals and small groups will be called together to help each other by being the audience and suggesting revisions for the writings of others, by helping with the editing of the writing (mechanics), and by providing encouragement and help, when needed. The groups should be fluid and flexible, changing as the needs of the individual group members change.

Because of the fluidity of the groups and the fact that each student will progress through the various stages of writing at different rates, it is important that each writing workshop segment includes a few minutes for the teacher and students to assess the goals for the specific day's workshop. The teacher may ask children individually what stage they are at and what they need to be doing that day. Some teachers prefer to have this planning session at the very end of the day's writing workshop so that they have some time to organize groups and schedule the events that must take place during the next day's workshop. At the beginning of the next day's workshop the teacher can help get the students started efficiently and promptly.

The workshop concept is based on the premise that students will write often but not every piece will be published or shared with others. Goals for publication and sharing must be set, however. Initially, a goal might be to have each student publish one piece of writing each school quarter. Students will need to select something they have written (most often a selection from their journal) and write it in a preliminary draft and then carry it through all of the polishing steps. Once the preliminary draft has been created the student may need assistance in knowing how to elaborate or expand the writing into something viable. They may need an individual, instructional conference with the teacher or they may need someone to listen to their writing and make suggestions for revising the piece to be more interesting. As the students express their writing needs for the day the teacher forms a strategy for continuing. She or he sets up conference groups and a schedule for the workshop segment of the day. For example, there may be two or three people who need individual conferences before they may go on. A schedule of those conferences can go on the board. While the first student is in his or her individual conference, two other students may listen and provide suggestions to the writing of a fourth student. Meanwhile other children may be rewriting, typing their work on the computer, editing their hard copy and asking a peer to proofread the piece for them, or binding their finished story and drawing the illustrations.

If the teacher is a careful observer and sets up a system to record her or his observations about what children can do with their writing, needs for small-group instructional conferences can be determined and scheduled and participants can be identified. The teacher will know what students would be ready to expand on their ability to use a particular skill, for example, the use of periods in writing. During these instructional conferences some modeling of the use of the identified skill is

I dɪad a Sies ICKE sqɑdMɼ Waih WaitR. The WɑItR Ih The CKNTdNR OVRFOTdd. And 5al Cam Alɑɪg And qaiht It DɑohwdlT Jɑsr Wait Daoɳ.

Jacob

Fig. 2.2.

often included along with some guided practice. Students can be assisted in the revision of a piece of their own writing, using the identified skill. Later, when the writing is ready to be edited, the teacher can remind the student that one of the skills that the student could use in his or her writing is the correct use of the punctuation mark.

Those who wish to read more about the organization of the writing workshop should read Jo-Anne Parry and David Hornsby's *Write On: A Conference Approach to Writing* (Heinemann, 1985). Their book is one of the most useful in terms of a practical application of the writing workshop.

Often, the model writing process time is an extension of a read-aloud session held during the reading workshop or of another activity that is part of another focus in a content area of the curriculum. During the model writing process time, innovations on the story grammar of books read earlier can be constructed as a group activity. Lists, for example, of animals, ideas, objects, and people related to other curricular areas can be generated. Letters to a class pen pal can be modeled. Eventually these modeling activities will result in some of the forms and techniques being assimilated into the writing of students. They will pick the bits of knowledge that they are ready to deal with and incorporate that information into their journal writing and then into the writings they choose to expand on for sharing or publication. Including the model writing process time in the activities of each day is very important to the students' continuing growth as writers. The modeling, however, need not always take place during the time designated for the writing workshop. Sometimes the modeling might be a natural outgrowth of activities in the reading workshop or in the content area workshops. Any use of writing activities within other disciplines will be one more step toward integrating the language arts across the curriculum.

As students read and are read to, literature (including information literature) gives student writers the foundation for their own writing. Student writers mimic patterns of writing, find universal themes, and discover new ways to express themselves. Frequent opportunities to write group papers will help learners identify their own topics for writing and will model techniques for developing sequential thoughts, adding details, editing, revising, and so on.

The instructional, sharing, and polishing time will generally blend together. In addition to the one or more daily model writing process times, each day of the writing workshop will include a journal time and a planning time. The needs expressed during the planning time will determine the frequency of the other components of the writing workshop. One student might spend the entire day in the writing workshop developing a piece of writing while another student might read his or her piece to a small group of students and then solicit suggestions for editing and revising. Another student might have a final conference with the teacher in preparation to make a final copy of a piece for publication. Other students may be in the school library media center searching out background information for writing that they wish to develop. Myriad writing activities may be going on at any one time during the writing workshop. The common element of all of the activities and conferences is that the focus of the workshop is writing.

Writing takes many forms—informal writing, reports, diary and journal entries, letters, written reports, etc. During the writing workshop period, student writers spend their time writing, sharing, seeking assistance, and responding to others. It is important that students are given choice—beyond topic choice. Student writers must be allowed to maintain editorial control over the content of their writing. Suggestions, questions, and comments can prompt changes, but the writer must be given the choice of rejecting or accepting suggestions and comments. The role of writing within the whole language classroom is addressed by Linda Leonard Lamme, a language arts instructor at the University of Florida, Gainesville, who suggests ways to build "a class of authors."[6] She suggests that one of the key facets of whole language instruction is authorship and that the goal of the whole language classroom is to help children become avid readers and writers. The sense of being an author comes about by viewing oneself as an author. That feeling can be promoted by creating a writing center where students can conveniently publish their writings.

---

[6]Linda Leonard Lamme. "Authorship: A Key Facet of Whole Language." *The Reading Teacher* 42, no. 9 (May 1989): 704-10.

GETTING STARTED

Organizing the writing activities and materials in your classroom will allow learners to focus more on writing than on locating materials and identifying topics to write about. Organizing both physical space and materials and giving learners a management system for their own ideas and writings will allow them to make the optimum use of their writing opportunities. Organizing and establishing a writing center and helping students produce personal writing folders are the first steps in creating an environment conducive to writing.

Establishing the Writing Center

A writing center will help accentuate the importance of both writing and sharing that writing with others. Students writers who choose to revise and polish a piece of writing will benefit from having a legitimate audience. During the time when the entire class is engaged in the writing workshop, most students will work at their desks or tables. During times when several (or all) in a class are working on writing projects, the center can become the place to go for supplies and for their own individual folders. The actual writing, however, will need to be done away from the center so that all students can maintain access to the supplies.

With encouragement the writing activities will extend beyond the actual designated writing workshop time. Students will become engaged in their writing and given the opportunity will choose to continue their writing at other times during the day. A writing center can provide a place where students can finish a piece, prepare it for publishing, and find an opportunity for sharing it. In addition, the writing center can serve as a convenient publishing center. As students progress through the writing process, they will reach the publishing stage at varying times and can proceed to the center one by one, or in small groups, to "publish" their manuscripts.

Almost any classroom can dedicate a corner with a table or desk to serve as a student writing center. Writing materials in the center should be interesting and varied. Types of writing tools that should be available include pencils, fat and skinny watercolor markers, colored pencils, and crayons. Various types of drawing and writing paper should also be available. A selection of materials that might be used to bind together the completed pieces of writing could also be included in the center. The center will serve as headquarters for organizing writing into a published format. Books written by the students can be displayed in the writing center.

The center can also serve as a place where students can store the writing folders holding their current writing projects (see next section). A portable file drawer should be provided for this purpose.

Writing resources such as dictionaries, posters, and books giving tips on writing should also be a part of center. Specifically recommended as writing resources are *Messages in the Mailbox: How to Write a Letter*, written and illustrated by Loreen Leedy (Holiday, 1991); *Writing for Kids* by Carol Lea Benjamin (HarperCollins, 1985); and *Where Do You Get Your Ideas?* by Sandy Asher, illustrated by Susan Hellard (Walker, 1987).

Once the center is organized, encourage students to work together at the center to revise, rewrite, and polish their pieces. Whenever individual students choose to write they may go to the center. Using the center can foster in students the attitude that writing is a continuing process.

Creating the Writing Folder

A writing folder can help students organize their own writing and can provide a place to record ideas, skills, and topics.

Once a book is read on a given topic and a writing activity modeled, children can choose to list that topic or ideas for future writing on writing charts (see appendix A, pp. 177 and 178). They can also record on the charts topics or pieces of writing they identify from their journals for rewriting and polishing. The writing charts can be printed on paper and stapled inside a file folder or printed on both sides of a letter-size manila file folder. As specific skills are taught to individuals or groups, and when the students feel comfortable using them, they can be recorded in the " " " ! ? Skills I Can Use in My Writing" section. The skills might include using quotation marks, punctuation, paragraphing, abbreviations, etc. Many of the entries in the "Ideas for Writing" section will evolve from topics discussed in class and from topics on which a child is an "expert." Children will become "experts" by reading and researching topics that interest them. When one section of the chart is filled, the folder can be turned inside out and the other side used or another chart paper stapled in the folder. The folder itself can be used to hold the student's current writing project.

The writing folder contains sections titled:

- Ideas for Writing

- My Expert Topics

- " " ! ? Skills I Can Use in My Writing

- Books I've Published

CONNECTIONS TO MAKE—A SAMPLER

These connections are not intended to be given to students as assignments but are designed to provide the impetus for group writing activities, brainstorming, and oral discussions. The books and writing suggestions that follow will provide some "Ideas for Writing" as students get used to recording those ideas in their writing folders.

Bayer, Jane. *A, My Name Is Alice*. Illustrated by Steven Kellogg. Dial, 1984. (Picture book)
Alliterative alphabet verses correspond to or accompany playground games like "Four Square"—a bouncing-ball game.

- Create alphabetical lists of countries, products, cities, states, etc.

- Use the alphabetical lists to write new versions of the alliterative verses, incorporating a specific type of information such as capitals of the states within the United States, animals in Asia, or countries of the world.

Blume, Judy. *The Pain and the Great One*. Illustrated by Irene Trivas. Bradbury, 1974. (Picture book)
"The Pain" is a six-year-old boy and "The Great One" is his eight-year-old sister. The book has alternating chapters that relate incidents from the viewpoint of each child.

- Tell about your brother or sister. Then write the story you have just told from your brother's or sister's point of view (or ask your brother and sister to write the story from their point of view).

- Make a list of reasons why your sister or brother is NOT a pain.

Brett, Jan. *Annie and the Wild Animals*. Illustrated by Jan Brett. Houghton, 1985. (Picture book)
Annie attempts to find her lost cat. She goes into the woods and tries to find a new animal pet—a woodland animal. Each of the animals goes back into the woods and eventually Annie's cat reappears. Contains beautiful illustrations with borders that foreshadow parts of the story.

- Choose a wild animal from the book and research information about the animal. Make a list of five interesting facts about the animal.

- Tell about a pet you have or would like to have. Describe the pet—how it looks, how it acts, what it eats, etc.

Briggs, Raymond. *Jim and the Beanstalk*. Illustrated by Raymond Briggs. Coward, 1970; Putnam, 1989.

Jim finds a beanstalk outside his window, climbs it up through the clouds, and reaches a castle. Because he is hungry he decides to see if the people who live in the castle have any cornflakes. His knock is answered by an old giant who turns out to be the son of the giant in "Jack and the Beanstalk." Jim finds this giant in need of eyeglasses (so he can read his poetry books), false teeth (so he can eat "something juicy"), and a wig (so he'll be "good-looking" once again). Each time Jim leaves to get the items the giant needs, the giant gives him a giant gold coin to use for the purchase.

- Make a list of other things the giant might need (see appendix A, p. 179).

- Draw a picture of a giant-size object that the giant will ask Jim to buy for him on his next visit.

- Create an episode that tells of Jim's return and the next object he will get next for the giant. Several episodes could be combined to make a book titled "Jim and the Beanstalk (Part II)." Some suggestions would include a giant-size glass to soak his false teeth in, a toothbrush, new shoes (notice the holes in the giant's shoes), a comb for his new red wig, etc.

Brown, Jeff. *Flat Stanley*. Illustrated by Tomi Ungerer. Harper, 1964; Scholastic, 1972.

Stanley has the horrible misfortune of having himself accidently flattened by a falling bulletin board. As he lives the life of a person who is flat, Stanley discovers that there are advantages of being flat. He can slip under doors and do many things ordinary people cannot do. But people stare at him when he walks down the street, and other problems arise. Soon Stanley's brother comes up with a solution to solve Stanley's flatness. He uses a tire pump to pump Stanley back to his plump shape.

- Make a picture of yourself as a flat person.

- How did you become flat? Tell about things that happened to you when you were flat. How did you become plump again? (See appendix A, p. 180.)

- Make a chart of the advantages and disadvantages of being flat.

Carlstrom, Nancy White. *The Moon Came Too*. Illustrated by Stella Ormai. Macmillan, 1987.
A trip to Grandmother's brings the moon along too.

- Make an alphabetical list of items you would take to Grandmother's house.

Carrick, Carol. *What Happened to Patrick's Dinosaurs?* Illustrated by Donald Carrick. Clarion, 1986. (Picture book)
A boy wonders what happened to the dinosaurs of long ago and forms several hypotheses about where they might be.

- Invent a new dinosaur and write a story about it. Give its name and details about where it lives, its family, its personality, etc.

- Make a list of adjectives to describe dinosaurs.

- Brainstorm a list of ideas under the heading "Dinosaurs Would Be a Problem If They Were Living Today."

- Describe the planet on which the dinosaurs landed.

Charlip, Remy. *Fortunately*. Illustrated by Remy Charlip. Parents, 1964; Macmillan, 1972. (Picture book)
Fortunately Ned is invited to a party in Florida. Unfortunately Ned lives in New York....

- Brainstorm and list situations that follow the pattern: Fortunately ... Unfortunately....

- Choose one of the situations from the brainstormed list and write the situation in correct sentence format (see appendix A, p. 181).

- If students choose to complete their own "Fortunately ... Unfortunately ..." sheets, compile them into a class book. Add a cover and a title page. The pages could be used on a bulletin board as a board story and eventually be bound together as a book.

Cole, Babette. *The Trouble with Mom*. Illustrated by Babette Cole. Coward, 1983. (Picture book)
The boy's mother in the story is a witch. When the boy's friends come to play at his house, his parents take them away. But all turns out find when it is discovered that the witch has rescued the children from a fire in the house.

- Make a list of characteristics of the boy's mom. Star those characteristics that most mothers would not share.

- Would you like to be a friend of the boy? Explain why or why not?

dePaola, Tomie. *Marianna May and Nursey*. Illustrated by Tomie dePaola. Holiday, 1983. (Picture book)
Marianna May is cared for by Nursey, who always dresses her in white dresses. But when Marianna eats orange ice she gets orange stains on her dress, and when she rolls in the grass she gets green grass stains on her dress. To keep her white dresses clean Nursey sits Marianna in the swing. Marianna does not like to sit in the swing when she could be playing. Mr. Talbot, the iceman, sets out to solve the problem. And he does.

- Before reading the book aloud, explain the problem to the children (be sure to discuss the concepts of "nursey/nursemaid" and iceman). Ask the children to brainstorm a list of solutions to the problem. Acknowledge all reasonable solutions as possibilities. Make a list.

- Read the story as dePaola wrote it, revealing the solution he thought of for the problem. Then reread the book and finish it with an ending that the children originated. Write the ending if possible and put it on an overhead transparency for all to read. In another session reread the story once more and let the children choose the ending that they would like to have read to them: dePaola's or their own.

Elting, Mary, and Michael Folsom. *Q Is for Duck*. Illustrated by Jack Kent. Clarion, 1980. (Picture book)
This is a unique alphabet book that promotes reverse thinking. "Q is for Duck. Why? Because a duck quacks." The illustrations are a clever addition to this alphabet riddle book.

- As the book is read aloud, let the students participate by providing the finishing phrases for each letter's riddle. Discuss the critical attribute that each riddle focuses on. In other words, how did those listening know each riddle's answer? Make a list of other animals and things that have recognizable critical attributes.

- Make a transparency of the pattern page (see appendix A, p. 183). Use the pattern page to model the sentence structure that evolves from the brainstormed list of animals and things and their critical attributes. The modeling can encompass the entire alphabet, or each student or pair of students can be asked to complete a riddle for a specific letter of the alphabet.

- If the format page is used (see appendix A, p. 183), fold each page between the center black lines. When the sheet is folded, the blank side should be on the inside. Arrange the folded sheets in alphabetical order. Make one copy of the cover page (see appendix A, p. 182). Bind the cover sheet with the folded sheets to create a book.

- As with any "book publishing" project this is a good time to discuss such things as cover, spine, title page, author, title, and publisher.

Ets, Marie Hall. *In the Forest: Story and Pictures*. Illustrated by Marie Hall Ets. Viking, 1976. (Picture book)
A little girl walks into the forest.

- Use the pattern of the story to write a similar imaginary walk—anywhere. Tell who follows you and what each of you takes along. Visit storyland, outer space, dinosaurland, or Africa.

Folsom, Marcia, and Michael Folsom. *Easy as Pie: A Guessing Game of Sayings*. Illustrated by Jack Kent. Clarion, 1985.
From "Straight as an Arrow" to "Tough as Nails" to "Shy as a Violet," this book contains 26 familiar sayings that make comparisons. There is a saying for each letter of the alphabet.

- Before using this book students should be introduced to some of the old sayings that their parents or grandparents might use. Give students some examples such as "wise as an owl," "light as a feather," and "old as the hills." Encourage students to interview their parents and to write down some of the sayings that are used in their family.

- In class, share the sayings gathered from the family interviews. Discuss the sayings and their meanings.

- After reading *Easy as Pie*, write an original alphabet book of sayings. The pattern is simple: _____ as _____ . The last blank will contain a word that begins with each letter of the alphabet. The class could brainstorm and write the new book as a group exercise, or individuals or pairs of students could concentrate on a specific letter.

- Correlate this writing with a class activity called "Old Proverbs Made New" (see appendix A, p. 184). Have some fun developing some new proverbs. Individual students or small groups might work with their own copies of the "Old Proverbs Made New" sheet, or a transparency of the sheet can be used to write the "new" proverbs as a class activity.

Gackenbach, Dick. *Mag, the Magnificent*. Illustrated by Dick Gackenbach. Clarion, 1985. (Picture book)

After putting on his "magical" suit, a boy hears a strange voice that says, "Draw me on your wall." The boy draws Mag, the Magnificent, a magical dragon. The dragon is able to carry out the boy's wishes and turns everything into chocolate; she also eats all the asparagus in the store so there won't be any left for the boy's mom to buy.

- Make a list of the wishes you would ask Mag to grant you.

- Describe your dragon (draw her if you wish) and tell where you would hide the dragon so that your mother or father would not find her.

Galdone, Paul. *The Teeny Tiny Woman: A Ghost Story*. Illustrated by Paul Galdone. Clarion, 1984. (Picture book). O'Connor, Jane. *The Teeny Tiny Woman*. Illustrated by Tomie dePaola. Random, 1986. (A Step into Reading book: Step 1; early reader)

The little old woman finds a bone and takes it home and puts it away. When she attempts to go to bed, a small wee voice demands, "Give me back my bone." Each time the demand is made the voice is somewhat louder and more demanding.

- Use the verse and form of the story to parody the tale. Perhaps the old woman has found a "big toe" or a "lock of hair." And maybe the main character is an old man or a little girl.

- Determine appropriate sound effects for each episode of the story: a creaking cupboard door, shuffling feet across the floor, etc. Use the sound effects as the parody story is being reread.

Hamilton, Virginia. "A Wolf and Little Daughter." In *The People Could Fly: American Black Folktales*, illustrated by Leo Dillon and Diane Dillon. Knopf, 1985. (Collected stories)

A. Delaney's retelling of *The Gunnywolf* (Harper, 1988) and *Gunniwolf* by Wilhelminia Harper (Dutton, 1967) have many of the same story elements as "A Wolf and Little Daughter."

- Use the story pattern to write another tale about a little girl that goes off into the woods and meets a "wolf."

Hofmann, Ginnie. *Who Wants an Old Teddy Bear?* Illustrated by Ginnie Hofmann. Random, 1978. (Picture book)

When Andy receives a package in the mail and discovers that it is a teddy bear, he throws it down asking, "Who wants an old teddy bear?" Later that night his dreams reverse the situation when a bear asks, "Who wants an old boy?"

- Brainstorm a list of gifts that you were not especially happy to receive. Choose one of the gifts and tell about your reaction to that gift.

- Discuss the concept of other stories with favorite characters; read Hofmann's *The Runaway Teddy Bear* (Random, 1986).

Hutchins, Pat. *Good-Night, Owl!* Illustrated by Pat Hutchins. Macmillan, 1972. (Picture book)

The owl could not sleep because all the animals were making too much noise. Bees buzzed, robins peeped, and all of them kept the owl from sleeping. When night came, the owl screeched and woke up all the animals.

- Brainstorm a list of animals and the sounds they make. Rewrite the story and use the brainstormed list to include other animals.

Kellogg, Steven. *The Mysterious Tadpole*. Illustrated by Steven Kellogg. Dial, 1970.

When a little boy receives a special package for his birthday, from his uncle in Scotland, the boy is thrilled. The gift appears to be a tadpole. Eventually the "tadpole" grows and grows and grows. After several efforts to find a suitable home for the tadpole, a librarian helps the boy and the mysterious tadpole uncover some buried treasure. The treasure funds the building of a swimming pool that provides a home for the tadpole and a swimming spot for the neighborhood children. Next year, for his birthday, the boy receives an "egg" from his uncle.

- Draw a picture of what you think will hatch from the egg and then write about what happens when the egg hatches (see appendix A, p. 185).

L'Engle, Madeleine. *A Wrinkle in Time*. Farrar, 1962; Dell, 1964. (Novel)

Meg, her brother, Charles Wallace, and Calvin attempt to travel through space to locate and rescue Meg's father. They visit several planets, including Camazotz where IT controls all minds.

- Keep a diary of the time the characters spend on Camazotz.

Lionni, Leo. *Alexander and the Wind-Up Mouse*. Illustrated by Leo Lionni. Pantheon, 1969. (Picture book)

Alexander longs to be a wind-up mouse like Willy. He wishes to be treasured and loved as Willy is. But in the end it is Willy who changes, when he becomes a real mouse like Alexander.

- Pretend you found a purple pebble that turns you into a mechanical toy. Who owns you? What can you do when you are wound up? What adventures do you have? Will you ever get to be a real person again?

- Compare and contrast Lionni's story with William Steig's *Sylvester and the Magic Pebble*, illustrated by William Steig (Windmill, 1969), and with Lionni's *Let's Make Rabbits* (Pantheon, 1982).

Littledale, Freya. *The Magic Fish*. Illustrated by Winslow Pinney Pels. Scholastic, 1966. (Picture book)

A fisherman catches a magic fish that grants his wishes. His wife is not satisfied with what she gets and demands something bigger and better each time the fisherman returns. Finally, the fish grows tired of the demands and returns the couple to their original abode.

- Brainstorm lists of three progressively greater wishes, for example: a nice house, a mansion, and a castle; or a wading pool, a family-size pool, and an olympic-size swimming pool.

- Use the brainstormed list to rewrite a version of the magic fish story.

Marshall, James. *George and Martha Encore*. Illustrated by James Marshall. Houghton, 1973. (Picture book)

Martha really does like George and George likes Martha and that friendship results in some funny happenings.

- When we do something for others we show our friendship for them. List some examples of things you can do to show others that you care about them.

- Continue the discussion of friendship by reading Marshall's *George and Martha* (Houghton, 1972), *George and Martha Back in Town* (Houghton, 1984), *George and Martha One Fine Day* (Houghton, 1978), *George and Martha Rise and Shine* (Houghton, 1976), and *George and Martha, Tons of Fun* (Houghton, 1980).

Martin, Bill, Jr. *Polar Bear, Polar Bear, What Do You Hear?* Illustrated by Eric Carle. Holt, 1991.
"Polar Bear, Polar Bear, what do you hear? I hear a lion roaring in my ear." In a parade of animals, elephants trumpet, zebras bray, leopards snarl, walruses bellow, and lions ROAR.

- Make a card for each of the animals in the story. Each animal card should have the animal's picture on the card. The name of each animal might be added, as you wish. Read the story aloud. By the time the story is read a second time the children will join in as soon as the page is turned to reveal the new animal. Distribute the animal cards. Make duplicates so that each child can have an animal card. Read the story once again, but this time do not show the illustrations. Start the action by asking, "Polar Bear, Polar Bear, what do you hear?" Those holding the polar bear card should stand and respond, "I hear a lion roaring in my ear." Those children not standing will ask, "Lion, Lion, what do you hear?" The children with the lion cards should then stand and respond with the next phrase until the entire story is completed. This exercise helps strengthen young children's memory, but it can be used with children of any age to set the stage for writing a book with a similar pattern (see next suggestion).

- After the story grammar has been thoroughly internalized, ask the children to write a story using the same story grammar (pattern). If the children choose to illustrate their stories, they may want to add a title page and bind the book. (Illustrations could be made using a tissue paper collage technique as Carle did for the illustrations for Martin's book.)

- As a pre-activity to the preceding suggestion, the class may wish to generate a list of animals and the sounds the animals make.

- Follow the procedure for the two preceding activity suggestions, but specify that the characters in this story are certain types of people, such as a football player, a scuba diver, a baby, a toddler, a schoolteacher, a doctor, a grandmother, etc. List the way each of these people would say something. Write a story. For example, the story could start with, "Grandmother, Grandmother, what do you hear? I hear a baby boy cooing at me. Baby Boy, Baby Boy, what do you hear? I hear a doctor whispering in my ear." Continue in the same manner as the other story.

- An earlier book created by Martin and Carle could be used with comparable activities— *Brown Bear, Brown Bear, What Do You See?* by Bill Martin, Jr., and illustrated by Eric Carle (Holt, 1983; 1992).

Mayer, Mercer. *Frog Goes to Dinner*. Illustrated by Mercer Mayer. Dial, 1974. (Wordless picture book)
A frog hides in a boy's pocket when the boy and his family go out to dinner. Inside the restaurant the frog creates havoc, which results in the family being ejected from the restaurant. The boy and the frog appear to be dejected until they are alone in their bedroom, and then they burst into laughter. This book is available as a 12-minute video or 16mm film from Phoenix/Bfa (1985).

- There are 16 characters in this book. Choose a character and tell about the happenings in the restaurant and afterwards from that character's point of view.

Mayer, Mercer. *Hiccup*. Illustrated by Mercer Mayer. Dial, 1976. (Wordless picture book)
Two hippopotamuses go out on a picnic and ride in a rowboat. The male hippopotamus attempts to help the female get rid of her hiccups. He only succeeds in pushing her out of the boat.

- The story has only two characters. Tell the story from the male's point of view and then from the female's point of view. How do the stories differ?

Mayer, Mercer. *There's a Nightmare in My Closet*. Illustrated by Mercer Mayer. Dutton, 1968. (Picture book)
This is a popular tale about all the monsters a little boy imagines are in his closet.

- Write a paragraph or more describing the monster in your attic, in your closet, or under your bed.

- Correlate responses with Mercer Mayer's *There's an Alligator Under My Bed* (Dutton, 1987), *There's Something in My Attic* (Dutton, 1988), and Robert Crowe's *Clyde Monster* (Dutton, 1976).

Mayer, Mercer. *What Do You Do with a Kangaroo?* Illustrated by Mercer Mayer. Scholastic, 1987. (Picture book)
Everywhere there is an animal, an animal that does not belong. What does one do?

- Imagine going in to take a bath and finding an animal in your bathtub. What would you do? Read the book and create more episodes in which animals create havoc with your life.

Miller, Moira. *Oscar Mouse Finds a Home*. Illustrated by Maria Majewska. Dial, 1985. (Picture book)
When the attic where Oscar lives becomes too crowded with little brothers and sisters, he searches for a home of his own.

- Write about other places Oscar might go to find a place to live: a church belfry, a house attic, a basement workroom.

- Make a list of other animals and match the animals to the names of their homes: pig:sty, sheep:fold, horse:stable, cow:barn, etc.

Most, Bernard. *If the Dinosaurs Came Back*. Illustrated by Bernard Most. Harcourt, 1978. (Picture book)
Imagine if the dinosaurs really did return to the modern world. What would they do? Where would they go?

- Introduce the concept of imaginative roles and uses for animals by reading Shel Silverstein's *Who Wants a Cheap Rhinoceros?* (Macmillan, 1983).

- Brainstorm other uses for the rhinoceros.

- Read *If the Dinosaurs Came Back* and suggest that students brainstorm ideas for using dinosaurs (see appendix A, p. 186). They could illustrate their ideas if they wish.

Nerlove, Miriam. *I Meant to Clean My Room Today*. McElderry, 1988.
Many excuses are given in this book for not completing tasks. (Junior novel)

- Make a list of excuses you have used, or wished you had had the courage to use, for not cleaning your room, taking out the garbage, coming home on time, or getting your homework finished.

Peet, Bill. *Cyrus the Unsinkable Sea Monster*. Illustrated by Bill Peet. Houghton, 1975. (Picture book)
Cyrus, a giant sea serpent, looks like a large fearsome monster but is actually gentle and considerate. Cyrus has a series of adventures on the high seas.

- Make a chart of Cyrus's characteristics.

- Research and write about one of the "real" monsters: Big Foot, Abominable Snowman, Loch Ness Monster.

- Create another adventure for Cyrus.

Roberts, Willo Davis. *The Girl with the Silver Eyes*. Macmillan, 1980; Scholastic, 1985. (Novel)
Ten-year-old Katie has a special power, a power that all who have silver eyes possess. She can move an object by simply thinking about it.

- What special power would you like to have? What would you do with that power?

- Does ESP really exist?

Rockwell, Thomas. *How to Eat Fried Worms*. Illustrated by Emily McCully. Dell, 1973. (Novel)
Billy makes a bet that he can eat 15 worms in 15 days. His first problem is whether or not he can swallow the worm. But after he conquers that problem, other obstacles come into play.

- Create a recipe using worms as one of the ingredients.

- Produce a commercial advertisement for the book. Record the advertisement onto a cassette tape or a videotape and share it with other students who might like to read the book.

Williams, Vera B. *Three Days on a River in a Red Canoe*. Illustrated by Vera B. Williams. Greenwillow, 1981. (Picture book)
A mom takes her youngsters on a camping trip by canoe in this book full of adventure and fun.

- If your dad or mom were taking you on a camping trip, what would you need to take? Make a list.

- Correlate with Mercer Mayer's *Just Me and My Dad* (Golden, 1977).

Wright, Jill. *The Old Woman and the Jar of Uums*. Illustrated by Glen Rounds. Putnam, 1990. (Picture book)
Magic spells abound.

- What type of magic spell would you like a fairy to cast on you?

GOING BEYOND

Writing topics must come from the writer. Because students come to expect that they will be given time each day to write, they will begin to plan for topics they can use in their writing. They can record those topics in their writing folders, in the "Ideas for Writing" section.

Gathering Writing Ideas from Books

Books can play a major role in providing ideas for children's writings. For example, during several sessions in the library media center, we were reading versions of the Grimm Brothers' "The Wolf and the Seven Little Kids." We read versions illustrated by Felix Hoffman (Harcourt, n.d.) and Svend Otto (Larousse, 1977) and newer versions adapted by Tony Ross, *Mrs. Goat and Her Seven Little Kids* (Atheneum, 1990), and by Eric A. Kimmel, *Nanny Goat and the Seven Little Kids*, illustrated by Janet Stevens (Holiday, 1990). The story grammar in each of these stories is similar: The mother goat warns her seven kids not to let the wolf in (they would know him by his gruff voice and his black paws), but the wolf manages to trick the kids and he eats them up, all except the youngest, who stays hidden until his mother comes. The littlest goat tells his mother where the others are and she goes to rescue them. She finds the wolf sound asleep, cuts open his stomach to release the kids, fills his belly with stones and sews the opening shut. When the wolf attempts to quench his thirst, he falls in the well or the stream and is never seen again. In one version, the wolf eats up all the children and hides under the table and eats Mother Goat when she returns. Mother Goat has scissors and thread in her apron pocket so she is able to cut open the wolf's stomach from inside and release herself and all her seven children. Ross's version has Mother Goat butting the wolf until he coughs up all her kids. One final butt sends the wolf flying so far away that nobody ever sees him again.

After his class had discussed the story grammar and compared and contrasted the stories, one second-grader decided to write a penguin story. A classroom discussion of animals (specifically penguins) and the experience with the several versions of the Grimm story came together as he told the story of Mother Penguin going away for the day. She warns her baby penguin to watch out for the walrus, "You will know him by his gray coat." But the walrus comes and the penguin is tricked into coming too close to him. Before long the baby penguin finds himself inside the stomach of the walrus. Fortunately, his mother has given him a packet of sleeping powder, which he sprinkles in the walrus's stomach. "And before long the walrus was asleep and the penguin crawled out of his stomach through his throat."

After sharing Mary Elting's and Michael Folsom's *Q Is for Duck* (Clarion, 1980), several children began to write their own alphabet book patterned after the author's pattern: "**Q** is for Duck. Why? Because a duck quacks." When they came to the **F** page they wrote **F** is for Stanley. Why? Because Stanley is flat." They not only succeeded in writing an innovation on the text by Elting and Folsom, but they had also included one of their favorite books, *Flat Stanley* by Jeff Brown (Harper, 1964; Scholastic, 1972).

Student writers will garner information from the books they read, find writing patterns to mimic, and develop their own thought processes as they begin to create innovations on the text. Good books of literature will provide a link from the child's experience to their written work by helping them realize how much of one's own experience goes into writing of any type.

Writing ideas generated by picture books are often evident as books are shared and connections are made to other books. Students will generate many of their own adaptations or innovations on the text. Whenever an innovation or adaptation is made clear, credit should be given to the original text and author/illustrator. The rights inherent in the copyright law and the concept of plagiarism is appropriate for discussion with even the youngest student. Reading and sharing novels or information books can also generate ideas for writing that relate directly to those titles.

Discussions of the setting can lead to speculation about how the book's action would change if the setting were 100 years earlier or 100 years later. Those who particularly like a book might wish to write recommendations to others suggesting that they read the book. A reader might even wish to write a letter to a film producer suggesting that the book be considered as the basis of a film.

Writing to Authors and Illustrators

When books are shared and the author's writing or illustrator's technique and illustrations are discussed, there are often questions that arise that only the creator can answer. In those instances, a letter to the author or illustrator is a valuable experience. For example, during one class's viewing of the video *A Visit with Bill Peet* (Houghton Mifflin, 1989), the students noted that Peet said the Whingdingdilly was a combination of seven animals, but they could only count six. They looked at that segment of the tape several times, reread *The Whingdingdilly* (Houghton, 1970; 1982), but still could not come up with the seventh animal. The children discussed ways they could find out what the seventh animal was. After much discussion they decided that the only viable solution was to ask Mr. Peet himself. They wrote him a letter and promptly got a letter in return. The students found out that they had forgotten to count Scamp, the dog. The Whingdingdilly still had Scamp's eyes and brain. Peet pointed out that the Whingdingdilly still thought like Scamp would have thought. Writing a letter to the author is a viable activity as long as the question or comment is legitimate. Some authors, such as Beverly Cleary, deplore the attitude some children display when they write letters to authors.[7] Cleary mentions the demands made for free books, articles to be auctioned as prizes for reading, and dictates about what kind of answers they want to be given. She once received 31 pounds of mail in a single day. If she spent time answering all the mail personally, she would not have time to write. Teachers can help children prepare for writing letters to authors by discussing some of the following points, which were compiled after several discussions with authors who share some, if not all, of Cleary's concern about what we are teaching children.

Tips for Teachers—Writing an Author or Illustrator

1. Help students decide why the letter is being written. Is the question sincere? Is it a question that cannot be answered using standard reference sources? Is the purpose of the letter to pay the author/illustrator a compliment? These reasons are legitimate; however, if you wish to give students experience writing book reviews (positive or negative), do not assign the review to be sent to the author or illustrator. Instead, provide a forum for those reviews, such as a book review column in the school newspaper or a Friday book discussion group, but do not assume that authors and illustrators want to read assigned reviews.

2. Ask students to do their own research first. They should not ask general questions that can be obtained from the book flap or from standard information sources. A student who is interested enough in an author's or illustrator's work should be interested enough to learn the basics about the author/illustrator.

3. Suggest to students that they use the same polite manners they would use with friends in a "formal" social situation. Do not ask for handouts: books, mementos, etc. Do not make demands or ask questions that would not normally be considered polite.

---

[7] Beverly Cleary. "Dear Author, Answer This Letter Now...." *Instructor* (November/December 1985): 22-23, 25.

4. Some authors/illustrators deplore the "write an author" assignment. Others feel that such an assignment is acceptable. If you decide to make the assignment, it is best to do so after a special focus on that author's work. Write a class letter, or if individual letters are written, include them in a single manila envelope with a cover letter from you explaining the focus and the assignment. If students are selecting individual authors/illustrators to whom to write, make sure that each student selects a personal favorite author or illustrator. And, of course, the student should have read one or more of the author's or illustrator's books.

5. Do not offer special grades or bonuses for those students who get a reply. Whether or not the student writer receives an answer has nothing to do with the student.

6. If you have the home address of the author/illustrator, you certainly may send the letter there; otherwise, enclose the letter in an envelope ready for the publisher's representative to complete the address and put that envelope in another envelope addressed to the attention of the "Publicist/Books for Children and Young Adults" at the company that published one of the author's or illustrator's most recent works. It is best to enclose a cover letter indicating that you would like the address completed and the envelope sent on to the author or illustrator.

7. Always include a self-addressed stamped envelope for the author's or illustrator's use in case he or she wishes to reply.

8. Remember that deceased authors have also made important contributions to the body of literature. Young readers should be encouraged to read good books of all periods, not just books that have an author/illustrator to whom they can write.

It is important to determine if a book creator is still living before writing the letter. Standard research books such as the Author a Month and Bookpeople titles from Libraries Unlimited and the Something About the Author series from Gale Research, and the series Junior Authors and Illustrators (the sixth volume was published in 1989) published by H. W. Wilson can provide information. But if the particular author/illustrator is not listed, or if the material is more than a year or two old, then you must look further. A letter of inquiry to the publisher (Attn: Publicity— Children's Books) could be sent. Publishers often have author or illustrator brochures available and will supply them if a return self-addressed stamped envelope is included with the inquiry. It is best to send a manila envelope, 5 by 7 inches or 8 by 10 inches, so that any brochures returned do not have to be folded.

In addition to writing letters to the author or publisher, students can learn much about the writing process and about putting real-life incidents into their written work by learning and writing about the author. Putting oneself in the place of the author helps the reader analyze the types of books that author has written and the aspects of the author's life that have become part of his or her work. Mavis Jukes, for example, writes about blended families—families mending after divorce, the arrival of a new stepparent, or the death of a grandparent. She has been part of many of the experiences that she writes about. She tells about those experiences in a videotape from Walt Disney, *Writing Progress with Mavis Jukes*.[8] A written (or oral) presentation about the author or illustrator and the bits and pieces of that person's life that are found in his or her work can help students understand that their own lives have bits and pieces that they might use in their own writing.

---

[8]Walt Disney Educational Media Company, distributed by Coronet/MTI Film and Video, 420 Academy Drive, Northbrook, IL 60062.

Researching a Topic

A major component of writing is the research necessary to accurately write about a topic. Some books clearly show that the author has done much research in order to produce the book. Students who have information about such research activities might be more motivated to research a topic and write about it. Assignments asking students to create sequels to stories, additional chapters for books, and even complete books must be viewed as long-term assignments. These assignments must be framed in the context of prior experience, and ample time must be provided to allow students to work through the process of writing: researching, creating a draft, reading and revising, editing, and creating the final manuscript.

Research is generally accepted as part of writing a book intended to give information, but research is equally important in writing books of fiction. The information on the book flap of *Ashanti to Zulu: African Traditions* by Margaret Musgrove (Dial, 1976) describes the "exhaustive research covering the thousands of details [Leo Dillon and Diane Dillon] have shown in their paintings." Research for a fiction book, *San Domingo, The Medicine Hat Stallion* (Rand, 1972; Aladdin, 1992), is discussed by Marguerite Henry in a 16-minute 16mm film, *The Story of a Book* (Pied Piper, 1979). Henry tells about receiving a letter from a young boy whose horse had been sold by his father and how that first letter evolved into a book idea that grew and changed as she changed the setting to protect the boy's identity. She eventually came to research the Pony Express in order to put the boy in an interesting context. Her research took her from her home in Rancho Santa Fe to the Huntington Library in San Marino, California, where she read dozens of diaries—first-hand accounts of westward treks that took place in the 1850s. She and the book's illustrator, Robert Lougheed, traveled back along the Oregon Trail, through Nevada territory, through Utah and the vast territory of Nebraska to the starting point of St. Joseph, Missouri. Along the way she gathered ideas for her characters and organized her chapters in folders; then, after months of research she sat down to write the book.

James and Christopher Collier discuss the research and writing of their books in a filmstrip/cassette, *Meet the Newbery Author: James and Christopher Collier* (American School Publishers, 1981).

* * *

The role of teacher is not to assign products to be created based on the reading of books but rather to serve as encourager and facilitator. In the role of encourager, the teacher will seize opportunities to encourage students to write and will suggest ways to make connections between the students' reading and their writing.

Chapter

3

Literature in Math or Vice Versa

Better that a small child should read Hans Andersen than worry his little brain over nine plus seven.

—Anonymous, National Education Conference, 1898

USING BOOKS AS SPRINGBOARDS

Whatever the sentiment of the 1890s, today's child is encouraged to read Hans Christian Andersen *and* to know the sum of nine plus seven. Sometimes both reading literature and learning mathematical concepts may be combined to bring both into the learner's life. Using appropriate literature within diverse subject matter provides a context for viewing, manipulating, and evaluating a tremendous range of experiences. Books provide situation-specific references that correspond to a student's life experiences. Many thinking skills and coping abilities are developed and practiced vicariously as literature is read for enjoyment and skill development. And in the case of literature in mathematics classes, it will serve to stimulate young learners to explore and manipulate mathematical concepts. Books can be springboards to motivating an interest in any content area, but the availability of suggestions for using books of literature to introduce mathematical concepts has been somewhat more limited than the availability of books to use in science and social studies integration schemes. In the past, writers have presented books that correlate nicely with science activities,[1] and writers of social studies textbooks frequently include references to biographies and informational books that can be correlated with subject matter within those textbooks. Resource books that focus on integrating social studies and literature are also more available.[2] Resource books that addresses

---

[1]One excellent source is *Science Through Children's Literature: An Integrated Approach* by Carol M. Butzow and John W. Butzow (Englewood, CO: Teacher Ideas Press, 1989).

[2]Three sources that will provide some model social studies activities are *Adventures with Social Studies (Through Literature)* by Sharron L. McElmeel (Englewood, CO: Teacher Ideas Press, 1991), *Social Studies Readers Theatre for Children* by Mildred Knight Laughlin, Peggy Tubbs Black, and Margery Kirby Loberg (Englewood, CO: Libraries Unlimited, 1991), and *Teaching Social Studies Through Children's Literature* by Anthony R. Fredericks (Englewood, CO: Teacher Ideas Press, 1992).

the use of literature in conjunction with mathematics are less available, suggesting that the integration of literature with mathematics is more elusive. There are, however, several possibilities for integrating literature with mathematics.

Trade books will not replace the mathematics textbook, nor will trade books actually teach the concepts that are important to the mathematical development of students. But they will play an important role in extending and enhancing the understanding of mathematical concepts. Many trade books can be used to motivate and stimulate interest in a concept.

Some of the books that can be used in conjunction with mathematical activities are general in nature, but others are relevant to a specific concept. Among the more general titles is Mitsumasa Anno's *Anno's Math Games* (Philomel, 1982). Anno has addressed the concept of one, comparison and classification, sets, combinations, mixtures, addition, subtraction, multiplication classification, sequence, position, ordinal numbers as contrasted with cardinal or set numbers, and several other math-related topics. The book has a section on tangrams and shapes. Since the first book, Anno has written two similar books, *Anno's Math Games II* (Philomel, 1990) and *Anno's Math Games III* (Philomel, 1991). All three provide stimulation for a varied array of mathematical activities. Another title in this general category is Marilyn Burns's *The I Hate Mathematics! Book* (Little, Brown, 1975). The book is filled with riddles that address probability, logic, time/measurement, the concept of dozen, and many other mathematical functions. Other books in this category include *Math Teasers: Mental Gymnastics* by Robert Muller (Sterling, 1989) and *Math for Smarty Pants* by Marilyn Burns (Little, Brown, 1983). And there are many books that can introduce or deal with specific concepts.

GETTING STARTED

Mathematical objectives for student learning are often written in terms of specific concepts. Organizing files using a standard list of concepts should facilitate coordinating the books and response suggestions with specific objectives within a district's prescribed curriculum. To facilitate identifying and discussing books that deal with a specific concept, titles have been grouped according to the following ten mathematical concepts.

Ten Mathematical Concepts

I.   Numbers and Enumeration

II.   Place Value

III.   Shapes

IV.   Addition and Subtraction

V.   Multiplication and Division

VI.   Telling Time

VII.   Probability, Estimation, Prediction

VIII. Fractions and Decimals

IX.   Measurement

X.   Money

CONNECTIONS TO MAKE—A SAMPLER

Concept I: Numbers and Enumeration

Numbers by definition are symbols or words that are used in counting or that tell how many or which one in a series. Enumeration, sometimes numeration, is the act or process of counting or naming one by one.

Some books are filled with many possibilities for counting activities. Mitsumasa Anno has created a book, *Anno's Counting Book* (HarperCollins, 1977), that is filled with numerical concepts. The basic book shows objects representing the numbers **0** to **12**. Each page has sets of objects and things in the appropriate number. On the left-hand side of the page the number is further emphasized by the use of building blocks depicting the focus number. The page depicting **1** is a January snow scene: one cloud, one crow, one snow-covered cedar tree, one sun, one house, one child beside one snowman (holding a flag with the numeral **1** on it), one bridge, one stream, one fox, etc. The page depicting **2** is a snow scene with patches of brown ground, two cedar trees, two children playing on the hill, two rabbits running, two trucks and two drivers, and two buildings. The

house from the **1** page has been joined by a church with a clock tower showing the time as 2:00, and the bridge now is spanned by a road that forks to make two roads. The **3** page continues in a similar vein: the church clock tower records the time as 3:00, groups of flowers sprout in bunches of threes, three canoes float down the stream, a stone house has been added to make three buildings in the scene, three people are in the picture, and three butterflies flutter above the hillside. By the time the pictures get to the numeral **10**, the colors are those of autumn, the building blocks have reached the top (concept of tens), and on the very next page (11) a second stack of blocks has to be started to the right of the first stack. The final double-page spread depicts **12**, and the scene shows snow falling. Twelve reindeer are flying above twelve buildings, eleven adults stand in front of the church, and the twelfth adult is crossing the bridge with twelve children on their way toward the church tower. The clock shows that the time is 12:00. Because of the positioning of characters and objects, some number problems can be constructed. For example: Eleven adults by the church plus one on the bridge equals twelve ($11 + 1 = 12$), or twelve adults less one standing with the children equals eleven by the church ($12 - 1 = 11$). Houses show appropriate numbers of openings. Six windows on one side plus five on the other side plus one door equals twelve ($6 + 5 + 1 = 12$), or twelve openings less one door equals eleven windows ($12 - 1 = 11$). Each page holds possibilities for similar numeric equations.

Other counting books are plentiful; some count up, some count down, and some count up and down. One nursery verse, "Roll Over," has been used in a variety of forms to provide exercises in subtraction. Some of the variations provide other elements that might be used in other ways. Merle Peek's *Roll Over! A Counting Song* (Clarion, 1981) is fairly standard. Mordicai Gerstein's *Roll Over!* (Crown, 1984) provides a countdown verse that has ten different animals rolling out (falling out) of bed: Papa Pig, Mama Mouse, Brother Beaver, Sister Seal, Aunt Alligator, Uncle Unicorn, Grandpa Goat, Grandma Goose, Cousin Camel. When the one boy is left alone in bed, he turns out the lights and settles down to sleep on the tenth pillow on the bed. But the next double-page spread shows that all the other animals have crawled back into the little boy's extra-wide bed from the other side. The last page has the animals (and the boy) all settled down in the bed; the spread shows only ten bumps in the bed. Stan Mack's *Ten Bears in My Bed: A Goodnight Countdown* (Pantheon, 1974) uses the verse with ten bears, but in Mack's version instead of falling out as the animals do in Gerstein's book, each of the bears has its own unique method for

getting out of the bed. The first bear "flew out"; the second one "galloped out"; and the subsequent bears "skated out," "roared out," "chugged out," "jumped out," "bounced out," "pedaled out," "tootled out," and finally "rumbled out."

So, in addition to the obvious countdown and subtraction aspect of the Gerstein and Mack books, the Gerstein book lends itself to a focus on alliteration, a literary device. That book not only counts down but can also serve as an exercise to create a list of other alliterative names that can be used to retell the "roll over" story. The Mack book can be used to focus on verbs. A list of verbs can be generated that can then be used to retell a version of the rhyme.

Aker, Suzanne. *What Comes in Twos, Threes, and Fours?* Illustrated by Bernie Karlin. Simon, 1990.
This book introduces the numbers **2**, **3**, and **4** by linking them to common objects.

- The concept in this book can be used to build another book identifying objects that come in fives, tens, twelves (a dozen), etc. Begin by brainstorming a list of objects that usually come in pairs; for example, shoes, stockings, mittens, earplugs. Then make other lists for dozens, and then list other objects and the number of items usually found in the unit. Drinking glasses are frequently purchased in boxes of eight. Dinner dishes often are sold in sets of four.

- Extend the concept of pairs by reading Bruce McMillan's photo essay, *One, Two, One Pair!* (Scholastic, 1991). In this book readers will count and match to find pair after pair: red socks, blue shoelaces, yellow mittens, and others.

- This book could also be used with Concept V, Multiplication and Division. As the lists are generated, multiplication problems could also be generated. For example, how many shoes would we have in ten pairs?

Aylesworth, Jim. *One Crow: A Counting Rhyme*. Illustrated by Ruth Young. Lippincott, 1988.

Beginning with **0** and counting to **10**, Aylesworth uses a verse enumerating various animals and their actions during the winter season; he then varies the verse to depict the same ten animals during the summer.

- Write the enumeration verse for autumn and for spring.

- Write another counting book using other animals. The counting phrases could include only the number and the animal, using the picture to depict the season of the year.

Bang, Molly. *Ten, Nine, Eight*. Illustrated by Molly Bang. Greenwillow, 1983.

Seashells, shoes, and other objects are included in the items counted in this countdown to bedtime until at last it is just one big girl ready for bed.

- Create your own bedtime countdown. Include rituals you include in your nighttime routine.

Base, Graeme. *The Eleventh Hour: A Curious Mystery*. Illustrated by Graeme Base. Abrams, 1988.

This intriguing mystery book shows a mystery involving eleven animals who have an eleventh birthday party for one of the animals. The book abounds with visual plays on numbers and words.

- Find all the occurrences of **11** within the book. Make a list of the "eleven" things.

- Each page has a specific number of hidden mice within the pages. Somewhere on each page is a numeral within a circle—this is the number of mice that one should be able to find in the picture.

Calmenson, Stephanie. *Dinner at the Panda Palace*. Illustrated by Nadine Bernard Westcott. HarperCollins, 1991.

An interesting group of patrons arrive at Panda's restaurant, from one elephant to a mother hen and her nine chicks. The final guest, a tiny mouse, makes 56 guests dining happily at the Panda Palace.

- Count the guests as they arrive; add as they arrive.

- Write about another day at the Panda Palace, this time including other interesting patrons in varying combinations of numbers, to total 56.

Christelow, Eileen. *Five Little Monkeys Sitting in a Tree*. Illustrated by Eileen Christelow. Clarion, 1991.

Mama Monkey and her five little monkeys take a walk down by the river for a picnic supper. While the little monkeys climb a tree, Mama takes a nap, and the monkeys tease the crocodile from the tree. "Can't catch me!" they tease, but Mr. Crocodile is undaunted as he snaps his mouth, leaving only four little monkeys swinging from the tree. A countdown book with surprise reappearances.

- Write the numerical equations that represent the action in the counting story. The first equations will subtract; the final equations will add.

- Read Christelow's earlier books about five little monkeys, *Five Little Monkeys Jumping on the Bed* (Clarion, 1989) and *Don't Wake Up Mama! Another Five Little Monkeys Story* (Clarion, 1992).

Coats, Laura Jane. *Ten Little Animals*. Illustrated by Laura Jane Coats. Macmillan, 1990.

A creative variation of the "roll over" verse. A small boy's toy animals tumble from the bed, bump their heads, and are comforted. Illustrations are gentle watercolors that make this book a calm book for laptime reading.

- Use the verse for the obvious counting and countdown activities.

- Compare and contrast this title with the variations of the verse by Mordicai Gerstein, Stan Mack, and Merle Peek.

- Draw your own illustration of ten animals (real or stuffed) in your bed.

Crews, Donald. *Ten Black Dots*. Illustrated by Donald Crews. Scribner, 1968; rev. ed., Greenwillow, 1986.

In this counting book and book of simple rhymes using everyday objects, the central question is: "What can you do with ten black dots?"

- Make your own version of Ten Dots. Think of new ideas for each set of dots **1-10**. Draw the illustrations and bind your pages into a book.

Dunbar, Joyce. *Ten Little Mice*. Illustrated by Maria Majewska. Harcourt, 1990.

Ten furry mice cavort in the country fields and then one-by-one take leave of the group and head homeward to a cozy nest. The full-color illustrations have an old-fashioned look.

- Write story problems reflecting the action in the book.

- Make mice-shaped bookmarks. Ask each student with a bookmark to visit the school library media center, use the catalog, and locate a book about mice (fiction or nonfiction). Write the name of the book and author on the bookmark. Either use the bookmark as a bookmark or display the bookmarks on a "Count the mice—Read a book" bulletin board.

Feelings, Muriel. *Moja Means One: Swahili Counting Rhymes*. Illustrated by Tom Feelings. Dial, 1971.

This book depicts rural Africa. Swahili number words are defined in English. Sepia-tone pencil drawings are effectively used.

- Learn to count in another language. Invite a parent who speaks a second language (or a primary language other than English) to help students learn to count to **10** in that language. If there are no parents or grandparents who can be invited, perhaps a high school foreign language student would visit your classroom.

Grossman, Virginia. *Ten Little Rabbits*. Chronicle, 1991.

Native-American costumes are worn by these charming rabbits as they share ten Native-American customs. Among the groups enumerated are five storytellers, eight fishermen, and ten sleeping weavers. In a final scene all ten rabbits come back wrapped in tribal blankets so that each of the distinctive designs can be enjoyed once more. Notes at the back of the book provide background on customs of ten tribes: Sioux, Tewa, Ute, Menominee, Blackfeet, Hopi, Arapaho, Nez Percé, Kwakiutl, and Navajo. Each tribe is represented in the text and illustrations.

- List the customs depicted in the book (weaving, fishing, storytelling, etc.) and collect more information about each of the traditions or lifestyles that surround the custom. Use the encyclopedia and books about Native Americans.

- Discuss various types of patterns. Use graph paper to create your own special blanket pattern.

- This title has been cited as presenting stereotypes about "Indians." Members of the American Library Subcommittee for Library Services to American Indian People reviewed the book with these observations: "Although the illustrations are beautiful, the messages conveyed are confusing. Each page shows the rabbits/Indians dressed in the manner of a different tribe, but this isn't explained until the end of the book, as an afterword. The impression given is one of generic "Indianness," and once again animals "become" Indians simply by putting on certain articles of clothing, relegating an entire race to the status of a role or profession." Discuss this book in relation to these comments.

Hayes, Sarah. *Nine Ducks Nine*. Illustrated by Sarah Hayes. Lothrop, 1990.

Nine ducks, each cunning and energetic, leaves the group one-by-one in an effort to lure a fox down to a rickety bridge where they outwit him and trick him into going away.

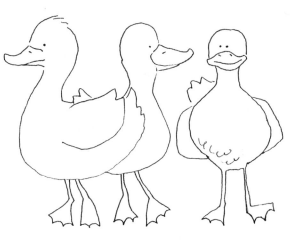

- Make a transparency of the endpapers showing the map of the fields, the rolling hills, the fence, the stream, and the rickety bridge. Use the map to show the route each duck takes to the rickety bridge.

- Use the text to generate number sentences.

- Make a fox puppet and nine duck stick puppets. Use them against a backdrop (created on a length of brown or colored butcher paper) to act out the action in the book.

Katz, Michael Jay, selector. *Ten Potatoes in a Pot: And Other Counting Rhymes*. Illustrated by June Otani. HarperCollins, 1990.

Jumping rope rhymes, finger games, and counting jingles are short and easily memorized.

- Try jumping rope to one of the rhymes.

- Create your own versions of the rhymes using the pattern or patterns in one of the rhymes.

Concept II: Place Value

Understanding place value involves understanding the value of each of the digits making up a number: ones, tens, hundreds, thousands, etc. Dr. Seuss's *The 500 Hats of Bartholomew Cubbins* is my favorite to focus on the hundreds concept, although there are several others that can be used to introduce the concept of numbers in the hundreds, thousands, etc.

Estes, Eleanor. *The Hundred Dresses*. Harcourt, 1974.

A young girl shows up in school each day in the same dress, all the while telling her classmates that she has a hundred dresses at home. Of course, the children do not believe her and do not treat her very kindly. When the girl abruptly leaves school, the others find that she really does have a hundred dresses—paper dresses for her paper dolls. This book will make a good read-aloud for late primary or older students.

- The primary theme of this book has to do with kindness toward our fellow human beings. Any use of this book should be preceded by a discussion of its real focus: the treatment of the girl by her classmates.

- Have the class make a total of 100 paper dresses. Students should first determine how many each student will have to make if each makes an equal number?

- Display the hundred dresses made by the students (group them by tens) to help advertise the book to other readers.

Gág, Wanda. *Millions of Cats*. Illustrated by Wanda Gág. Coward, 1928.

In this classic tale, more cats and more cats arrive until millions and millions of cats arrive at the house of the old man and woman.

- How many groups of ten would make a million cats? How many groups in a hundred? How many groups of ten in a thousand? Make a graph showing 5 million cats, 10 million, etc. How many cats will one cat on the graph represent?

- Is it realistic to think that one couple could actually have a million cats? Why or why not? (Note: How much cat food would a million cats eat on any one day?)

- Build on the concept of a million by using other books focusing on that number. Use David M. Schwartz's *How Much Is a Million?* illustrated by Steven Kellogg (Lothrop, 1985) and Bernice Myers's *The Millionth Egg* (Lothrop, 1991).

Hoberman, Mary Ann. *A House Is a House for Me*. Illustrated by Betty Fraser. Viking, 1978.

Sets of objects within each illustration depict various types of homes. In one double-page spread, characters and objects from Lewis Carroll's *Alice in Wonderland* are part of the illustration.

- List the sets that are found on each page (and note the number of objects in each set). Group the sets into groups of tens. How many sets are depicted in the entire book?

- How many objects are in each set? What is the total number of objects in all the sets? What is the average number of objects in each set?

- Tally the different kinds of houses that the class identifies.

- Brainstorm other types of houses.

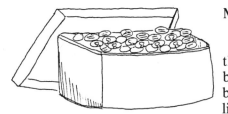

Mathis, Sharon Bell. *The Hundred Penny Box*. Illustrated by Leo Dillon and Diane Dillon. Viking, 1975.

A young child and a hundred-year-old woman talk about the memories brought about by the woman's hundred penny box. For each year of her life she has put one penny into the box. Each penny represents an episode or a memory from her life.

- Make your own penny box and put in it one penny for every year of your age. Try to obtain pennies dated with the years that correspond to the years of your life. Write a paragraph or two about a special memory or episode from each year of your life.

- Use a hundred pennies for math activities—for adding, subtracting, grouping in sets, etc. If actual pennies are not available to use, use cardboard facsimiles.

- Collect family stories. Other books that might be used in conjunction with building a collection of family stories is Deborah Kogan Ray's *My Daddy Was a Soldier: A World War II Story* (Holiday, 1990) and Kathryn O. Galbraith's *Laura Charlotte*, illustrated by Floyd Cooper (Philomel, 1990).

Seuss, Dr. *The 500 Hats of Bartholomew Cubbins.* Vanguard, 1938; Random, 1988.

Bartholomew, a boy from the cranberry bog, happens to be in town when the king and his entourage are passing. Bartholomew attempts to remove his hat in respect, but each time he removes one hat, another one takes its place. One of the king's men takes Bartholomew to the castle, where the king and his court attempt to use every means possible to remove the simple one-feathered hat from Bartholomew's head. As a last resort, Bartholomew is to be thrown from the top of one of the castle's turrets. On the way up the steps, Bartholomew frantically removes hat after hat. Each hat that appears is more and more glorious, until the 500th hat remains. The king buys that hat, paying Bartholomew gold for it. Bartholomew returns home to the family cranberry bog with enough money to help his family.

- Encourage students to participate as the book is read aloud. They might help count the hats as Bartholomew is removing them and mimic the process of taking off the hats one-by-one. As each ten hats are counted, ask a student to stand in a line. When the first hundred hats are counted, ask one child to move over to the hundredths place. The tens would need to sit down until another ten were counted, and then when ten tens are counted, they can be replaced by a second hundred. To solidify the connection ask students to stand in a row representing the value of the numbers.

- After the first 250 hats or so are removed, each hat becomes somewhat fancier than the original, until finally the 500th hat is very brilliant, colorful, and decorated with many fancy jewels. Make a list of the hats (by number) showing the relationship between the number of the hat and its decorations. See what if any pattern can be identified.

- Categorize the various hats by hundreds. How does the 100th, 200th, 300th, 400th, and 500th hat compare with the others? Do they follow the pattern?

- Tally the hats as Bartholomew removes them from his head.

- Write a hat adventure for a modern-day Bartholomew.

- Write a newspaper account of Bartholomew's hat episode. Be sure to include who, what, when, and where. Newspaper articles are usually written with the most important parts of the story in the beginning paragraphs so that if cuts need to be made for late-breaking news, the last paragraphs of the story can be chopped off without destroying the sense of the story.

- Write the story of the 500 hats with *Betsy* Cubbins as the heroine. Perhaps it was a curtsey that was causing the problem.

Concept III: Shapes

Shapes are the way things look because of their outline—their outer form. Some common shapes that are traditionally part of mathematical studies include circles, triangles, squares, and rectangles. Recognizing shapes helps students build a schematic background for the study of geometry and other related mathematical disciplines. Activities that encourage learners to identify shapes in their own environment, and other activities using tangrams, can emphasize the relationships between shapes.

Hoban, Tana. *Circles, Triangles, and Squares*. Macmillan, 1974; *Shapes and Things*. Macmillan, 1970.

Tana Hoban is noted for her photographic investigative books focusing on concepts and objects.

- Use photographs to emphasize the shapes of things in everyday life. After sharing Hoban's books, begin a search for specific shapes in the classroom, house, school, etc. Record the objects that include the targeted shape.

- If possible, take photographs of "circles, triangles, and squares" or of "shapes and things."

- List all the objects that have circle components, triangular components, square components, etc.

Paul, Ann Whitford. *Eight Hands Round: A Patchwork Alphabet*. Illustrated by Jeanette Winter. HarperCollins, 1991.

Twenty-six American patchwork quilt patterns are shown. Each pattern introduces a letter of the alphabet and explains the origin of the design, including whether it was based on an event, activity, or object.

- Use this book to motivate students to create original quilt patterns. Provide graph paper with 1-inch squares to help them develop their patterns. The patterns can range from a simple alternating of colors to more intricate designs.

- Incorporate other quilt books during the focus on patterns and shapes (see the list below). Some books use the pattern of the quilt as an element in the story, whereas others show quilts in the illustrations. The patterns shown in the quilts can serve as examples of patterns and designs that can be made using shapes.

Quilt Books

Chorao, Kay. *Kate's Quilt*. Dutton, 1982.

Coerr, Eleanor. *The Josefina Story Quilt*. Harper-Collins, 1986.

Daly, Niki. *Joseph's Red Sock*. Atheneum, 1982.

Ernst, Lisa Campbell. *Sam Johnson and the Blue Ribbon Quilt*. Lothrop, 1983.

Flournoy, Valerie. *The Patchwork Quilt*. Illustrated by Jerry Pinkney. Dial, 1985.

Martin, Jacqueline Briggs. *Bizzy Bones and the Lost Quilt*. Illustrated by Stella Ormai. Lothrop, 1988.

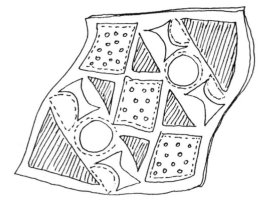

Moncure, Jane Belk. *My "Q" Sound Box*. Children's, 1979.

Moore, Clement C. *The Night Before Christmas*. Illustrated by Tomie dePaola. Holiday, 1980.

Vincent, Gabrielle. *Ernest and Celestine's Patchwork Quilt*. Greenwillow, 1982.

Willard, Nancy. *The Mountains of Quilts*. Illustrated by Tomie dePaola. Harcourt, 1987.

- Use crayons or felt-tip markers to create a pattern on 1-inch graph paper. Put the patterns together to make a paper quilt banner. Discuss the repetitive patterns of 1-2-1-2 and the 1-2-3-1-2-3 patterns. As this exercise is repeated, the patterns will become more and more complex.

- Integrate math patterning activities with an activity creating advertisements for favorite books. Make a miniposter for a favorite book on a 6-x-6-inch square of paper. Affix the miniposter in the center of one of the patterned graph pages to create book advertising poster with a patterned border. A quilt-patterned border is shown in dePaola's illustrated version of *The Night Before Christmas* and in Lisa Campbell Ernst's *Sam Johnson and the Blue Ribbon Quilt*.

- Use the book advertising posters created in the previous activity to form a paper banner; hang the banner in the hallway or stairwell to advertise books and to display the varied patterns created by students.

Silverstein, Shel. "Shapes." In *A Light in the Attic*. HarperCollins, 1981.
This poem can be used to focus on the shapes that will be studied in mathematics class.

- Correlate the study of shapes with the reading of some of the following books that use shapes as an element in the story.

Shape Books

Chermayeff, Ivan, and Jane Clark Chermayeff. *First Shapes: Premières Formes, Primeras Formas, Erste Formen, Prime Forme*. Abrams, 1991.

Ehlert, Lois. *Color Farm*. Illustrated by Lois Ehlert. HarperCollins, 1990.

Goor, Nancy, and Ron Goor. *Shadows, Here, There, and Everywhere*. Crowell, 1981.

Hutchins, Pat. *Changes, Changes*. Illustrated by Pat Hutchins. Greenwillow, 1971.

Kuskin, Karla. *Square as a House*. HarperCollins, 1960.

Stephen, Oliver, photographer. *My First Look at Shapes*. Random, 1990.

Tompert, Ann. *Grandfather Tang's Story: A Tale Told with Tangrams*. Crown, 1990.
Tompert successfully combines the use of shapes to make shapes with a narrative that tells a story. The author's notes at the end of the book explain the origin of the tangrams and the specific shape that a tangram takes.

- Use a transparency of the tangram chart (see appendix A, p. 187). Make the transparency from colored transparency stock or use a permanent transparency marker to color in the tangram shapes so that the shapes project clearly on the overhead. To demonstrate the manner in which the shapes can be combined to create other images, cut apart the pieces and create animal shapes on the overhead.

- Encourage students to experiment with tangram shapes. Allow them to use the overhead tangram and individual paper or cardboard tangrams at their desks or workstations.

- Use the shapes the students make to create the illustration for a group or individual tangram story.

- One section of *Anno's Math Games* (Philomel, 1982) uses tangrams to show how different animals can be created. Use Anno's book in conjunction with these tangram activities.

Concept IV: Addition and Subtraction

Addition is the adding of numbers to get a sum or total. Subtraction is the reverse operation—the act of taking away, as a part from a whole or one number from another. Many of the books in the section dealing with Concept I: Numbers and Enumeration could be utilized for creating addition and subtraction equations based on the cumulative effect of the characters' actions.

Anno, Mitsumasa. *Anno's Counting House*. Philomel, 1982.
Ten children are shown in a cutaway of the inside of a house. The children are going to move, one at a time, to a house on the other side of the street. The second house is also shown in a cutaway. Each time one of the children moves, he or she takes something along for the new house.

- Use the various illustrations to compose equations to determine how many children are still in the first house and how many have moved. Add equations representing the objects they take, etc.

- On a large sheet of butcher paper print all the equations that can be derived from the action in the story. Show that each equation results in the same sum (**10**).

- Make 10 paper doll-type figures from overhead transparency film. Use the figures to represent the equation created (e.g., 2 paper dolls + 3 paper dolls = 5).

- Have students write word problems to fit each equation or situation in the book. When each child reads his or her word problem aloud, ask the other students to identify the page in the book that is being described.

- Use the book to classify. For example: How many boys and how many girls? How many children wear blue? How many wear green? Graph the classifications.

Calmenson, Stephanie. *Dinner at the Panda Palace*. Illustrated by Nadine Bernard Westcott. HarperCollins, 1991.
A number of guests gather at the Panda Palace.

- Make a list of type of animal and the number arriving at Panda's. As the list grows, add up all the numbers to find out how many animals came to eat at Panda's.

Giganti, Paul, Jr. *Each Orange Had 8 Slices: A Counting Book*. Illustrated by Donald Crews. Greenwillow, 1992.
Donald Crews's bright and graphic illustrations help the reader focus on a large variety of objects to be counted. Not only can the objects be counted, they also provide opportunities to multiply the number of tricycles times the number of wheels, etc. The final nursery rhyme verse, "On the Way to Saint Ives," focuses the reader on the mathematical problem inherent in the verse—but, of course, any computation is unnecessary because the only one going to Saint Ives is the person asking the question. All the others are going in the opposite direction.

- Calculate the number problems on each page. Develop the mathematical equations for each question and display the equations on the overhead or on the chalkboard.

- Use the book as a model to create innovative number pictures. Create the pictures and then ask the questions.

Concept V: Multiplication and Division

Multiplication is a method of finding the result of adding a constant figure to itself a certain number of times. Division, the reverse of that process, is subtracting a constant figure from itself a certain number of times.

Fairy tales often use multiple objects or attempts in threes or sevens; Rumpelstiltskin spins gold for the woman three different times, the woman is taken to three rooms, the queen is allowed to guess names three different times, etc. Other stories, such as "Snow White and the Seven Dwarfs," use the number **7**. Threes and sevens can help focus on multiplication in any fairy tale being read by using word problems such as: How many names did the queen guess if she was allowed three guesses on each of the three nights?

Anno, Mitsumasa. *Anno's Mysterious Multiplying Jar*. Philomel, 1983.

In a format similar to other Anno books dealing with mathematical concepts, this book focuses on various multiplication activities.

- Formulate equations to represent some of the actions shown in the book. The equations could be multiplication or division equations.

- Use the actions shown in the book to formulate some additional multiplication or division activities. Write the story problems to accompany the actions in the activities created.

Hutchins, Pat. *The Doorbell Rang*. Greenwillow, 1986.

Two children are about to share a plate of cookies from their grandmother when the doorbell rings. Another guest shows up and the children must figure out how to divide the cookies on the plate. Before the children can begin to eat the cookies, the doorbell rings again. The scene is repeated several times until there are more children than cookies. Finally, the doorbell rings one more time. It is Grandmother with another plate of cookies.

- Each time the doorbell rings and a new guest or guests arrive, write the equation representing the number of cookies that each child will be given.

- Create original scenarios as an outgrowth of Hutchins's story. For example, if the plate of cookies Grandmother brings at the end of the story has the same number of cookies as the first plate, how many cookies will each guest be given?

Lobel, Anita. *A Treeful of Pigs*. Illustrated by Arnold Lobel. Greenwillow, 1979.

A farmer refuses to help around the farm and his wife must find a way to get him into action.

- Establish from the illustrations groups of pigs to be used in mathematical equations.

Concept VI: Telling Time

The traditional idea of "telling time" generally focuses on recording the passage of time. *Anno's Counting House* could provide an introduction to mechanized means of recording the passage of hours. Other books focus on clocks and telling time, whereas others deal with the passage of days, weeks, etc.

Anno, Mitsumasa, ed. *All in a Day*. Philomel, 1986.

This book presents another dimension of the time of day concept. Different parts of the world are in different time zones. Each page shows the activities that are occurring simultaneously in eight different parts of the world: Australia, Brazil, China, England, Japan, Kenya, the United States, and the country formerly known as the USSR. Eight separate illustrations depict the activities. Readers are able to observe the movement of daylight and darkness around the earth and its effect on the time of day. Each of the eight country scenes is drawn by a noted illustrator representing that country: Mitsumasa Anno, Raymond Briggs, Ronald Briggs, Gianvittore Calvi, Eric Carle, Zhu Chengliang, Diane Dillon and Leo Dillon, Akiko Hayashi, and Nicolai Popov.

- Introduce the concept of time zones and discuss the concept of the book. Because of the small size of each of the eight scenes, this book is better suited to small-group rather than whole-group activities.

- Create some story problems focusing on the element of time in various places in the world. If it is 8:00 P.M. in England, what time is it in Japan?

Carle, Eric. *The Grouchy Ladybug*. Illustrated by Eric Carle. Crowell, 1977.

A grouchy ladybug, who thinks she should have all the aphids to eat, gets into an argument with another ladybug. When she finds out she can't have them all, the ladybug flies away, encountering various animals that she challenges to fight. None accepts her challenge, and she eventually returns to the leaf and the aphids ready to share and be friends with the other ladybug. Each of the ladybug's challenges to fight takes place at a specific hour that is shown on the face of a small clock in the corner of each page.

- Make a transparency of a clock. Attach black clock hands to the transparent clock with paper fasteners. As the story is read, move the clock hands to reflect the time each encounter takes place.

- At the end of the story the action happens in quarter hours. Discuss that concept and use the transparency clock to show quarter hours.

- Use in conjunction with Marilyn Singer's *Nine O'Clock Lullaby*, illustrated by Frané Lessac (HarperCollins, 1991), to establish a focus on the time of day.

Carle, Eric. *The Very Hungry Caterpillar*. Illustrated by Eric Carle. Crowell, 1969.

This book covers the life cycle of a butterfly but also regards the passage of time as it relates to the days of the week. On the first day of the week the egg hatches in the sun, and then on each day of the week the caterpillar eats something different—from one apple to many different good things to eat. After the passage of two weeks the caterpillar emerges from the cocoon as a "beautiful butterfly."

- The sequence of the days can be matched with the foods the caterpillar eats. Construct a calendar with the food objects in the appropriate blocks for each day. Since the number of objects increases (one apple, two pears, etc.) as the days of the week go by, a sense of the ordinal order of the weekdays can be introduced.

- Make butterflies of all types—with fingerpaints, watercolors, crayon shavings ironed between sheets of waxed paper, and folded tissue paper.

- Share Christina Rossetti's poem "Brown and Furry."

      Brown and furry
      Caterpillar in a hurry;
      Take your walk
      To the shady leaf or stalk.
      May no toad spy you;
      May the little birds pass you;
      Spin and die
      To live again a butterfly.
                    —Christina Rossetti

de Regniers, Beatrice Schenk. *How Joe the Bear and Sam the Mouse Got Together.* Illustrated by Bernice Myers. Lothrop, 1990. (Originally published by Parents in 1965; illustrated by Brinton Turkle.)

One day Joe and Sam meet and decide to be friends. They want to do things together and are delighted to find that each is looking for a house to live in. But Joe needs a large house and Sam needs a small house. So they can't live together. Other ideas of things to do together continue in the same vein until they discover that both like to eat ice cream at three o'clock, every day.

- Focus on the time element in the story. Begin by making clocks of every type (digital clocks, Roman numeral clocks, clocks with dots instead of numerals, Arabic numeral clocks, grandfather clocks, clock radios, etc.) that show the time to be three o'clock. Then have your own ice cream party at three o'clock.

- Discuss other things that Joe and Sam might be able to do together (and at what time). Perhaps both like to read and at two o'clock each day they would meet at the library and read together. If the clocks made for the three o'clock ice cream party were made with movable hands or number rolls, each of the clocks could be set to reflect the new activity time.

- Write an innovation on the text. What happens if Joe and Sam discover that they like to recite the alphabet, do math problems, or eat Mexican food?

- Joe and Sam like to eat different flavors of ice cream. List the kinds of ice cream that Joe and Sam could eat. Take a class vote to establish students' three most popular flavors of ice cream. Using those three most popular flavors, create a bar graph using dips of ice cream (made from paper) depicting the popularity of each of the flavors. Paper cones are placed at the bottom with the flavor name on it. Children can "vote" by writing their names on individual dips of ice cream and placing them on the appropriate cone. The result should be three multidipped ice cream cones that represent the relative popularity of each flavor.

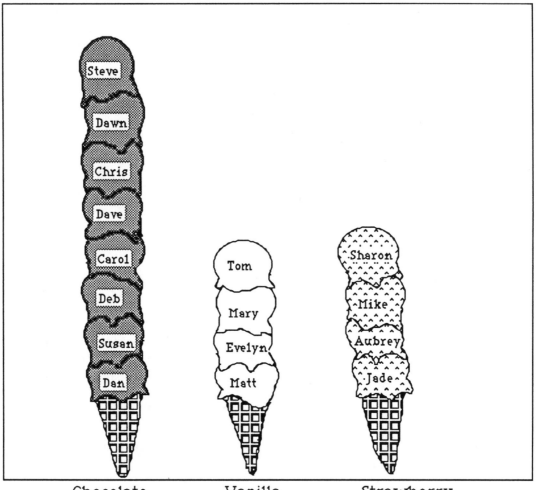

- Read Jack Prelutsky's poem "Bleezer's Ice Cream" in *The New Kid on the Block* (Greenwillow, 1984) and "Eighteen Flavors" by Shel Silverstein in *Where the Sidewalk Ends* (HarperCollins, 1974). Then create original ice cream flavors. Convince others to try the new flavors by writing descriptive paragraphs introducing the new concoctions.

- Create a large backdrop of an ice cream store. Students can create pictures of themselves eating ice cream. The pictures can be placed collage style in the foreground of the ice cream store. (During a parent visitation night, parents can attempt to match their own child with one of the pictures drawn. Number the people in the picture for ease of matching.) Make sure the clock in the ice cream store shows the time to be three o'clock.

Fritz, Jean. *And Then What Happened, Paul Revere?* Coward, 1973; *Can't You Make Them Behave, King George?* Coward, 1977; *What's the Big Idea, Ben Franklin?* Coward, 1976; *Where Was Patrick Henry on the 29th of May?* Coward, 1975; *Why Don't You Get a Horse, Sam Adams?* Coward, 1974; and *Will You Sign Here, John Hancock?* Coward, 1970.

These titles are well-researched and humorously written biographies of six revolutionary war figures: King George, Paul Revere, Benjamin Franklin, Patrick Henry, Samuel Adams, and John Hancock.

- Introduce the books as a unit, emphasizing how these men's lives and the events of the period in which they lived were interrelated. Weston Woods has a video presentation, *Jean Fritz: Six Revolutionary Heroes*, in which Fritz introduces her books and emphasizes the relative time periods of her subjects' lives and the time of significant events in relation those lives and the revolutionary war.

- Using the dates Fritz mentions in the video (or dates gleaned from the books), construct a timeline showing how the lives of the six men were interrelated. Tom Snyder Productions has a computer program, *Timeliner*, that assists in building timelines. A similar timeline procedure might be utilized with other books of history or biography.

Gibbons, Gail. *From Path to Highway: The Story of the Boston Post Road*. Illustrated by Gail Gibbons. Crowell, 1986.

Over a period of 500 years, a well-traveled narrow path served as a post road traveled in the 1600s by post riders; a road for colonists and their wagons in the 1700s; a train track bed in the 1800s; and eventually the Boston Post Road in the 1900s.

- Make a timeline showing the development of the highway.

- A note at the end of the book ties the road's history to the lives of notable people who traveled the road: Paul Revere, George Washington, Sarah Knight, Henry Wadsworth Longfellow, and Mark Twain, who often used the road when he lived in Connecticut. On the timeline created earlier, indicate the period during which each of these people would most likely have used the road.

Gibbons, Gail. *New Road!* Illustrated by Gail Gibbons. HarperCollins, 1983.

This book details the actual building of a superhighway and covers a much shorter time span than *From Path to Highway: The Story of the Boston Post Road*.

- Make a timeline showing the building of the new road.

- Use the notes and chart at the end of the book that detail different types of roads. The Romans constructed roads of broken tiles or bricks in 300 B.C., and in the nineteenth century roads were made from many types of materials, such as cobblestone, wooden blocks, tree trunks (these were called corduroy roads), planks, and gravel. Another type of popular road was the macadam, a road made of broken stone and cement or asphalt, invented by John L. McAdam. Today we have concrete and recycled roads.

- Use the timeline created for the evolution of the types of roads as a model to create a time chart for other historical developments.

Hall, Donald. *The Ox-Cart Man*. Illustrated by Barbara Cooney. Viking, 1979.

As time progresses so do the activities of a New England family. The setting of the book is 1832, when beards were in fashion, turnpikes were an essential means of travel, and the brick market in Portsmouth, Maine, was still standing. Each scene shows a season of the year.

- Discuss the time span of the book's story. How many months or seasons pass from start to finish? How many days is Father away from home when he goes to sell the family's wares?

- View the videocassette version of Hall's *The Ox-Cart Man* from Live Oaks or the Reading Rainbow® program featuring the same story.

Hogrogian, Nonny. *Apples*. Collier-Macmillan, 1972.

This wordless book depicts a man who throws the core of an apple on the ground. Over a period of time the birds carry the seeds away, where they fall and grow into a new apple tree. New apples grow, and the cycle is repeated until over time a grove of trees is established.

- To establish a realistic sense of time, discuss how long it would take an apple tree to grow from a seed, to a seedling, and finally to a tree that bears fruit. How many years would it take to establish a grove of trees like the one pictured in the illustration?

- Create a timeline depicting the events in the book.

- Correlate with a reading of Gail Gibbons's *The Seasons of Arnold's Apple Tree* (Harcourt, 1984).

- Use apples to provide data for mathematical computation. Ask each student to bring an apple to be cut open.
  - Count the number of seeds in each apple.
  - Figure the total number of seeds in all the apples.
  - Compute the average number of seeds per apple.
  - Estimate how many apple trees would grow from the seeds if it took five seeds to produce each tree.
  - Create additional computations based on the number of seeds, the slices per apple, the weight of the apples, etc.

Sendak, Maurice. *Chicken Soup with Rice*. HarperCollins, 1962.

Rhythmic verses focus on sharing chicken soup with rice through each month of the year. Delightful rhymes are included for each month.

- Read the book orally, then invite students to participate in a second reading of the book.

- To give students a visual clue as to the month that is the focus of each stanza and to give an idea of the passage of time, use a large calendar of the current year. As each of the poems is recited, move the calendar to the appropriate month.

- Highlight the identification of each month by asking students to stand during the stanza written for the month of their birth.

Concept VII: Probability, Estimation, Prediction

Probability assesses whether or not a certain fact or event is probable. Something is probable if it seems that from what is known there is a strong chance something may turn out a certain way. The probable answer in mathematics is based on estimation — the ability to make a general but careful guess about size, value, cost, etc. — and on prediction — the ability to make a judgment about what will happen next or about the outcome of a mathematical problem. These related concepts involve not only numbers and numerical concepts but the whole realm of critical thinking.

Allen, Pamela. *Who Sank the Boat?* Illustrated by Pamela Allen. Coward, 1982.

A cow, donkey, sheep, pig, and mouse climb aboard a boat before it sinks. Each animal wants to think that the other animal sank the boat. Estimation, prediction, and mathematical calculation of the weight of each animal must be used in the attempt to find a logical answer to the book's primary question: Who sank the boat?

- Discuss the relative size of each animal and then estimate its weight. After researching the weight of each animal, compare the estimations with the actual established weight of each.

- Re-create the story, by using weights, to scale, to represent the weights of each of the animals, a toy boat, and a water table. Graph, predict, and record results and validate those predictions.

Balian, Lorna. *Humbug Potion: An A B Cipher*. Abingdon, 1984. Hicks, Clifford. *Alvin's Secret Code*. Chapter 4. Holt, 1963.

Codes and ciphers are one way that critical thinking, estimation, and prediction can join literature and math. Balian's book introduces a cipher, and chapter 4 of Hicks's book introduces the idea of a secret code.

- Discuss the difference between a code and a cipher. A code is a system of symbols used in secret writing. Letters, symbols, etc., are arbitrarily given certain meanings, whereas a cipher assigns certain values, as in a = 1, b = 2, etc. A cipher message is based on a cipher key. Anyone who figures out the cipher can figure out the message. Develop a numerical cipher key. Mathematical equations can be part of the key. Use that key to write a message to others.

Brett, Jan. *The Mitten*. Illustrated by Jan Brett. Putnam, 1989.

A young boy, Nicki, wears his newly knitted white mittens outside to play. One mitten is lost and left behind on the ground. While it is on the ground animals squeeze inside. The mitten stretches and stretches to accommodate a mole, rabbit, hedgehog, owl, badger, fox, and bear, who scrunch inside. But when the meadow mouse comes by and settles on the bear's nose, the bear sneezes and the force of the sneeze pops the mitten off the animals and scatters them in all directions.

- Research the size of each of the animals to establish how big the mitten would have to have been to have held all the animals. Is it probable that all the animals could have fit into the mitten? Finding the solution to this question will involve work with estimation, probability, and spatial relationships.

- Estimating the size of the mitten can be based on the sizes of the animals. Full-scale models of the animals and the mitten might be created. If full-scale models are not feasible, then perhaps one-half, one-quarter, or other scaled representations might be created, giving students experience in using ratio and fractions.

- Alvin Tresselt illustrated an earlier retelling of the tale in his *The Mitten* (Lothrop, 1964). Tresselt's version could be used with activities similar to those suggested for Brett's book. In Tresselt's version a boy, while picking up sticks, loses his yellow mitten. While the mitten is on the ground, various animals squeeze inside. The animals—a little mouse, a green frog, an owl, a rabbit, a fox, a wolf, a wild boar, and a bear—squeeze into the mitten one-by-one until a little black cricket puts her "first scratchy foot inside." This causes the old yellow leather to crack, which in turn causes the red lining to split in half and all the animals to pop out into the snow. The boy never does find his mitten.

- The level of response to these two titles will vary according to the sophistication and experience of the reader. One kindergartner's response included the drawing in figure 3.1. The animals' names are represented only by their first letter: **S**, skunk; **B**, bear; **F**, fox; **M**, mouse; and **D**, dog. Kindergartners might respond at the counting level—counting the animals that the mittens held—whereas older students will be able to compute the dimensions for a scale model of the animals and the mitten.

    Another kindergartner, who portrayed three animals walking toward the mitten, wrote a text to accompany the illustration in figure 3.2 on page 64. The text in the figure reads as follows: "One day a boy went outside and played and lost his mitten. Then a fox came and a dog came and a cat came. The End."

Hooper, Meredith. *Seven Eggs*. Illustrated by Terry McKenna. HarperCollins, 1985.

This simple flap book moves through the days of the week. "On Monday the first egg cracked and out came a baby penguin." The flaps (and the eggs) get larger as a crocodile hatches on Tuesday, an ostrich on Wednesday, a frilled lizard on Thursday, a turtle on Friday, and a barn owl on Saturday. On Sunday the seventh egg yields seven chocolate eggs—one for each of the six animals and "one for you."

- Brainstorm a list of animals that hatch from eggs; use the size and characteristics of the eggs to predict what will hatch from the egg pictured.

- Continue the focus by sharing *Chickens Aren't the Only Ones* by Ruth Heller (Dunlap, 1981).

- Use Hooper's and Heller's books to begin a combined science/mathematical focus on the relativity of egg size to the size of the animal that is hatched from it. Research to find out the sizes of animals and their eggs and to determine any patterns that can be established between size of egg, size of baby animal, and size of adult animal.

Lobel, Arnold. *Uncle Elephant*. Illustrated by Arnold Lobel. HarperCollins, 1981.

This is a gentle story about the relationship of a young elephant and his elderly uncle who is caring for him while the young elephant's parents are away at sea. The story provides several opportunities for using mathematical concepts.

(Text continues on page 65.)

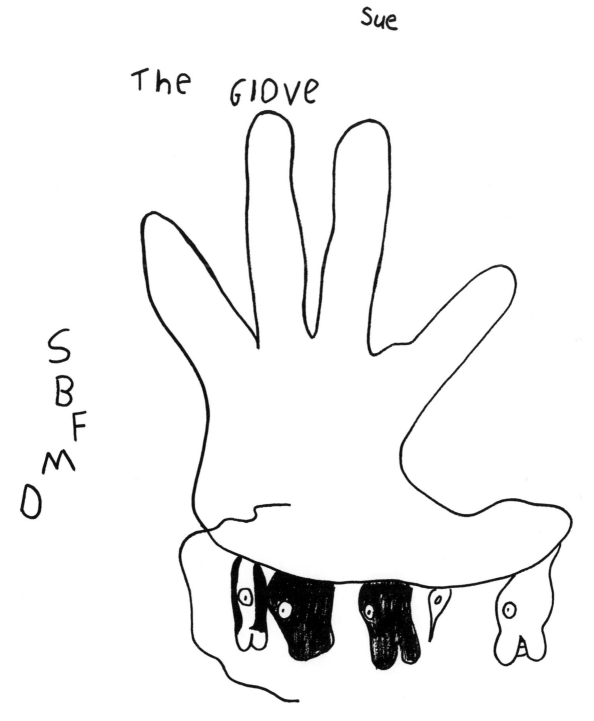

Fig. 3.1.

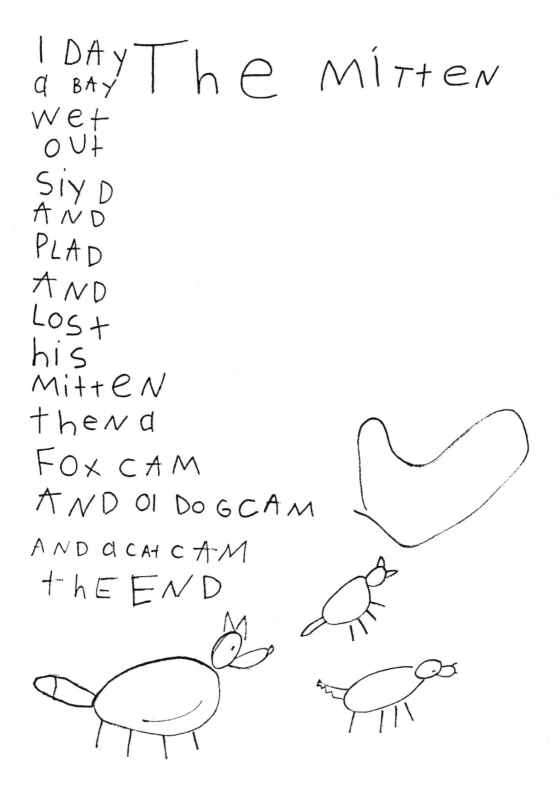

I DAY The Mitten
a BAY
wet
out
Siy D
AND
PLAD
AND
Lost
his
Mitten
thend
Fox CAM
AND OI DOGCAM
AND a CAt CAM
thE END

Krystal H

Fig. 3.2.

- In the chapter "Uncle Elephant Counts the Poles," the poles are moving by the train window too fast, so the two elephants end up counting peanuts. Use a sack of unshelled peanuts and count them by twos, threes, etc. After counting the peanut shells in one container, estimate the number of peanut shells in other containers—containers that are larger, smaller, or similar in size to the original.

- A "talking lamp" is introduced in one segment of the story. Let children become the "magic" voice of the lamp (the "voices" can hide under the table); then give the other children word and number problems.

- Focus on the concept of aging. Cut pictures of people out of magazines, arrange each picture chronologically, and record an estimation of the ages of the people under each picture. Focus on chronological age sequencing by reading Juliet Bawden's *One One-Year-Old: Counting Children One to Ten* (Holt, 1990). Bawden's book features photographs of children ages one to ten. This might provide a pattern for creating another book that extends through more ages.

Parker, Tom. *In a Day*. Houghton, 1984.

Parker has amassed statistics about Americans: the number of pencils they buy each day, the amount of paper they throw away, etc.

- Use Parker's book as a model to gather statistics about your own classroom. Make a list of those things students in the class want to know. For example, how many pieces of paper are used each day in your classroom? How many total drinks of water are taken by members of the class each day? After making the list of questions, estimate the answers—how many pieces of paper, how many drinks, etc. After recording the estimates compile the actual statistics. Compare the estimates with the compiled statistics.

- Compile a book of data for your classroom or school. Publish it and sell copies during your next school book fair.

Concept VIII: Fractions and Decimals

The word *fraction* comes from a Latin word meaning "to break." A fraction is one of the parts broken from the whole. Some examples of fractions are 1/2, 1/3, 1/4, 3/4, and 9/25. The denominator (or bottom number) represents the number of parts into which the whole has been divided. The numerator (or top number) is the number of parts that is being considered in the fraction. Thus, a fraction written as 9/25 tells us that the whole has been divided into 25 parts and that we have nine of those parts. A decimal number is a fractional number based upon the number **10**, counted by tens. A decimal number can represent a fraction with a denominator of 10, 100, 1000, etc. A fraction such as 1/10 is written as .1; 3/10 as .3; 4/100 as .04; and 5/1000 as .005, etc.

This is a difficult topic on which to locate books for inspiration. Any book that mentions pies could be manipulated to involve activities with fractions, and cookbooks can provide some experience in using fractional measurements to create a food dish. Many of the activities in chapter 4 of this book will correlate with fraction activities.

Bradfield, Jolly Roger. *Pickle Chiffon Pie*. Illustrated by Jolly Roger Bradfield. Rand, 1967.

The king in this story has two loves: his daughter and pickle chiffon pie. The king promises the hand of his daughter to the person who brings him the most unusual thing. Three would-be princes set out to seek their opportunity. The story is a literary fairy tale in which goodness and kindness prevail. The fraction focus comes with the king's love of pickle chiffon pie. The story is enough fun that the book is worth searching out in libraries.

- Create a green circular pie (in felt or as an overhead transparency) that can be manipulated into pie-shaped fractional pieces. Use the pie and its fractional pieces to discuss fractions.

- Serve real "pickle chiffon pies" that the children will cut and serve in equal portions to each person in their group. How much of the pie does each person get if there are eight people in the group? Six people? Two people? The following "recipe" for pickle chiffon pie is actually a secret recipe that should be given out only in special circumstances. Fill prepared graham cracker piecrusts with instant pistachio pudding, and sprinkle a few bits of sweet pickle relish on top. The pickle relish will cause students to wrinkle up their noses, but it really doesn't affect the taste of the pie. And serving this delicacy will usually evoke a lively discussion about whether or not it is really a "pickle chiffon pie."

- Another book that can provide for similar pie-cutting activities is Peggy Parrish's *Amelia Bedelia* (Harper-Collins, 1963). In this book Amelia Bedelia makes reference to her special lemon meringue pie. If one wanted to use an actual pie, one could be made using a prepared graham cracker piecrust and lemon pie or pudding filling.

Mathews, Louise. *Gator Pie*. Illustrated by Louise Mathews. Dodd, 1979.
Alvin and Alice do not want to share their pie with the other alligators.

- Read the story to introduce a focus on fractional parts. Use a felt or cardboard pie to allow students to represent the action of the story.

McMillan, Bruce. *Eating Fractions*. Photographs by Bruce McMillan. Scholastic, 1992.
Children of all ages "eat fractions" in this book designed to stimulate interest in fractions.

- Share the book and then make a list of all the ways fractions can be part of our everyday life.

- Make a list of other foods that are often cut into fractional parts before eating: watermelon, pizza, cakes, pies, sandwiches, etc.

Pillar, Marjorie. *Pizza Man*. Photographs by Marjorie Pillar. Crowell, 1990.
This black-and-white photo essay demonstrates the steps involved in making pizza, from dough to customer.

- Use various size cardboard pizzas to work with fractions, allowing learners to manipulate the fractional parts of the pie. Discuss story problems involving fractions, and use the parts to visualize the problem solving.

- Make pizzas for lunch, but before eating them, work with fractional parts. Simple pizzas are made by spreading small amounts of thawed frozen bread dough on greased pizza pans or cookie sheets. Canned pizza sauce and grated cheese top off the pizzas.

Concept IX: Measurement

Measurement is the system of measuring length, size, or amount. To determine the length of an object is to compare the length of the object to a standard definitive length or to the length of another object. A unit or standard of measure most often provides the comparison point.

Many books will present opportunities to use and practice measurement. When reading a story about a giant, determine how tall a giant would be and help students visualize the height by measuring the height against a wall or stairwell. When reading a story about mice, such as *Bizzy Bones and Uncle Ezra* by Jacqueline Briggs Martin (Lothrop, 1984), make full-scale models of the mice and their home. Whenever a distance, size, or weight is mentioned in a story, investigate what other objects might represent a similar size, distance, or weight. Make comparisons and measurement recordings when the opportunity arises.

Asch, Frank. *Bear Shadow*. Illustrated by Frank Asch. Prentice, 1985.
A young bear finds that his shadow gets in his way. He tries to capture it so that it won't bother him, but he cannot. Then his shadow disappears—but not for long.

- Choose a day and every hour measure a shadow from the same spot. Record the height of the shadow. Use the data to create a bar or line graph.

- Read other books that focus on shadows.

Shadow Books

de Regniers, Beatrice Schenk. *The Shadow Book*. Illustrated by Isabel Gordon. Harcourt, 1960.

Tompert, Ann. *Nothing Sticks Like a Shadow*. Illustrated by Lynn Munsinger. Houghton, 1984.

Wolcott, Patty. *My Shadow and I*. Addison, 1975.

Brown, Marc. *Your First Garden Book*. Illustrated by Marc Brown. Little, 1981.
This book contains everything young people need to know to plant and tend their own garden plot: what to plant, how to plant, and how to care for various types of plants.

- The growth of plants can provide measurement activities as seeds are planted and their growth is measured, recorded, and charted.

- Reading other books can stimulate an interest in seed planting and growing activities.

Growing Plants

Carle, Eric. *The Tiny Seed*. Illustrated by Eric Carle. Picture Book, 1987.

Cole, Joanna. *Plants in Winter*. Illustrated by Kazue Mizumura. Crowell, 1973.

Gibbons, Gail. *From Seed to Plant*. Illustrated by Gail Gibbons. Holiday, 1991.

Krauss, Ruth. *The Carrot Seed*. Illustrated by Crockett Johnson. HarperCollins, 1945.

Freedman, Russell. *The Wright Brothers: How They Invented the Airplane*. Photographs by Wilbur and Orville Wright. Holiday, 1991. Provensen, Alice, and Martin Provensen. *The Glorious Flight: Across the Channel with Louis Blériot, July 25, 1909*. Viking, 1983.
Each of these books recounts important events in the history of flight.

- Use one or both of these books to establish a focus on flying and to develop activities dealing with estimation and measurement. Freedman's chapter titled "The Art of Flying" may inspire students to create original planes that fly—paper airplanes.

  —Share Seymour Simon's *Paper Airplane Book*, illustrated by Byron Barton (Viking, 1971), to investigate the art of making paper airplanes. Experiment with making airplanes.
  —After each student has created a paper airplane, hold a fly-off. Each contestant has three opportunities to fly an original folded plane. The contestant may choose which attempt should be used in the contest statistics. Hold competitions for the longest flight in terms of time in the air and the longest flight in terms of distance traveled.

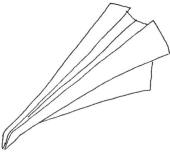

Other categories may be designated. Hold trial runs and average the length of all the flights in terms of time and distance. Determine which entrants beat the average times and which entrants' entries flew the longest time and the longest distance.

Galdone, Paul. *The History of Mother Twaddle and the Marvelous Achievements of Her Son Jack*. Clarion, 1974. (Reprinted by Clarion in paperback as *Jack and the Beanstalk*.)
This is a traditional retelling of the classic "Jack and the Beanstalk."

- Use Galdone's version or any of the many versions of this tale to focus on growing plants. Use the information in the story to fill in a chart patterned on a chart found on an actual bean seed packet. Read the Jack and the Beanstalk selection carefully to determine such bits of information as days to germination, color of leaves and stalk, and depth for planting. From that information determine, for example, the height of the plants in "Jack and the Beanstalk" and the length of the growing season (see appendix A, pp. 188 and 189).

- Make scale models of the plants grown from the "Shamrock Bush Beans" and those grown from "Old Mother Twaddle Beans."

Lopshire, Robert. *The Biggest, Smallest, Fastest, Tallest Things You've Ever Heard Of*. Illustrated by Robert Lopshire. Crowell, 1980.
This book, which is in a question-and-answer format, presents facts about animals, geographic features, human-made structures, and other topics. Included in the book is information about the biggest, smallest, fastest, and tallest animal in the world, the coldest and hottest place on earth, and the two words used most often by people who are writing and speaking.

- Discuss and list pairs of antonyms relating to size: tallest-shortest, biggest-smallest, fastest-slowest, etc.

- Make a list of the biggest animal, tallest animal, fastest fish, shortest snake, etc.

- Practice substituting numbers for spelled-out figures. For example: The Grand Canyon is over two hundred miles long: 200 miles; the Sears Tower is fourteen hundred and fifty-four feet high: 1,454 feet.

- Many geographical locations are mentioned in the book. Locate one of those places on a map, and determine who is farther from that location—someone who lives in New York City, San Francisco, Chicago, or your hometown. If this book is used with students with more advanced skills, they could use the map's scale to determine how far, in miles, they live from the location.

- Read other books that focus on comparison sizes.

Biggest and Smallest in Books

Caple, Kathy. *The Biggest Nose*. Illustrated by Kathy Caple. Houghton, 1985.

Kroll, Steven. *The Biggest Pumpkin Ever*. Illustrated by Jeni Bassett. Holiday, 1984.

Lionni, Leo. *The Biggest House in the World*. Illustrated by Leo Lionni. Knopf, 1963.

Most, Bernard. *The Littlest Dinosaur*. Illustrated by Bernard Most. Harcourt, 1989.

Simon, Seymour. *The Smallest Dinosaurs*. Illustrated by Anthony Rao. Crown, 1982.

Myller, Rolf. *How Big Is a Foot?* Illustrated by Rolf Myller. Atheneum, 1962.
This book aptly introduces the concept of standard measurement. The story is set in a time before standardized measurement was developed. A king orders a big bed made. He requests that the bed be 6 feet long and 3 feet wide. When the bed is completed it is much too small because the carpenter has used his own, much smaller, feet to measure the length and width of the bed. To

obtain the size bed he really wants the king has his foot outline traced, and that length becomes the standard for the "foot" measurement.

- Use the story to illustrate the importance of having standard measurements.
- Set up a measurement center where students are allowed to measure familiar objects and to record their length and width, weight, circumference, etc.
- After much actual practice with measuring, begin to focus on estimating size and weight and then verifying the estimations by using standard measuring tools.

Norton, Mary. *The Borrowers*. Chapter 1. Harcourt, 1953.
The first chapter establishes the setting of the Borrowers' home. It describes the objects used to create their home.

- Use chapter 1 to introduce measurement and the idea of scale models.
- Use cardboard and objects described in the book to create a full-scale model of the Borrowers' home.

Watson, N. Cameron. *The Little Pigs' First Cookbook*. Little, 1987. Stallworth, Lyn. *Wond'rous Fare: A Classic Children's Cookbook*. Calico, 1988. Wilkes, Angela. *My First Party Book*. Knopf, 1991.
The three little pigs share their favorite culinary dishes in recipes that young readers can prepare. *Wond'rous Fare* includes recipes from classic stories in children's literature. *My First Party Book* presents directions for making not only party favors and decorations but also funny-face dips and sandwiches — including cheesy pig sandwiches, pinwheel sandwiches, and munching caterpillars.

- Develop measuring skills (and practice following directions) by actually preparing some of the treats suggested in one of the cookbooks.
- Often books will contain possibilities for incorporating some cooking activities in the classroom. Making stone soup is a favorite activity, as is making Pippi Longstocking's pancakes or the cookies she rolled out on her kitchen floor. Look for cooking opportunities in books shared in the classroom.
- Chapter 4 of this book, "Gourmet Reading," provides many more cooking connections.

Concept X: Money

Coins of gold, silver, and other metal, and paper bills, are issued by a government for use in buying and selling. Some cultures use other items in place of coins and paper bills. For example, some Indian tribes used shells or beads as items of value that they used to barter for goods.

Money used in the United States is founded on the base ten system, and an understanding of the value of money and exchange values is an important mathematical concept.

Mathis, Sharon Bell. *The Hundred Penny Box*. Illustrated by Leo Dillon and Diane Dillon. Viking, 1975.
An old woman has a box containing a hundred pennies, each representing a memory from one of the hundred years that she has lived.

- Use this book to stimulate inquiry about coin collecting and kinds of coins.
  - Make your own hundred penny box. Search for a penny for each year of your life. The first penny in your box should have a mint date that coincides with your birth year. Other coins should carry the year of each of the other years of your life up to and including the present year.
  - Locate a set of coins: penny, nickel, dime, quarter, half-dollar, dollar — all minted in the year of your birth or some other significant year.

Schwartz, David M. *If You Made a Million*. Illustrated by Steven Kellogg. Lothrop, 1989.

Provocative bits of information, questions, and data about money are presented. The book provides much information that will lead to money manipulation and measurement. Included in the books are questions such as, "How many miles high would a stack of 1 million dollars worth of pennies reach?" and "Describe how you would prove that 1 million dollars worth of quarters would weigh as much as a whale."

- Ask the question, "Would you rather have a 5-foot stack of pennies, a 15-inch stack of nickels, a 5-inch stack of dimes, or a 3¼-inch stack of quarters? Discuss and allow students to work in cooperative groups to determine the stack that would be worth the most. Critical thinking will help students determine ways they can establish the value of each stack.

- Use other questions from the book to pique interest in working together to solve the questions using measurement and mathematical computation.

Silverstein, Shel. "Smart." In *Where the Sidewalk Ends*. HarperCollins, 1974.

A young boy is given a dollar bill by his father and through a series of trades ends up with five pennies. Because five is more than one he feels he has been very successful; in fact, when he tells his father what he has done and his father gets "all red in the face," the young boy just knows it is because his father is "too proud of me to speak."

- Use this poem to examine the humor created by the boy's failure to understand the value of money.

- Calculate how much money the boy lost in each trade.

- Rewrite the poem to make its outcome favorable to the boy.

Viorst, Judith. *Alexander Who Used to Be Rich Last Sunday*. Illustrated by Ray Cruz. Atheneum, 1978.

Alexander is given a dollar by his grandparents and he proceeds to spend it on a variety of things. The text could be a source of a continuous subtraction problem.

- Use the dialogue and story line in the book to construct the money problem that appears in the story.

    $1.00 − .15 (bought bubble gum) = .85
    .85 − .15 (lost bet with Nicky) = .70
    .70 − .12 (rented a snake) = .58
    .58 − .10 (fined for saying forbidden words) = .48
    .48 − .03 (flushed down toilet) = .45
    .45 − .05 (fell down crack) = .40
    .40 − .11 (paid for candy bar) = .29
    .29 − .04 (lost in vanishing money trick) = .25
    .25 − .05 (fined for kicking) = .20
    .20 − .20 (spent at garage sale) = 0

All Alexander had left was a "dopey" deck of cards, a one-eyed bear, a melted candle, and some bus tokens.

- Use Alexander's story to model another dialogue involving money. If the person getting the money had been someone other than Alexander, perhaps the money would have been invested and would have actually increased in value. Or perhaps the money would have dwindled away just as Alexander's did.

GOING BEYOND

There are some number activities that can bring numbers into book discussions regardless of the specific book. Each opportunity should come about as a natural outgrowth of the book discussion. However, listing some of the opportunities may help stimulate some spontaneous activities.

Building Graphs

1. As different versions of a tale are shared over a period of time, discuss the elements in each — the illustrations, the use of language, and so on. And when each book is the focus, discuss the notable aspects of that particular book. In the final discussion, review the comments about each of the books and discuss which books are favorites (and why). Allow children to vote for their favorite book by making a human graph (lining up) next to the appropriate book. The length of the lines will indicate the popularity of each title. Count the number of people in each line.

2. As a second step, re-create the graph on a piece of butcher paper. At the bottom of each column place a photocopy of the cover of one of the books being discussed. Then in the appropriate columns indicate which book is each student's favorite title. It is most effective if each child can place on the graph a small photocopy of his or her own school picture or perhaps a 2-by-2-inch piece of paper with the child's name on it.

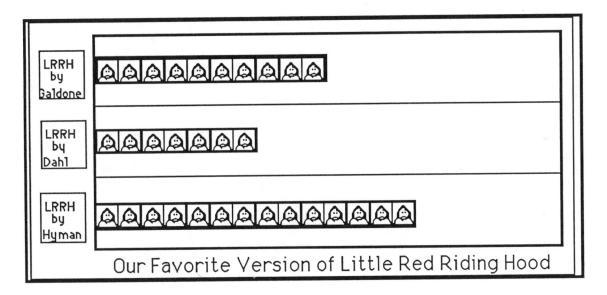

Our Favorite Version of Little Red Riding Hood

3. Eventually the graph can become more abstract, moving from actually standing in line to representing the vote with a picture or name placed in the proper column to creating a bar graph on which each vote is represented by a colored square.

Copyright Date

1. The copyright date can be utilized to determine when a book was published. Could moms and dads have read the book as a child? Was the book published before or after students were born? Other comments that focus on publication years include: This book was published when you were two years old. This book won the Caldecott Award the year [name of person] was born. (Also show a picture of the person.)

2. Use the copyright date to discuss the appropriateness of the information. For example, if the book is one about life in Mexico and the copyright date is 20 years ago, it is reasonable to assume that the information may not be representative of life in Mexico today.

3. Celebrate anniversaries of favorite book characters. How old are Curious George (author: H. A. Rey), Clifford the Big Red Dog (author: Norman Bridwell), Anastasia (author: Lois Lowry), and the Wild Things (author: Maurice Sendak)? The age of a character can be determined by the copyright date of the first book published with that character in it.

One Hundred Days of School Festival

From the first day of school count forward to the 100th day of school and plan a festival. Devote the day to activities that lend themselves to a connection to the number **100**. Below is a list of 25 activities you may wish to implement in your schoolwide or classroom celebration.

1. Read for 100 minutes during the day.

2. Have a special recess 100 minutes into the day.

3. Send a traveling book cart, with 100 books, from room to room. When the book cart arrives in the room, everyone must "drop everything and read."

4. Have each student bring 100 pieces of an ingredient for trail mix, such as M & Ms, peanuts, sunflower seeds, and raisins.

5. In gym class bounce the ball 100 times, skip rope 100 times, collectively make 100 free throws on the basketball court, do 100 push-ups, and run 100 laps around the gym or track field.

6. Read books that include a focus on **100**, such as Sharon Bell Mathis's *The Hundred Penny Box*, Eleanor Estes's *The Hundred Dresses*, and Keiko Kasza's *The Wolf's Chicken Stew*.

7. Discuss a specific event in history that took place approximately 100 years ago. Introduce the book *Trouble at the Mines* by Doreen Rappoport (Crowell, 1987) by role-playing the character of Mother Jones, who in 1898 lead the struggle in Arnot, Pennsylvania, to bring better working conditions to the coal mines of the area.

8. Invite artists that practice crafts of 100 years ago to visit the school and share their crafts.

9. Make a time chart showing what life was like 100 years ago.

10. Involve staff by asking that they wear something that reflects the number **100**. Participants could wear clothing with 100 items sewed on, such as ties with 100 buttons, hats with 100 feathers, or T-shirts with 100 signatures of students.

11. Make a list of 100 authors whose books we like to read.

12. Create mathematical story problems using the number **100**.

13. Solve 100 multiplication, division, addition, or subtraction problems.

14. Count backward from **100**.

15. Count to **100** by twos, fives, and tens.

16. Write a paragraph about any topic using exactly 100 words.

17. Make a list of 100 important people in the history of the United States during the past 100 years.

18. Make other lists of 100 things that correlate with whatever topics are being studied in class at the time. For example, if the class is studying animals, make a list of 100 animals; if the class is studying a region of the United States, make a list of 100 cities with a population of 100,000 or more located in that region.

19. Determine how many 100 days you are old. Don't forget that leap years have one extra day.

20. Measure and make a list of things whose length, width, or height is 100 inches, 100 feet, or 100 yards.

21. Make a list of objects whose combined weight would equal 100 pounds.

22. Collectively write 100 letters or postcards to people in your community or to relatives, thanking them for something they have done.

23. Make 100 puppets; tell 100 stories.

24. Count 100 marbles, 100 feathers, 100 pickup sticks, 100 pennies, 100 nickels, 100 pencils, etc. Compare the weights and volumes of these objects.

25. During each day of school, beginning with the first day, put one kernel of popcorn into a can. On the 100th day the can should contain 100 kernels of popcorn. Measure the volume of the kernels. Pop the corn, measure the volume of the popped popcorn, and have a 100th day popcorn party—a read-and-feed.

Chapter

4

Gourmet Reading

Children like stories that make
them laugh, are frightening, are
sentimental, and are about eating.
— Jim Trelease

TASTING GOOD LITERATURE

A friend once told me that children had to taste a book before it would become theirs. I thought he meant that figuratively, but soon afterward I had an experience with one of my sons, then three years old, that convinced me of the literal value of that comment. Matthew fell in love with *The Gingerbread Boy* by Paul Galdone (Clarion, 1975). He would tuck our borrowed library copy under his arm and toddle up and down the street until he found a likely person sitting on the porch enjoying the afternoon quiet. He would convince that person to read the story to him (often several times), and then he would toddle back home to convince someone there to read the book to him once more. We borrowed this book often, and after the same scenario occurred time and time again we purchased the book for Matthew's own personal library. The very first day he owned the book he immediately chewed the spine; he tasted the book and it was his.

Children enjoy books that make them laugh, frighten them, appeal to their emotions, and satisfy their sense of taste. The goal of any activity with books is to leave children with a positive memory, and in this chapter the goal is to leave the reader with a positive "taste" for books and for reading. Activities with food are just one more type of hands-on experience that children can associate with a book. Such activities can serve to link something new with a familiar experience, to build opportunities for cooperative activities, to develop organizational skills, to provide practice in following directions, and to encourage children to share books and savor the joy and pleasure of reading with others.

GETTING STARTED

Involving children in reading, and including their families in the process, can bring many benefits to the young reader. Sending home recipes that focus on a favorite book can foster interaction between a child and other members of the family. Trying recipes in the classroom can bring together comprehension and organizational skills. A search through cookbooks to locate recipes for foods mentioned in a particular book can promote more reading and provide students an opportunity to refine research skills, specifically the use of library catalogs, indexes, and tables of contents. Picture books are an invaluable tool to use with students, especially for brief introductions to hands-on activities that will leave readers with a good taste for books. Not every response to a book containing references to food needs to involve cooking or eating. There are stories behind favorite recipes to gather, writing projects to undertake, and other books to read.

Cooking at school can be an expensive proposition if it falls upon the teacher to supply all the ingredients and the cooking utensils. In communities where students are unable to contribute ingredients for cooking projects, there are other alternatives. In some schools classrooms are allowed to plan a school lunch menu for a specific day. If that is possible in your school, suggest that the class plan a "literary lunch." One possible menu might include spaghetti from *Strega Nona* by Tomie dePaola (Harcourt, 1975); garden vegetables (celery, carrots, etc.) from *The Giant Vegetable Book* by Nadine Bernard Wescott (Little, 1981); peaches from *Each Peach Pear Plum* by Janet Ahlberg and Allan Ahlberg (Viking, 1979; Puffin, 1986); and chocolate pudding from *Charlie and the Chocolate Factory* by Roald Dahl (Knopf, 1964; Bantam, 1979) or *Chocolate Fever* by Robert Kimmel Smith (Dell, 1986; Putnam, 1989). If it is not possible to actually plan a menu, use advance school menu information to plan to read some books that correlate with the foods that will be served. When the menu includes celery sticks, introduce your students to James Howe's *Celery Stalks at Midnight* (Macmillan, 1983; Avon, 1984). On the day "monster cookies" are served, read *Maggie and the Monster* by Elizabeth Winthrop, illustrated by Tomie dePaola (Holiday, 1987) or *The Monster's Ring* by Bruce Coville (Pantheon, 1982). When the school breakfast menu includes pancakes, rename them flapjacks and hold a Flapjack

and Folklore Festival. If children bring birthday treats for their classmates, ask that they plan a literary treat. Arrange to share the connecting book. Recipes can be used for mathematical calculations: double the recipe, decide how many batches would have to be baked for the entire school, etc.

Take every opportunity to read and taste books.

CONNECTIONS TO MAKE—A SAMPLER

Tasty Books

Adler, David A. *Malke's Secret Recipe: A Chanukah Story*. Illustrated by Joan Halpern. Kar-Ben, 1989.
Berel tries to make Malke's recipe for latkes but his wife, Yentel, does not think Berel will succeed so they use Yentel's recipe. Both Yentel and Berel are surprised when the latkes taste the same as usual. This book is described as a "Chelm variation on 'stone soup.'" Yentel's recipe is included so that readers can try making latkes.

- Discuss what is meant by "Chelm variation on 'stone soup.'"

- Make latkes using the recipe in the book.

Adoff, Arnold. *Eats*. Lothrop, 1973.
These poems celebrate a delicious feast of verse.

- Write a poem about one of your favorite eats.

- Share the recipes for your favorite foods.

Asch, Frank. *Popcorn*. Parents, 1979.
Bear's friends all bring popcorn to his Halloween party. They pop it and eat it all.

- Pop a big batch of popcorn. Read and feed.
- Read Tomie dePaola's *The Popcorn Book* (Holiday, 1978).

Barrett, Judi. *Cloudy with a Chance of Meatballs*. Illustrated by Ron Barrett. Atheneum, 1978. (The text of this story can also be found as a selection in Caroline Feller Bauer's *Rainy Day: Stories and Poems*, Lippincott, 1986.)
In this funny tale, set in the town of Chewandswallow, citizens receive food from the cloudy sky.

- Focus on the skill of skimming for specific information by asking students to skim the story and to make a list of the foods that fall from the sky. Classify the foods on the list according to the five food groups in the New Food Guide pyramid.
- List the foods that would fall in your community on the very sunniest of days, the dreariest of days, etc.

Blume, Judy. *Freckle Juice*. Four Winds, 1971.
Plagued by freckles, Sharon sets out to discover the secret in a concoction dubbed freckle juice.

- Make your own version of freckle juice (see recipe in appendix B, p. 196).

Carle, Eric. *Pancakes, Pancakes!* Illustrated by Eric Carle. Knopf, 1970; Picture Book, 1990.
Eric Carle was a struggling artist and author in Greenwich Village in New York City when he developed an invitation to invite his friends to a pancake dinner. He used his favored collage technique. The invitation was later expanded to become the book.

- Correlate reading this book with Tomie dePaola's wordless *Pancakes for Breakfast* (Harcourt, 1978), which includes a recipe for pancakes.

- After sharing either of the books, serve up a special readers' lunch or breakfast of silver dollar pancakes with strawberry jam and butter (see strawberry jam recipe in appendix B, p. 197).

Caseley, Judith. *Grandpa's Garden Lunch*. Illustrated by Judith Caseley. Greenwillow, 1990.
Grandpa and Sara plant and tend a garden of herbs, flowers, and vegetables. One day the two of them have a "garden lunch." The table is set with a bouquet of flowers and they enjoy iced tea flavored with mint, a garden salad, spaghetti with basil, and a zucchini cake.

- Have your own garden lunch. Invite one of your grandparents to eat lunch with you and read a book together.

Conford, Ellen. *What's Cooking, Jenny Archer?* Illustrated by Diane Palmisciano. Little, Brown, 1989.
Jenny encounters problems when she attempts to sell her creative school lunches to her friends.

- Correlate with a reading of *Bread and Jam for Frances* by Russell Hoban (HarperCollins, 1964). In Hoban's book all Frances wishes to eat is bread and jam until she is given only bread and jam. Finally, Frances wants nothing to do with bread and jam and begins to take creative lunches to school.
- Hold your own Creative Lunch Day.

Cooper, Jane. *Love at First Bite: Snacks and Meal Time Treats the Quick and Easy Way*. Knopf, 1977.
Recipes include many no-cook items.

- Use the recipes in this book to make one or two of the treats.

dePaola, Tomie. *The Knight and the Dragon*. Illustrated by Tomie dePaola. Putnam, 1980.
A knight and a dragon face off in a duel after reading books about fighting each other. But they find that fighting is not the way to live, and they go back to reading for information. The knight reads how to make a grill and uses his armour to make it, and the dragon learns how to utilize his flaming breath to heat the grill. Together the knight and the dragon open the K & D Grill.

- Introduce the story and share "burger bites" with the listeners. The burger bites are actually cookie treats made with green-tinted flaked coconut, chocolate mint patties, vanilla wafers, and sesame or poppy seeds. Try the following recipe to make 24 burger bites: Tint ¼ cup flaked coconut by putting a few drops of green food coloring into a plastic bag or jar. Add the coconut and shake. Place 24 vanilla wafers, flat side up, on an ungreased cookie sheet and top each with a chocolate mint pattie. Place wafers and patties in a 350 degree oven for about one minute or until the chocolate begins to soften. Remove the wafers/patties and sprinkle each with approximately ½ teaspoon tinted coconut. Top each with another vanilla wafer. Press gently. Use a clean pastry brush to brush the top of the vanilla wafers with just enough water to moisten (so the seeds will stick). Sprinkle each cookie with sesame or poppy seeds and serve.

dePaola, Tomie. *Tony's Bread*. Illustrated by Tomie dePaola. Putnam/ Whitebird, 1989.
This literary folktale tells how the delicious Italian bread shaped like a flower pot came to be called *panettone*, Tony's bread.

- Make panettone by using a sweet dough recipe and the ingredients mentioned in the story.

- Make up your own legends about the origin of a favorite family or ethnic dish.

- Interview parents or grandparents to uncover some real legends or stories about foods enjoyed in individual families. As a long-term project collect the stories into a "heritage cookbook."

dePaola, Tomie. *Watch Out for Chicken Feet in Your Soup*. Illustrated by Tomie dePaola. Prentice, 1974.
In this story from dePaola's childhood, dePaola's Italian grandmother makes chicken broth by boiling chicken feet. To accompany the soup she makes bread twists.

- Use frozen bread to make bread twists of your own. If you wish the tops to be very brown, brush the tops of the twists with diluted egg yolk before baking. Dilute the egg yolk with water to make a thin yellow mixture.

Dragonwagon, Crescent. *This Is the Bread I Baked for Ned*. Illustrated by Isadore Seltzer. Macmillan, 1989.
This cumulative verse has Glenda preparing a delicious meal for her husband, Ned. Numerous friends savor the meal with Ned and Glenda.

- Write your own cumulative verse detailing the dinner you will make for Ted, Ed, Jed, Red, or Zed.

Gilson, Jamie. *Can't Catch Me I'm the Gingerbread Man*. Lothrop, 1981. (Novel)
Mitch attempts to win a national baking contest with his Healthy Nutty Gingerbread. Tofu shakes are also featured.

- Create a recipe for Healthy Nutty Gingerbread and make some following the recipe.

- Use the recipe in the book to make a banana tofu shake: Blend 3 frozen bananas, 6 ounces tofu, 1 tablespoon honey, 2 tablespoons peanut butter, a pinch of nutmeg, and ¼ cup cold milk.

Gwynne, Fred. *A Chocolate Moose for Dinner*. Simon, 1987.
This book shows figurative expressions as they might be interpreted literally.

- Make chocolate mousse (see recipe in appendix B, p. 198).

- Interview parents to find and record figurative phrases. Use those phrases to create your own book of figurative expressions; illustrate the book to show *literal* interpretations of the expressions.

Kaska, Keiko. *The Wolf's Chicken Stew*. Illustrated by Keiko Kaska. Putnam, 1989.
A wolf's efforts to obtain a fat chicken for his dinner is thwarted when the chicken gives his food offerings to her 100 little chicks. At the end of the story the wolf decides that maybe he'll make them 100 scrumptious cookies.

- Make 100 scrumptious cookies (see recipe in appendix B, p. 199).

Kellogg, Steven. *Pinkerton, Behave!* Illustrated by Steven Kellogg. Dial, 1979.
A lovable Great Dane responds to simple commands by doing just the opposite thing. But when burglars arrive, Pinkerton's master figures out a way to communicate with him.

- Make a batch of puppy chow (a no-bake classroom activity). The puppy chow is for people only; chocolate is hazardous to the health of dogs.

  Puppy Chow for People

  1 cup chocolate chips
  1 cup peanut butter
  1 stick margarine
  1 box Crispnix™ (12 ounces)
  1 pound powdered sugar
  Melt chocolate chips, peanut butter, and margarine. Pour over cereal and mix to coat. Put powdered sugar in a plastic bag, add cereal, and shake until coated.

Kline, Suzy. *Orp and the Chop Suey Burgers*. Putnam, 1990.
Orville Rudemeyer Pygenski, Jr., Orp for short, finds himself in the middle of a cook-off competition when he enters his chop suey burgers.

- Hold your own cook-off with no-bake recipes.

Lee, Dennis. "Alligator Pie" in *The Random House Book of Poetry for Children*, selected by Jack Prelutsky, illustrated by Arnold Lobel. Random, 1983.
This is a rhyming patterned verse that is easy to mimic.

- Write new verses for this poem.

- Make an alligator pie (using any kind of green filling in a prepared graham cracker piecrust), alligator bread (bread baked from dough colored green), alligator cake (white cake tinted green with green frosting), etc.

- Publish a book filled with alligator pie verses and read them to others.

Lord, John Vernon, and Janet Burroway. *The Giant Jam Sandwich*. Houghton, 1973.
    To get rid of mosquitoes the community decides to make a giant jam sandwich to attract and trap the insects.

- Read the story and make a giant jam sandwich. Order a 5-foot loaf of bread from the bakery and ask each child to bring some jam. Build the sandwich to share while you reread the book.

Manushkin, Fran. *Latkes and Applesauce: A Hanukkah Story*. Illustrated by Robin Spowart. Scholastic, 1990.
    An affectionate family caught in a storm is able to, with the help of a kitten and a dog, find the ingredients for the traditional potato latkes and apples for fresh applesauce.

- Use the cookbook section of your library to locate a recipe for making latkes. Make latkes and applesauce. You can cook the apples in a crock pot.

McCloskey, Robert. "The Doughnuts." In *Homer Price* by Robert McCloskey. Viking, 1943. (Also available as a videotape from Weston Woods.)
    Young Homer is helping in his uncle's doughnut shop when the automatic doughnut-making machine goes wild and a woman loses her diamond bracelet — it's probably baked inside one of the doughnuts.

- Read or view this story and make doughnuts from tube biscuits. Just cut holes out of the biscuits, deep-fry in hot shortening, roll in granulated or powdered sugar, and serve warm.

Pinkwater, Daniel. *The Frankelbagel Monster*. Dutton, 1986.
    Only bagels will do.

- Make bagels from scratch, or thaw and bake frozen bagels.

Pinkwater, Jill. *The Natural Snack Cookbook: One Hundred and Fifty-One Good Things to Eat*. Four Winds, 1975.
    Dozens of recipes and hints about eating healthily are included in this book.

- Select a recipe to make just one of the treats.

Polacco, Patricia. *Thunder Cake*. Illustrated by Patricia Polacco. Philomel, 1990.
    A young girl's fear of thunder and storms is quieted by her grandmother's story about baking a "thunder cake."

- Use the recipe in the book to make your own thunder cake.

Prelutsky, Jack. "Bleezer's Ice Cream." In *The New Kid on the Block* by Jack Prelutsky. Greenwillow, 1986.
    A myriad of flavors is the focus of this poem.

- Mix vanilla ice cream with your choice of flavorings or added ingredients to develop an innovative flavor of your own and then settle back and enjoy a cone with your new ice cream flavor.

Rockwell, Thomas. *Oatmeal Is Not for Mustaches*. Holt, 1984.
    Many unusual uses for food are investigated. One of the two children's discoveries is that a really fine mustache is created with ketchup, not oatmeal.

- Serve up little cups of oatmeal, brown sugar, and milk. Portions should be small unless children really love oatmeal.

- Have students make a book with their own unusual uses for their favorite foods.

Rylant, Cynthia. *The Relatives Came*. Bradbury, 1985.
A great deal of food is necessary when all the relatives stay for weeks and weeks.

- Plan a meal for a reunion. Bring favorite family recipes for potluck dishes. Compile a cookbook and prepare copies for each student's family.

Seuss, Dr. *Scrambled Eggs Super!* Random, 1953.
A search is conducted for special eggs to put into "Scrambled Eggs Super Dee-Dooper-dee Booper Special deluxe à-la-Peter T. Hooper.

- Write down your recipe for your very own Scrambled Eggs Super.

- Compile a "Super Dee Dooper" cookbook to share.

Snow, Pegeen. *Eat Your Peas, Louise!* Children's, 1985.
Father finally gets Louise to eat her peas by saying "please."

- Hold a pea-tasting party. Include cooked peas from various canned and frozen brands. Put drained peas from each variety on separate paper plates. Label the plates A, B, C, etc. (Keep track of which variety is represented by which letter.) Each student should "spear" with a toothpick one pea from each plate, taste it, and record their evaluation (1 to 10) on a record-keeping chart. Sips of water should be swished in the mouth between each of the taste tests, so that the tastes don't mix. At the conclusion of the sampling exercise, rate favorites and chart the class results.

Zabar, Abbie. *Alphabet Soup*. Illustrated by Abbie Zabar. Stewart, 1990.
Antipasto, borscht, couscous, and 23 other interesting foods from around the world are featured in this book. Drawings, anecdotes, and histories of the foods are included.

- Use the alphabet format to write your own book of foods in your state, country, or city.

- Try some of the foods from *Alphabet Soup*.

Two Not-So-Tasty Books

Naylor, Phyliss Reynolds. *Beetles Lightly Toasted*. Atheneum, 1987.
Naylor's story is set in Iowa (West Union) and centers on Andy's entry in a contest sponsored by the *Cedar Rapids Gazette* and Iowa State University. To enter an agriculture contest Andy and his friend develop a recipe for Beetles Lightly Toasted—a new food product.

- After reading Naylor's book develop some new food recipes with unusual ingredients. Develop only recipes you are brave enough to try.

Rockwell, Thomas. *How to Eat Fried Worms*. Illustrated by Emily Arnold McCully. Dell, 1973.
Billy sets out to win a bet by eating 15 worms, one each day. At first he has difficulty swallowing the worm. He finally does, but then his problem becomes more complex as the days go by.

- Introduce Rockwell's book by reading "Willy Ate a Worm Today," a poem by Jack Prelutsky in Prelutsky's *Rolling Harvey Down the Hill* (Greenwillow, 1984).

- As Billy eats his 14th worm, serve chocolate-covered worms (Chinese noodles covered with melted chocolate); or serve gummy worms, which are more squirmy.

CHOCOLATE AND BOOKS—A CELEBRATION

Chocolate has long been a popular confection and food flavor. Its popularity spread from the ancient Aztecs and Mayans to the Spanish conquerors. By 1707 cocoa had become a fashionable beverage in London. Today, chocolate is popular in most parts of the world. Some believe that Americans eat more chocolate than the people of any other country, although citizens of Germany, Great Britain, France, the Netherlands, and Switzerland also consume great quantities of the confection.

Declare a day, week, or month to honor all lovers of chocolate. Introduce young readers to books that connect with chocolate. Drink hot chocolate, eat chocolate cookies, and read as many "chocolate" books as possible. This celebration might be particularly appropriate during American Chocolate Week (usually the third week in March), a week sponsored by the Chocolate Manufacturers Association of the USA.[1] Another opportunity might come the week prior to St. Valentine's Day, when you could hold a festival similar to the one sponsored the Saturday before St. Valentine's Day by the Firehouse Art Center in Norman, Oklahoma.[2] That festival features chocolate as art and as a delectable food. All types of chocolate foods and chocolate art are displayed. Include books from the booklist on pages 82-83 in *your* festival activities.

Celebrating Authors—Chocoholics

Many people enjoy chocolate, some so much that they consider themselves chocoholics. Two such chocoholics are authors James Howe and Robert Kimmel Smith. Include a focus on one or both of these authors in your celebration of chocolate and chocolate lovers. Organize a Chocolate Club and invite Howe and Smith to become members. Members can spend time reading, writing, and sharing chocolate recipes.

James Howe—Author and Chocoholic

James Howe is the author of *Bunnicula: A Rabbit-Tale of Mystery* (Atheneum, 1979), which includes many puns and references to food. It is a talking-animal story featuring the dog Harold—shaggy, reluctant, part Russian wolfhound—and his fellow pet, Chester—a cat with high self-esteem and a flair for drawing conclusions. Two sequels followed: *Howliday Inn* (Atheneum, 1982) and *The Celery Stalks at Midnight* (Atheneum, 1983). The same animal characters appear in junior novel *Hot Fudge* (Morrow, 1990). *The Celery Stalks at Midnight* discusses the possibility that vegetables throughout the neighborhood may have been "vampirized" by Bunnicula, a rabbit who acts mysteriously. Howe has also written a series of Sebastian Barth mysteries. *What Eric Knew* (Atheneum, 1985) began the series. In *Eat Your Poison, Dear* (Atheneum, 1986), Sebastian saves Miss Swille's reputation and her 25th anniversary party at school. Miss Swille, the school's head cook, is suspected of serving food that makes Milo Groot throw up, not once but several times. The finger of suspicion is pointed toward Miss Swille, the creator of such dishes as tuna fish dreamboats, apple chili dogs, apple lasagna, and even apple-cadabra. But Sebastian solves the mystery and saves the day.

James Howe's first books were written with his first wife, Deborah, who died of cancer in 1978. He is now married to Betsy Imershein-Howe who serves as Howe's in-house editor. Howe is a self-described chocoholic (just like Harold from his books); others who know him add that he is tall and friendly. Howe feels that writing for children includes a lot of responsibility, so it is no mistake that in *Bunnicula*, Chester is a cat that reads a lot and that Toby stays up late reading *Treasure Island*. And when Harold doesn't understand a word, he looks it up in a dictionary.

---

[1]Chocolate Manufacturer's Association of the USA, 450 Park Avenue South, New York, NY 10016.

[2]Firehouse Art Center, 444 S. Flood, Norman, OK 73069.

Howe lives with his wife in a cozy home in Hastings-on-Hudson, New York, in a quiet neighborhood just a few miles north of New York City. He writes his books using a word processor in a sunny room filled with book shelves; on the shelves sit many rabbits made of all sorts of materials—cloth, ceramic, glass, etc.

Robert Kimmel Smith—Author and Chocoholic

Robert Kimmel Smith wrote *Chocolate Fever*, illustrated by Gioia Fiammenghi (Putnam, 1972, 1989; Dell, 1986). When Smith's daughter, Heidi, was seven, she asked him to tell her a bedtime story. It was a story about a young boy who gets a rash from eating chocolate. That story was later published as *Chocolate Fever*. In describing where he got the story idea, Smith says that the boy was he himself, who had been a chocolate lover ever since he was "knee-high to a Hershey bar." *Chocolate Fever* was Smith's first book for young readers and is one of two of his books that have sold over a million copies.

Smith also wrote *Jelly Bean*, illustrated by Bob Jones (Delacorte, 1981), a story about what it means to be a fat kid. He knows about being fat from the first-hand experience of being the fattest kid in fifth grade. He includes his own emotions in the book, even though he never went to camp or had a family like the one in the book.

The idea for another book, *The War with Grandpa*, illustrated by Richard Lauter (Delacorte, 1984), actually came from Smith's son, Roger, who at the age of 10, said he loved their house, their neighborhood, and especially his room and he *never* wanted to live anywhere else. That statement became the nucleus for the book. Roger is now in his mid-20s and does live somewhere else, but his emotions concerning his boyhood home are reflected in his father's book.

Mostly Michael, illustrated by Katherine Coville (Delacorte, 1988), became Smith's fourth book for young readers. Michael Marder receives a diary for his 11th birthday and considers it a dumb present. Eventually, as Michael writes in the diary he begins to like it very much; it is one place where he can put his private thoughts. And even though Michael realizes he is changing his attitude toward his family, the biggest change is yet to come. This book was written because some fifth-graders asked Smith to write a book about an average kid who does not like school a lot.

Smith has been married to his wife Claire Medney Smith for over 35 years. They met on a blind date and have been talking about books ever since. Claire, who is associated with a writing agency in New York, is her husband's agent. Robert Smith has been writing full-time since 1970. He writes five days a week, from 9:30 A.M. to 2:00 P.M. He does much of the cooking during the week and Claire cooks on the weekends. He enjoys Chinese cooking, traveling, going to movies, eating chocolate, and reading thrillers. They live in a big old Victorian house in Brooklyn.

Books for Chocolate Lovers

Ammon, Richard. *The Kid's Book of Chocolate*. Atheneum, 1987.

Catling, Patrick S. *The Chocolate Touch*. Illustrated by Margot Apple. Morrow, 1979 (1952).

Claret, Maria. *The Chocolate Rabbit*. Barron, 1985.

Cobb, Vicki. *The Scoop on Ice Cream*. Little, Brown, 1985.

Cormier, Robert. *Beyond the Chocolate War*. Knopf, 1985. (For older readers)

Cormier, Robert. *The Chocolate War*. Pantheon, 1974. (For older readers)

Dahl, Roald. *Charlie and the Chocolate Factory*. Knopf, 1964; Bantam, 1979.

D'Ignazio, Fred. *Chip Mitchell: The Case of the Chocolate Covered Bugs*. Edited by Rosemary Brosnan. Lodestar, 1985.

Douglass, Barbara. *The Chocolate Chip Cookie Contest*. Illustrated by Eric Jon Nones. Lothrop, 1985.

Gwynne, Fred. *Chocolate Moose for Dinner*. Simon, 1987.

Hatchigan, Jessica. *Count Dracula, Me and Norma D.* Avon, 1987.

Simmonds, Posy. *The Chocolate Wedding*. Knopf, 1990.

Smith, Robert Kimmel. *Chocolate Fever*. Dell, 1986; Putnam, 1989.

Ziefert, Harriet. *Chocolate Mud Cake*. Illustrated by Karen Gundersheimer. HarperCollins, 1987.

GENERAL COOKBOOKS TO USE WITH LITERATURE

Many cookbooks written for children can be correlated with thematic units or used with specific individual book titles or with books by a specific author. *The Little House Cookbook* and *The Louisa May Alcott Cookbook* can be used with the books by those authors and in some cases can be used with books whose setting is approximately the same in terms of time period. *The Wild Wild Cookbook* can be used with almost any outdoor adventure book or with books dealing with nature. *Cooking the Australian Way* and other similar books can be connected with a study of a particular geographical region, and books such as *Clever Cooks: A Concoction of Stories, Charms, Recipes and Riddles* can be used with the specific stories referenced in the book. Almost any "gourmet" reader will enjoy the following cookbooks.

Cookbooks for Almost Any Gourmet Reader

Anderson, Gretchen. *The Louisa May Alcott Cookbook*. Illustrated by Karen Millone. Little, Brown, 1985.

Barchers, Suzanne I., and Patricia C. Marden. *Cooking Up U.S. History: Recipes and Research for Children*. Teacher Ideas Press, 1991.

Better Homes and Gardens New Juvenile Cook Book. Better Homes and Gardens, 1979.

Cobb, Vicki. *Science Experiments You Can Eat*. Illustrated by Peter Lippman. Lippincott, 1972.

Ellison, Virginia H. *The Pooh Cook Book*. Dell, 1975.

George, Jean Craighead. *The Wild Wild Cookbook*. Illustrated by Walter Kessell. Crowell, 1982.

Germaine, Elizabeth, and Ann L. Burckhardt. *Cooking the Australian Way*. Illustrated by Robert L. Wolfe and Diane Wolfe. Lerner, 1990.

Greene, Ellin, compiler. *Clever Cooks: A Concoction of Stories, Charms, Recipes and Riddles*. Lothrop, 1973.

Hayward, Ruth Ann, and Margaret Brink Warner. *What's Cooking? Favorite Recipes from Around the World*. Little, Brown, 1981.

Henry, Edna. *Native American Cookbook*. Messner, 1983.

Hughes, Helga. *Cooking the Austrian Way*. Illustrated by Robert L. Wolfe and Diane Wolfe. Lerner, 1990.

Krementz, Jill. *The Fun of Cooking*. Knopf, 1985.

MacGregor, Carol. *Fairy Tale Cookbook*. Illustrated by Debby L. Carter. Macmillan, 1982.

Moore, Carolyn E., Mimi H. Kerr, and Robert J. Shulman. *Young Chef's Nutrition Guide and Cookbook*. Barron, 1990.

Nguyen, Chi, and Judy Monroe. *Cooking the Vietnamese Way*. Lerner, 1985.

Paul, Aileen, and Arthur Hawkins. *Kids Cooking*. Doubleday, 1970.

Penner, Lucille Recht. *The Colonial Cookbook*. Hastings, 1976.

Pillar, Marjorie. *Pizza Man*. Illustrated by Marjorie Pillar. Crowell, 1990.

Rockwell, Anne. *The Mother Goose Cookie-Candy Book*. Random, 1983.

Sobol, Donald J., and Glenn Andrews. *Encyclopedia Brown Takes the Cake! A Cook and Case Book*. Four Winds, 1984.

Stallworth, Lyn. *Wond'rous Fare: A Classic Children's Cookbook*. Calico, 1988.

Walker, Barbara M. *The Little House Cookbook: Frontier Foods from Laura Ingalls Wilder's Classic Stories*. Illustrated by Garth Williams. Harper, 1979.

Watson, N. Cameron. *The Little Pigs' First Cookbook*. Little, Brown, 1987.

Wilkes, Angela. *My First Cookbook*. Knopf, 1989.

Wilkes, Angela. *My First Party Book*. Knopf, 1991.

PUBLISHING A COOKBOOK

Favorite recipes can be gathered and combined to produce a classroom or school cookbook. Combine research, reading, and writing in a family heritage unit by asking each student to select a favorite family recipe and investigate the background of the recipe. For example, one child who submitted his grandmother's chocolate chip cookie recipe told a story about when his father was young. When his mother (the child's grandmother) would bake a big batch of delicious cookies, he would take some to school and sell them. Another child submitted his grandfather's recipe for fried pheasant. His grandfather was an avid hunter but believed in hunting only what one would eat or use. A variety of family stories evolve in connection with foods. Both the family stories and the recipes could be included in the "Heritage Cookbook." Special holiday dishes could be included and a special "book treats" section might include recommendations for food-related books.

As a culmination to the cookbook publishing activity, hold a family classroom book luncheon or try a Literary Potluck Night at School. Each family could bring a potluck dish that was included in the cookbook or connected with a book. The event could be a prelude to a school open house or a special parents' night just for your class.

Throughout the year classroom treats might come from tidbits in books; or books might be coordinated with lunchroom menus. Some of the following food activities are suggested in the books cited.

- Prepare some "munchings and crunchings," which Gurgi is associated with in Lloyd Alexander's Prydain series. A popcorn, peanuts, and chocolate chip mixture or a trail mix would qualify as "munchings and crunchings."

- Make a dessert inspired by Betsy Byars's *The Pinballs* (Harper, 1977); that book includes references to Carlie's Famous Mayonnaise Cake.

- Brew some herbal tea, made from an herb gathered by Mary Call Luther in Vera Cleaver and Bill Cleaver's *Where the Lilies Bloom* (Harper, 1969).

- Make liverwurst and cream cheese sandwiches or tomato sandwiches. Meg offers the liverwurst and cream cheese sandwiches in Madeleine L'Engle's Time trilogy (the first book in the series is *A Wrinkle in Time* [Farrar, 1962]). Tomato sandwiches are Harriet's favorite in Louise Fitzhugh's *Harriet the Spy* (HarperCollins, 1964). These sandwiches could be made in miniature on party rye bread.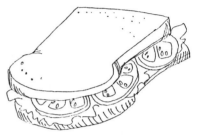

- Locate some Turkish delight, which proved to be Edmund's downfall in C. S. Lewis's *The Lion, the Witch, and the Wardrobe* (Macmillan, 1968); the treat is similar to white taffy but is more gelatin-like.

- Make banana pops inspired by the Curious George books by H. A. Rey (see recipe in appendix B, p. 200).

- Bake cherry tarts (using small tart shells and cherry pie filling) from the Mother Goose rhyme "The Queen of Tarts."

- Prepare a cranberry treat from one of the books by Harry Devlin and Wende Devlin. The stories take place in Cranberryport, and each book includes a recipe for cranberry bread, or some other cranberry treat; *Cranberry Thanksgiving* by Wende Devlin and Harry Devlin (Four Winds, 1971) is one of my favorite titles.

- Cook some spaghetti after reading "Spaghetti" by Shel Silverstein in *Where the Sidewalk Ends* (HarperCollins, 1974) or *More Spaghetti, I Say!* by Rita Golden Gelman, illustrated by Jack Kent (Scholastic, n.d.).

- Have some bread and butter, from Anne Colver's *Bread-and-Butter Journey*, illustrated by Garth Williams (Avon, 1971).

- Enjoy some fresh or canned peaches from Roald Dahl's *James and the Giant Peach*, illustrated by Nancy Burkert (Knopf, 1961).

- Hold an afternoon tea party as in Lewis Carroll's *Alice's Adventures in Wonderland*, illustrated by John Tenniel (Macmillan, 1963 [1865; 1872]), where a tea party is given by the Hatter and attended by the March Hare and the Dormouse. The tea party from Carroll's book is also featured in Betty Frazer's illustrations for *A House Is a House for Me* by Mary Ann Hoberman (Viking, 1978).

- Have a class picnic on the riverbank as in Kenneth Grahame's *The Wind in the Willows*, illustrated by E. H. Shepard (Scribner, 1940, first published in 1908); *The Wind in the Willows*, illustrated by Michael Hague (Holt, 1980); or *The River Bank* from *The Wind in the Willows*, illustrated by Adrienne Adams (Scribner, 1977). Mole and Rat's luncheon basket is filled with "cold chicken," and "coldtonguecoldhamcoldbeefpickledgherkinssaladfrenchrollscresssandwidgespottedmeatgingerbeerlemonadesoda-water."

- Make pepparkakor cookies as Astrid Lindgren often does and as Pippi Longstocking does in Lindgren's *Pippi Longstocking*, illustrated by Louis S. Glanzman (Viking, 1950) (see recipe in appendix B, p. 201). Pippi and her friends also make or eat pancakes, cakes in odd shapes, and buns.

- Join Mary Poppins for crumpets, coconut cakes, plum cake with pink icing, bread and butter, or tea in the air from P. L. Travers's *Mary Poppins*, illustrated by Mary Shepard (Harcourt, 1934). Uncle Alfred Wigg has the peculiar problem that whenever his birthday falls on a Friday, even a funny thought will so fill him with laughing gas that he floats right up into the air. When Mary Poppins takes Jane and Michael to have tea with this fellow on such an occasion, what is there to do but join him and enjoy the crumpets, coconut cakes, plum cake with pink icing, bread and butter, and tea in the air.

- Enjoy Amelia's famous lemon pie from Peggy Parish's *Amelia Bedelia*, illustrated by Fritz Siebel (Harper, 1963).

- Whenever the luncheon menu includes cheese, peas, or chocolate pudding, read Betty Van Witsen's *Cheese, Peas, and Chocolate Pudding* (Scott, Foresman, 1971).

- Make a Chincoteague Pot Pie as enjoyed by the Beebe family in Marguerite Henry's *Misty of Chincoteague*, illustrated by Wesley Dennis (Rand, 1947) (see recipe in appendix B, p. 202).

- Read Rudyard Kipling's *The Elephant's Child*, illustrated by Lorinda B. Cauley (Harcourt, 1983), then enjoy "elephant legs," made by stacking pancakes high enough that the stack reminds one of elephant legs.

- From *Roll of Thunder, Hear My Cry* (Dial, 1976), which tells of traveling through the South with a picnic lunch, prepare an outdoor meal, including fried chicken and other picnic-type food items.

If you do not want to have a real luncheon, make a luncheon bulletin board by creating the food items in three-dimensional form. Papier-mâché, clay, or scrap art might be combined to form a realistic depiction of the food item that connects with a favorite book. Accompanying the representation should be an explanation of the connection and the recipe for the "real thing."

GOING BEYOND

Declare celebrations on special days. On Laura Ingalls Wilder's birthday, February 7, serve her favorite gingerbread (with chocolate frosting) and lemonade. The recipe for Laura's gingerbread appears in *Adventures with Social Studies (Through Literature)* by Sharron L. McElmeel (Teacher Ideas Press, 1991), p. 35. That book contains many other activity suggestions in conjunction with the reading of books by Laura Ingalls Wilder, specifically in the chapter "In the Past (Books with a Historical Setting)." Celebrate March 1, National Pig Day, by sharing a recipe or two from *The Little Pigs' First Cookbook* by N. Cameron Watson (Little, Brown, 1987). Sometimes just discussing what a particular dish is made of will extend the schema of the students.

Food can always help connect children with authors and books. When the school kitchen staff bakes fresh bread for lunch, mention that it is Sandy Asher's favorite food and share books she has written. On days when you treat the children in the classroom to popcorn, mention Tomie dePaola and his love of popcorn. One of his books, *The Popcorn Book* (Holiday, 1978), tells the history of his favorite food. Make s'mores, a chocolate, graham cracker, and marshmallow treat, and read Kristi Holl's *The Haunting of Cabin 13* (Atheneum, 1987). On a specific author's birthday share the author's favorite food or find a recipe for it. Take advantage of any opportunity to read (and taste) one more book.

A Few Authors/Illustrators and Their Favorite Foods

Author/Illustrator	Birthday	Favorite food
Sandy Asher	October 16 (1942)	fresh-baked bread
Marc Brown	November 25 (1946)	pies (that he himself has baked)
Paula Danziger	August 18 (1944)	sushi
Tomie dePaola	September 15 (1934)	popcorn
Harry Devlin	March 22 (1918)	cranberry breads, cranberry cakes, etc.
Wende Devlin	April 27 (1918)	blueberry pancakes
Kristi Holl	December 8 (1951)	s'mores (graham cracker, chocolate, and marshmallow "sandwiches")
Tony Johnston	January 10 (1942)	chocolate chip cookies
Steven Kellogg	October 26 (1941)	ice cream or anything chocolate
David McPhail	June 30 (1940)	nutmeg mousse
Tony Ross	August 10 (1938)	lamb cutlets
George Shannon	February 14 (1952)	strawberries and chocolate
Laura Ingalls Wilder	February 7 (1867)	gingerbread with chocolate icing and lemonade
Elizabeth Winthrop	September 14 (1948)	brownies

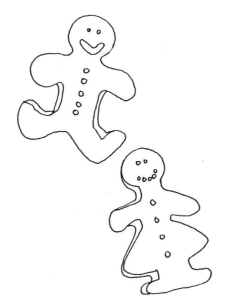

Chapter

5

Literature and the Arts

I hear, and I forget;
I see, and I remember;
I do, and I understand.
— Chinese Proverb

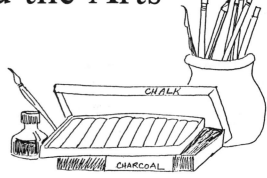

IDEAS TO "DRAW ON"

Children are frequently encouraged to respond to their reading through writing and speaking. Those who want to further encourage young readers to build memorable experiences with books will find ways to encourage the exploration and understanding of books through many other avenues within the curriculum, including art, music, and drama.

With the sentence "Draw a picture of your favorite part of the story," teachers often ask students to respond to a book artistically and expressively. Although this activity can be appropriate if not overused, there are other ways to promote expressive activities in connection with books. For example, during one first-grade class's focus on the collage art of Eric Carle, the children learned how to make marbleized paper using an alternative chalk method.[1] To teach the method to another class, a young writer created his own directions for the process (see figure 5.1).

Later, individuals in the class used Keats's collage techniques and created illustrations using marbleized paper as backgrounds for their illustrations and as endpapers for their own published writings. Through working with the art techniques in connection with their own writings, students were usually able to identify various techniques in the work of published authors and illustrators. In the case of the Keats study, students were able to recognize the subtle differences in techniques and materials used by various artists. Some collages (as those of Eric Carle) are created with tissue paper and brushed with paint for texture; other artists use more opaque paper. Differences within the basic technique were noted in the work of Carle, Keats, Leo Lionni, and Gerald McDermott. Paper was sometimes cut and sometimes torn. Some artists used plain paper and others used patterned paper to create the effect they wanted.

---

[1]See discussion of Ezra Jack Keats and his work in *My Bag of Book Tricks* by Sharron L. McElmeel (Englewood, CO: Libraries Unlimited, 1989), 119-22.

Put a Boll get the Chalk that Comes of fon Yor hands. tac Ser Sr S ScraP it in the Boll. Bloo the Chalk Put a Peec of PaPr in.

Fig. 5.1.

Students who were given the opportunity to respond to Keats's books through an expressive activity developed an awareness of the art form, improved their ability to recognize the art technique, expanded their own experiences through the medium, and broadened their writings by incorporating illustrations they had created with the technique they had studied. By encouraging the students to share with other students their information about an artist's work and technique, the readers were given the opportunity to summarize and sequence the information they had gained, resulting in an integration scheme that brought writing, speaking, listening, thinking, and the expressive arts together with reading.

Activities suggested in the following section will need to be adapted and implemented in different ways with different level groups. The sophistication of the responses to the activities will vary with the artistic sophistication of the group or individual; however, the process and thinking inherent in creating the product should be the constant and main consideration at all levels. When a mural is suggested, a group activity is implied—an activity that will take planning, organization, and group cooperation in addition to the expected artistic endeavors. When a new artistic technique is introduced, there will be opportunities for investigation, experimentation, and verification as well as opportunities for summarizing, analyzing, synthesizing, and evaluating.

CONNECTIONS TO MAKE—A SAMPLER

Albert, Burton. *Where Does the Trail Lead?* Illustrated by Brian Pinkney. Simon, 1991.
A boy follows a trail through buttercups and snapdragons, over sand and crunchy pine needles. He climbs over dunes and past honking geese—enjoying the smell of the salty sea.

- Simulate Pinkney's scratchboard technique by crayoning heavily on shiny-surfaced cardboard and covering the crayon with India ink (dabbed on with a cotton ball). After the ink has dried, scratch through the ink with pin or scissor points. This process is more appropriate for older students.

- Simulate the scratchboard technique using a procedure that is less sophisticated, but more appropriate for younger students:

  - Color a sheet of white paper with a thick layer of color. All white crayon may be used if you wish to have a black-and-white picture, but if you want colors to show through, color the paper with bands of the desired colors across the width of the paper.
  - Cover the entire paper with a thick coat of black crayon.
  - Use a round toothpick or any pointed object to scratch (or etch) out a drawing. In some cases a pencil can be used for the drawing. As the black layer is scratched, the under layer of white or color will show through, creating the desired image.

- Share other books that feature scratchboard illustrations:

Books with Scratchboard Illustrations

Agard, John. *The Calypso Alphabet*. Illustrated by Jennifer Bent. Holt, 1989.

Chauncer, Geoffrey. *Chanticleer and the Fox*. Illustrated by Barbara Cooney. Crowell, 1982.

Cooney, Barbara. *The Little Juggler*. Illustrated by Barbara Cooney. Hastings, 1961.

Fisher, Leonard Everett. *The Railroads*. Illustrated by Leonard Everett Fisher. Holiday, 1979.

Hooks, William H. *The Ballad of Belle Dorcas*. Illustrated by Brian Pinkney. Knopf, 1990.

Joseph, Lynn. *A Wave in Her Pocket: Stories from Trinidad*. Illustrated by Brian Pinkney. Clarion, 1991.

Kennedy, Richard. *The Song of the Horse*. Illustrated by Marcia Sewall. Dutton, 1981.

Baylor, Byrd. *Your Own Best Secret Place*. Illustrated by Peter Parnall. Scribner, 1979.
Special places are the focus in a lyrical verse.

- Make a diorama of "your own best secret place."

- Share other books about a special place, such as:

de Regniers, Beatrice Schenk. *Little House of Your Own*. Illustrated by Irene Haas. Harcourt, 1954.

Livingston, Myra Cohn. *I'm Hiding*. Illustrated by Erik Blegvad. Harcourt, 1961.

Bonners, Susan. *Pandas*. Illustrated by Susan Bonners. Delacorte, 1978. Yagawa, Sumiko. *The Crane Wife*. Translated by Katherine Paterson. Illustrated by Suekichi Akaba. Morrow, 1981.
Bonners's book brings us a gentle view of the panda, and Yagawa's story is a traditional tale from Japan. Both are illustrated with traditional Japanese-style paintings.

- Use dampened rice paper, ink, and watercolor to emulate the gentleness of the traditional Japanese paintings. This is a very appropriate technique to use to illustrate original haiku poetry.

Brown, Marcia. *Once a Mouse: A Fable Cut in Wood.* Illustrated by Marcia Brown. Scribner, 1961.
The illustrations in this tale of power and pride from India are woodcuts.

- Distinguish between woodcuts and linoleum cuts or linocuts. For each color to be printed, a separate wood or linoleum plate must be cut with the portions to be printed in a specific color left raised. The other parts of the wood or linoleum block are cut away. Once the block or plate is made, it is inked with a special printing ink, the paper is placed on top of the plate, and then the paper is pulled off the plate. Illustrations pulled from woodcuts can usually be identified by the wood grain visible in the finished illustration. Illustrations pulled from linoleum cuts do not show those texture lines.

- Woodcuts and linoleum cuts are generally not safe activities for elementary students. But a similar process can simulate the process. Use a foam meat tray. Wash the tray thoroughly and cut away the edges of the tray so there remains a flat rectangular piece of foam. Trace designs on the back side of the foam tray with a dull pencil or a ballpoint pen. Roll a water-based printing ink onto the tray and press onto it a piece of paper. Once the paper is pulled off there should be a printing of the image that had been drawn on the tray. Several printings can be made and various colors of printing ink used.

- Share books that are illustrated with linoleum cuts and woodcuts.

Linoleum Cuts

Brown, Marcia. *Dick Whittington and His Cat.* Illustrated by Marcia Brown. Scribner, 1950.

Fisher, Aileen. *Feathered Ones and Furry.* Illustrated by Eric Carle. Crowell, 1971.

Haley, Gail E. *A Story, A Story.* Illustrated by Gail E. Haley. Atheneum, 1970. (Haley explains her illustrative technique in the Weston Woods filmstrip/cassette *Gail E. Haley: Wood and Linoleum Illustration.*)

Woodcuts

Brown, Marcia. *How, Hippo!* Illustrated by Marcia Brown. Scribner, 1969.

Emberley, Barbara. *Drummer Hoff.* Illustrated by Ed Emberley. Prentice, 1967.

Emberley, Barbara. *One Wide River to Cross.* Illustrated by Ed Emberley. Prentice, 1966.

Emberley, Ed. *Green Says Go.* Illustrated by Ed Emberley. Little, 1968.

Ness, Evaline. *Josefina February.* Illustrated by Evaline Ness. Scribner, 1963.

Ness, Evaline. *Sam, Bangs, and Moonshine.* Illustrated by Evaline Ness. Holt, 1966.

Ness, Evaline. *Tom Tit Tot.* Illustrated by Evaline Ness. Scribner, 1965.

Rose, Anne. *Akimba and the Magic Cow.* Illustrated by Hope Merryman. Four Winds, 1976.

Cleary, Beverly. *Ramona and Her Father.* Illustrated by Alan Tiegreen. Morrow, 1977.
Ramona and her friends continue their escapades. In this story Ramona enjoys making "the longest picture in the world" and old-fashioned tin-can stilts.

- Make tin-can stilts.

- Use any media to create an original version of "the longest picture in the world."

Coerr, Eleanor. *The Josefina Quilt Story*. Illustrated by Bruce Degan. Harper, 1986.

Faith and her family set out across the prairie to settle in the West. Faith begs to take Josefina, her hen that is too old to lay eggs and too tough to eat. Eventually, Josefina demonstrates her usefulness as a member of the wagon train. During the journey Faith makes quilt patches commemorating events that take place during the trip, including Josefina's death.

- Replicate some of the quilt blocks that Faith makes during her journey. Make paper quilt blocks using crayon, cloth blocks using textile paints or markers, or appliquéd blocks using cloth scraps.

- Create your own story quilt using a favorite book to inspire designs for the quilt blocks.

Books About Quilts

Ernst, Lisa Campbell. *Sam Johnson and the Blue Ribbon Quilt*. Lothrop, 1983.

Flournoy, Valerie. *The Patchwork Quilt*. Illustrated by Jerry Pinkney. Dial, 1985.

Johnston, Tony. *The Quilt Story*. Illustrated by Tomie dePaola. Putnam, 1985.

Jonas, Ann. *The Quilt*. Illustrated by Ann Jonas. Greenwillow, 1984.

Polacco, Patricia. *The Keeping Quilt*. Illustrated by Patricia Polacco. Simon, 1988.

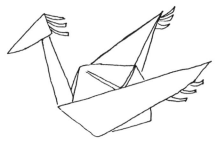

Coerr, Eleanor. *Sadako and the Thousand Paper Cranes*. Illustrated by Ronald Himler. Putnam, 1977.

A young girl suffering the aftereffects of the bombing of Japan is now dying. Before she dies she attempts to fold a thousand paper cranes in order to reap the benefits told of in an ancient legend. She is not able to complete the task, but after her death her friends continue folding and her memorial is surrounded by the thousand cranes.

- Fold paper cranes. Instructions are contained in origami books, which can be located by using the catalog in your library or library media center.

dePaola, Tomie. *Bonjour, Mr. Satie*. Illustrated by Tomie dePaola. Putnam, 1991.

Mr. Satie, a sophisticated cat, and his rat friend and traveling companion, Ffortusque Ffollet, Esq., have returned to the United States from their most recent trip to Paris. When Mr. Satie's niece and nephew receive a postcard announcing their visit, the title page of the book cleverly shows the steamer crossing the ocean from Paris to New York and the train chugging from New York to Rosalie and Conrad's home in Centerville. The vintage automobile sets the time period as the 1920s or 1930s. Uncle Satie tells stories of seeing his friend Pablo (Pablo Picasso) and of meeting Gertrude (Gertrude Stein) and Alice (Alice B. Toklas) in Paris. Henri (Henri Matisse) is also part of the story, which includes the depiction of several parodies of Matisse's and Picasso's work.

- Compare dePaola's depiction of Henri and Pablo with photographs of Matisse and Picasso.

- Read biographies of Picasso and Matisse. What real facts about these two artists did dePaola include in his book?

- Many people gathered at Gertrude's salon. In one illustration several well-known personalities are shown: James Joyce, Edith Sitwell, Isadora Duncan, Mabel Dodge, George Gershwin, Calvin Coolidge, B. Top, Josephine Baker, Ezra Pound, Ernest Hemingway, Zelda Fitzgerald, Paul Robeson, Claude Monet, and Virgil Thomson. On the jacket flap, dePaola identifies the people pictured, by first name and last initial. Two that I could not identify were Stephen S. and Olga P. DePaola included in the studio scene people who were close to Gertrude Stein prior to her move to England during World War I and others who were in her circle of friends upon her return to Paris after the war.

—Identify the period during which each of the characters pictured would likely have known Stein and been present in her studio.
—Locate some information about the relationship Stein had with each of these people.
—Identify the time setting for this story and profile life during that period.
—Identify some of the art masterpieces that are parodied in the illustrations.

Grimm, Jacob, and Wilhelm Grimm. *The Devil with the Three Golden Hairs*. Illustrated by Nonny Hogrogian. Knopf, 1983.
The endpapers of this book have been created with marbleized paper, recalling the backgrounds Ezra Jack Keats created for his illustrations.

• Share other books that feature marbleized papers.

Books with Marbleized Paper

Grimm, Jacob, and Wilhelm Grimm. *The Glass Mountain*. Illustrated by Nonny Hogrogian. Knopf, 1985. (Endpapers)

Keats, Ezra Jack. *Dreams*. Illustrated by Ezra Jack Keats. Macmillan, 1974. (Background for illustrations)

Lewis, Richard, ed. *In a Spring Garden*. Illustrated by Ezra Jack Keats. Dial, 1976. (Background for illustrations)

• Create marbleized paper. Swirl oil paints in a pan of water. Lay a piece of paper on the surface of the water. Lift it out and lay or hang to dry. If you do not wish to use oil paints, scrape colored chalk shavings into the water, swirl the shavings, and proceed in a manner similar to the steps you would take if you were using oil paints. More detailed instructions are available in *My Bag of Book Tricks*.[2]

Hoberman, Mary Ann. *A House Is a House for Me*. Illustrated by Betty Fraser. Viking, 1978.
Real and fanciful homes are featured in lyrical verses.

• Search for literary houses in favorite books and use them in a mural. Make sure to include Baba Yaga's chicken-footed house, the candy house of Hansel and Gretel, and Cinderella's castle.

• Create three-dimensional models of an unusual house from literature. Don't miss the cement block house from Robert O'Brien's *Mrs. Frisby and the Rats of NIMH* (Atheneum, 1971) and Sam's treehouse from Jean Craighead George's *My Side of the Mountain* (Dutton, 1975).

Hutchins, Pat. *Rosie's Walk*. Illustrated by Pat Hutchins. Macmillan, 1968.
Rosie, a red hen, is strutting through the barnyard seemingly unaware of the fox who is stalking her. At several points the fox is ready to pounce but is held back by happenstance: Rosie steps on a rake and the handle hits the fox in the face, etc. The fox never does get the hen.

• Create a map of Rosie's journey through the barnyard.

• Make cutouts of the story figures and move them along the map as the story is retold.

• Back cutouts of the figures with sandpaper and use the figures on a feltboard to aid in storytelling.

---

[2]See pages 119-22, *My Bag of Book Tricks* by Sharron L. McElmeel (Englewood, CO: Libraries Unlimited, 1989).

Lionni, Leo. *Swimmy*. Illustrated by Leo Lionni. Pantheon, 1963.
A group of small fish learn how to band together to scare away the threatening tuna.

- To emulate the watery illustrations used by Lionni in this title, use lace paper doilies and shapes whittled from erasers as objects for printing on paper that has been washed with watercolor.

Norton, Mary. *The Borrowers*. Illustrated by Beth Krush and Joe Krush. Harcourt, 1965.
This novel depicts the life of little people who live in a grandfather clock in a house.

- Construct a model of the Borrowers' rooms. Include walls papered with a "borrowed" letter, postage stamps hung as pictures on the wall, thimbles that serve as pails, bottle caps used for dishes, and gauze that serves as towels.

- Read other books about little characters that live in an object (e.g., shoe, dollhouse, clock) or in someone else's house.

Little Characters in Books

Andersen, Hans Christian. *Thumbelina*. (Many versions are available. Among the most popular is one retold by Amy Ehrlich and illustrated by Susan Jeffers (Dial, 1979), and one translated by M. R. James and illustrated by Kaj Beckman (Van Nostrand, 1973); also popular are a version titled *Thumbeline*, translated by Anthea Bell and illustrated by Lisbeth Zwerger (Picture, 1985), and one translated by Richard Winston and Clara Winston and illustrated by Lisbeth Zwerger (Morrow, 1980).)

de Regniers, Beatrice Schenk. *Penny*. Illustrated by Betsy Lewin. Lothrop, 1987. (An earlier edition illustrated by Marvin Bileck was published by Viking in 1966.)

Petersen, John. *The Littles*. Illustrated by Roberta C. Clark. Scholastic, 1970.

Peet, Bill. *How Droofus the Dragon Lost His Head*. Illustrated by Bill Peet. Houghton, 1971.
This fairy tale of sorts tells in rhyme about a lovable dragon named Droofus.

- Create large-scale papier-mâché dragons.

- Read other books about dragons.

Dragons in Books

dePaola, Tomie. *The Knight and the Dragon*. Illustrated by Tomie dePaola. Putnam, 1980.

Domanska, Janine. *King Krakus and the Dragon*. Illustrated by Janine Domanska. Greenwillow, 1979.

Hodges, Margaret. *Saint George and the Dragon: A Golden Legend*. Illustrated by Trina Schart Hyman. Little, 1984.

Karl, Jean. *The Search for the Ten-Winged Dragon*. Illustrated by Steve Cieslawski. Doubleday, 1990.

Kellogg, Steven. *Ralph's Secret Weapon*. Illustrated by Steven Kellogg. Dutton, 1983.

Seidelman, James, and Grace Mintonye. *The 14th Dragon*. Harlin Quist, 1968.

Williams, Jay. *Everyone Knows What a Dragon Looks Like*. Illustrated by Mercer Mayer. Four Winds, 1976.

Roy, Ron. *Three Ducks Went Wandering*. Illustrated by Paul Galdone. Houghton, 1979.
Three wandering ducks encounter a bull, foxes, a hawk, and a snake before ending up where they began—back home in their nest, safe with their mother.

- Create a map of the action, showing the duck's excursion.

Zemach, Harve. *The Judge*. Illustrated by Margot Zemach. Farrar, 1969.
The judge doubts the existence of the monster being described in his court; but finally he is convinced—just before he makes a hasty exit.

- Use large sheets of butcher paper and newspaper to stuff large-scale monsters.

- Use cardboard tubes, boxes, and so on to form all kinds of monsters.

- Search for other books that feature monsters. Among those that should be included is Maurice Sendak's *Where the Wild Things Are* (Harper, 1963).

FOCUS ON ENDPAPERS

Illustrators who are concerned with the total design of a book often design endpapers that complement or highlight the theme of the book or focus on a major character or element in the book. After reading a book with interesting endpapers, discuss the reasons the endpapers are the color and design they are. Learners who attempt to explain why the design or color of the endpapers is significant will gain experience in using critical thinking skills. Using as an example a book that has been read, continue to discuss how a critical element of the story might have suggested the design or the color of the endpapers. Or prepare endpapers for an original book that is to be published. Sometimes a "stamp" made from an eraser, a wooden block, or a stencil can be used to hand-make the endpaper.

Any focus on endpapers will help direct readers to a critical element of a book. Share the following books and discuss the significance of the endpapers created by the illustrators for the books.

Endpapers in Books

Ayres, Pam. *When Dad Cuts Down the Chestnut Tree*. Illustrated by Graham Percy. Knopf, 1988.
Endpapers depict a huge chestnut tree in the center of the double-page spread. A wall and other structures are depicted behind the massive tree.

Ayres, Pam. *When Dad Fills in the Garden Pond*. Illustrated by Graham Percy. Knopf, 1988.
A full view of the pond is shown on the endpapers.

Banks, Kate. *Alphabet Soup*. Illustrated by Peter Sis. Knopf, 1988.
Endpapers show a brown broth scattered with white letters reminiscent of the white alphabetical letters found in alphabet soup.

Barton, Byron. *Dinosaurs, Dinosaurs*. Illustrated by Byron Barton. Crowell, 1989.
Endpapers are a brilliant purple with large brightly colored silhouettes of dinosaurs. Four different dinosaurs are block-printed on each of the front and back endpapers. Each silhouette is identified with the dinosaur's name in white letters along with information on pronunciation of the name.

Brown, Marc. *D.W. All Wet*. Illustrated by Marc Brown. Little, 1988.
Endpapers are alternating blocks of yellow and white. Within each block is an object that could be part of a beach excursion: thonged sandals, a tube of sunscreen, popsicles, fudgesicles, a small shovel, a thermos, a picnic basket, snorkeling goggles, a seashell, a star shell, and a pair of sunglasses.

Hearn, Michael Patrick. *The Porcelain Cat*. Illustrated by Leo Dillon and Diane Dillon. Little, 1987.
Endpapers are an optical puzzle. Dark silhouettes show cats and mice in various poses. An overall pattern of dark and light space is created with one triad of cat images forming a light space between images that silhouette a bird. The endpapers show the most obvious characters that are part of the story from the beginning: the cat and the mouse. Only in the shadows of the cat does the figure of the bird emerge. That foreshadows the text of the book, which in the end has a bird coming to life from the broken figure of the porcelain cat.

Hogrogian, Nonny. *Noah's Ark*. Illustrated by Nonny Hogrogian. Knopf, 1986.
Endpapers in the front of the book show the inner structure of the ark with the vents, windows, and animal subdivisions located.

Jakes, John. *Susanna of the Alamo: A True Story*. Illustrated by Paul Bacon. Harcourt, 1988.
Endpapers show a map of Texas with a detail of the "places in the story. Important events at each place are given with dates."

Kherdian, David, and Nonny Hogrogian. *The Animal*. Illustrated by Nonny Hogrogian. Knopf, 1984.
Star-filled endpapers focus on the origin of *The Animal*, which in the lyrical story is said to have come "to them from a distant planet."

Martin, Jacqueline Briggs. *Bizzy Bones and Uncle Ezra* (1984); *Bizzy Bones and Moosemouse* (1986); *Bizzy Bones and the Lost Quilt* (1988). Illustrated by Stella Ormai. Lothrop.
Endpapers in the first title depict a map of the countryside where the story takes place. The original map, with the location of Moosemouse's house added, forms the endpapers for the second book. The home of the Orchard Mice, who play a pivotal role in the third book, is added to the map for that book's endpapers.

Most, Bernard. *Four & Twenty Dinosaurs*. Illustrated by Bernard Most. HarperCollins, 1990.
Endpapers depict various dinosaurs in the role of a nursery rhyme character. The same dinosaurs are found inside the book as part of an illustration accompanying a fractured nursery rhyme.

Segal, Lore. *The Story of Old Mrs. Brubeck and How She Looked for Trouble and Where She Found Him*. Illustrated by Marcia Sewall. Pantheon, 1981.
Various silhouettes of Old Mrs. Brubeck who is searching for trouble focus on the amusing theme.

Williams, Linda. *The Little Old Lady Who Was Not Afraid of Anything*. Illustrated by Megan Lloyd. Crowell, 1986.
The plain orange endpapers highlight the main character in the story, a character made with a pumpkin head.

Ziefert, Harriet. *Chocolate Mud & Cake*. Illustrated by Karen Gundersheimer. HarperCollins, 1988.
Molly and Jenny make a chocolate mud cake at their grandma and grandpa's house. But when the cake is done (baked in the sun) and they sit down to eat, both prefer a pretzel to the cake they have baked. The endpapers repeat a pattern of a yellow sun and a pretzel.

Ziefert, Harriet. *Me Too! Me Too!* Illustrated by Karen Gundersheimer. HarperCollins, 1988.
Two delightful little girls enjoy playing dress-up on a rainy day. The endpapers of this book reflect the season with a repeated pattern of a yellow rain hat and a bright blue flower.

GOING BEYOND

Many books lend themselves to using expressive art activities to provide the manipulation of story characters and setting. By allowing students to reconstruct portions of the story or story elements, we can help facilitate their understanding of the setting, identification of the story grammar, and visualization of story elements. The ability to manipulate the characters and setting of a story will enable the learner to develop innovations on the text, change the focus of the writing through styles and types of illustration, and develop a clearer understanding of the role of each character. Some suggestions for activities that involve creative and artistic expression follow.

1. Make a puppet representing one of the book characters. Use cloth, old socks, buttons, paper sacks, crayons, cardboard cutouts, popsicle sticks, or any other materials appropriate to the type of puppet to be made. Put on a puppet play.

2. Using mathematical computation to compute the size of a scale model, make papier-mâché models of characters—full-scale, larger than real, or smaller than real. When reading a book about whales, make a scale model of a whale. When reading about frogs, make a scale model of a frog.

3. Make a pop-up version of a scene in the story. Helpful suggestions to use with young readers are included in Joan Irvine's *How to Make Pop-Ups*, illustrated by Barbara Reid (Morrow, 1988), and *How to Make Books with Children* by Joy Evans and Jo Ellen Moore (Evan-Moor, 1985).

4. Make a story box to assist in retelling the story. Fill a flip-top school box (or an old cigar box) with miniature figures that represent characters in the story and small replicas of objects that are important to the story.

5. Use permanent magic markers to outline and draw characters onto pieces of felt. Cut out the felt characters and use them to retell the story on a feltboard.

6. Use clay or a salt and flour dough to make story tree ornaments or to create a three-dimensional illustration for the book.

    Craft Dough Figures

    4 cups flour
    1 cup salt
    Approximately 1½ cups warm water

    Mix ingredients together and knead the dough for at least 5 minutes, or until it is smooth. Shape the dough into figures. Place the figures on a foil-lined baking sheet and bake at 350 degrees for one hour. If the figures are to be hung, be sure to poke the hole in them before baking. After removing the figures from the oven, cool and paint them. Dipping the painted, dried figures in shellac or varnish will prevent them from cracking.

7. Make a game board for the story. The board could incorporate a map of the story area, cards relating to the book's action, and instructions for how to play the game.

8. Make endpapers for a favorite book. Be sure to focus on some aspect of the story when designing endpapers.

9. Make a new cover for a rebound book. Be sure to include the name and author on the book's spine.

10. Make a sequence of "movie" frames on a long horizontal roll of butcher paper. Starting at the last frame, roll the paper around a dowel stick and attach the other end to another stick. Before an audience unroll your movie while the story is retold live or by cassette tape.

11. Dramatize a story. The teacher or adult in the classroom can be the narrator who manages the impromptu "scripting." No props are necessary. Simply appoint parts and start reenacting the story. Ad lib the dialogue. For simple tales, such as "The Little Red Hen," several people can portray a single character and say the dialogue in unison.

12. Find a song that makes one think of the story's theme. With a group of friends sing the song to your class or another audience.

13. Write and perform a rap song or a poem that expresses an aspect of the story.

14. To develop perspective and the ability to visualize, make a three-dimensional model of a scene from the story. Use boxes, papier-mâché, clay, Styrofoam®, wooden blocks, and so on. This is especially helpful when the physical setting of a story is to be mapped. For example, a three-dimensional map of the setting through which Little Red Riding Hood traveled from her house, through the woods, and to her grandmother's house will help young readers visualize the setting. A two-dimensional map of the setting could be drawn to help students progress from the more concrete map to one that requires more visualization.

Part
II
Building More Connections

Chapter

6

The Bookshelf

Few children learn to love books by themselves.
Someone has to lure them into the wonderful
world of the written word; someone has to show
them the way.

—Orville Prescott

A READING TROVE

Reading aloud to children is still thought to be the single most effective activity to help children learn to read and enjoy reading. Orville Prescott wrote about the topic in his book *A Father Reads to His Children: An Anthology of Prose and Poetry* (Dutton, 1965), and Jim Trelease does the same in his book *The New Read-Aloud Handbook* (Viking, 1989). Reading aloud does much to lure students into the world of books. And reading books is the primary component in encouraging students to read and enjoy reading.

Reading aloud will allow a specific title to be shared with a group of children. Children respond to what has been read in many different ways, but by sharing a common reading experience children can join together to dramatize an event from the book, to share their favorite episodes, to explore and discuss the information presented in the book, and to focus on the story grammar and other stories. Often the only response to the reading of the book is to read another book. A good read-aloud of one author will often promote the reading of other books by the same author or will become the stimulation for reading a group of books tied together with a thematic thread.

Books with strong narratives are important in the elementary years because the narratives are compatible with the speaking patterns familiar to students and with students' listening experiences. A child's listening vocabulary and familiarity with speech patterns aid in the child's ability to read. A child's basic ability to read does much to facilitate that same child's ability to read for information and for other purposes. The response suggestions emphasized in the many literature-based reading series developed for the 1990s have continued to include an overwhelming number of suggestions for focusing on personal response, and even in the later grades the emphasis has been on works of fiction and personal responses to those works.

Yet, concepts about reading are changing. Dr. Willard R. Daggett, director of the International Center for Leadership in Education, speaks of the changes that educators need to address. In his many presentations from coast to coast Daggett cites studies that support his assertions that students in today's schools need to be encouraged to read more for information and critical analysis and less

101

for personal response. We must begin to prepare students for living in the twenty-first century, and the skills they will need as adults include skills that will enable them to

- understand written material

- follow written instructions

- put readings in context

- summarize main ideas and subsidiary ideas

- locate specific facts and details

- distinguish fact from inference

- interpret information in charts and tables

- use operating manuals

- understand technical and abstract material

Learners will also need skills in the other language arts areas that will enable them to

- write clearly and legibly

- take notes and develop outlines

- organize information into logical paragraphs

- compose letters, reports, and memoranda

- proofread and edit material

- locate sources of information

- cite reference sources correctly

- draft a project proposal

- respond appropriately to oral directions

- present oral information and directions

- observe verbal and nonverbal cues

- participate in a discussion

Literature, including information literature, provides children with models of good writing and presents opportunities for building writing skills through innovations on the text and extensions of the concepts within the text. Oral reading helps children develop an appreciation for well-written literature and extends their thinking skills. Books with a strong narrative, such as works of fiction, do not need to be abandoned completely in favor of books devoted to providing information. There are many opportunities to build needed skills through all types of literature.

In the bookshelf entries that follow I have tried to include a variety of titles that lend themselves to developing the skills listed in the preceding paragraphs. One must find the content interesting and must develop skills inherent in the reading of all types of written material. It is the skills that can be developed through the activities that is the key component. For example, in chapter 3, I suggested that Russell Freedman's book *The Wright Brothers: How They Invented the Airplane* (Holiday, 1991) be introduced and that as a follow-up response Seymour Simon's *Paper Airplane Book*, illustrated by Byron Barton (Viking, 1971), be used to encourage readers to investigate the art of making paper airplanes. This activity not only gives students a perspective of history and of the value of creativity, thinking, and persistence, but by following up with the Simon book, teachers also give young readers an opportunity to develop their ability to *follow written instructions* and to use their own thinking skills and creativity.

Other response suggestions, such as having readers make a list of animals in a book, helps readers *locate specific facts and details*. Response suggestions that encourage students to investigate a topic further provide the opportunity for the students to *locate sources of information* and *to cite those sources correctly*. Reading a book of fiction and collaborative factual information helps students *distinguish fact from inference*. Suggestions to create maps of the story action that takes place in a specific book of fiction can assist students in *interpreting charts and tables*. Graphing class preferences for specific books or lists of books can also provide opportunities for students to develop the ability to interpret graphs. Discussions following the reading of a book present students with the opportunity to *participate in a discussion* and thus increase their ability to organize and articulate their thoughts and ideas.

Other responses have similar goals. Response suggestions that include the writing of letters, summaries, etc., provide opportunities for students to practice *organizing material, composing letters, writing legibly and clearly*, and *proofreading and editing*.

Most of the title suggestions given in this chapter are appropriate for oral reading. For each I have also provided suggestions for response activities whose purpose is to develop in groups of children an active and cooperative response to literature, both fiction and factual. In many cases, the activity suggestions can be used to simply model a type of activity. After a type of activity is modeled successfully with readers and they are given a chance to respond in guided situations, they will be more confident and successful in developing their own ideas for books they have read. It will be that success that promotes more reading.

In the following section, in addition to book annotations and suggestions for response activities that promote a new focus on reading for information and critical analysis, I have included "Connections" for some of the titles. The connecting points include a variety of information, depending on the information that was available or ideas that seemed to connect naturally with the title cited. Some of the connections include tidbits about the author of a cited title and often titles of other books by that author. By using those connections in conjunction with the cited title, teachers can motivate students to read further. Other connections suggest related activities or books or simply approaches to use for getting started with a specific title. Each time a connection is made, a new opportunity for wide reading is presented. As connecting points are brought into focus, readers are challenged to think in new terms and to identify universal themes and topics.

Some responses suggested seem simple on the surface but take a great deal of background building and planning on the instructor's part. For example:

- To create an innovation on a text a child must have a thorough knowledge of the original. That is not accomplished with one reading or one experience with a single version. In many ways an innovation on a text is a personal response, but the play with the verse and the words helps one to understand the use of language. Eventually the thorough command of the language and its use will aid students in writing technical reports and other communications.

- Making a list of objects or animals in a story helps a reader search out specific facts in a text. Later when that reader must search out significant dates or events from an article about a historical period, the reader will find that his or her previous experience with skimming is very valuable.

Inherent in all of the responses suggested are skills that need to be introduced, practiced, or further developed, depending on the audience. If students begin with books dealing with experiences with which they can identify, they can start to focus on those skills in a comfortable setting. As each student's experience with the skills becomes more sophisticated and his or her ability to read is confirmed, that student will be able to apply those skills to reading information books and books with a more difficult reading level.

The most important response to any book, however, is the reading of another book. Therefore, many connecting points suggested include other titles by the author or books on a connecting theme. I have also tried to include response suggestions that are simply fun, because children must learn to associate reading with pleasure and enjoyment. As the pleasure grows so does the reader's desire to read more books.

It is within the power of every teacher, library media specialist, or public librarian to give children a rich experience with literature. We must teach children to read, but more important we must help them want to read—and the very best way to do that is to give children *time to read and the inspiration to enjoy and learn*.

BOOKS AND IDEAS FOR EXPRESSIVE RESPONSES

Abercrombie, Barbara. *Charlie Anderson*. Illustrated by Mark Graham. McElderry, 1990. (Picture book)

Two sisters own a cat, Charlie. Charlie is often gone and the girls do not know where he is, but he always comes back. A young man and woman also own a cat, Anderson. Anderson is often gone and the couple do not know where he is, but he always comes back. One day the girls' cat doesn't come home and they go searching for him. They find that Charlie has another home and another name, Anderson. The four of them decide to call the cat Charlie Anderson and to keep two homes for him. Charlie Anderson has two homes and two family portraits (as displayed in the illustration on the last page of the book).

- Discuss the similarity between Charlie Anderson's living arrangements and the living arrangement of the girls in the story. The girls also have two homes: one with their father and stepmother and one with their mother.

- Compare the girls' relationship with Charlie Anderson with Annie's situation in *Annie and the Wild Animals* by Jan Brett (Houghton, 1985). In *Annie and the Wild Animals*, Annie finds that her cat has gone away. She misses her pet and decides to attract a new one by leaving treats at the edge of the clearing near the forest. She succeeds in attracting all sorts of wild animals but none that would be an appropriate pet. Finally, Annie's cat comes home, with a litter of baby kittens born while she is away.

Ackerman, Karen. *Just Like Max*. Illustrated by George Schmidt. Knopf, 1990. (Picture book)

Seven-year-old Aaron idolizes his great-uncle Max, a tailor. When Max has a stroke Aaron visits him. Finally Aaron coaxes Max out of his sickbed and puts him on the path to recovery when he (Aaron) begins a sewing project of his own.

- Aaron shows a great deal of concern for his great-uncle, much as Tanya does in Valerie Flournoy's *The Patchwork Quilt* (see entry on p. 133). Compare and contrast Aaron's actions with Tanya's in *The Patchwork Quilt*.

- Ackerman's book can be described as one of intergenerational sharing, a book that shows the link between generations of people. Another book that does this superbly is Eve Bunting's *The Wednesday Surprise* (see entry on p. 118). Discuss the concept of caring and sharing with someone of another generation.

- Identify and read other books that portray intergenerational sharing:

Intergenerational Stories

Flournoy, Valerie. *The Patchwork Quilt*. Illustrated by Jerry Pinkney. Dial, 1985.

Fox, Mem. *Wilfrid Gordon McDonald Partridge*. Illustrated by Julie Vivas. Omnibus, 1983; Kane-Miller, 1983, 1985.

Kimmelman, Leslie. *Me and Nana*. Illustrated by Marilee Robin Burton. HarperCollins, 1990.

Polacco, Patricia. *The Keeping Quilt*. Illustrated by Patricia Polacco. Simon, 1988.

- Brainstorm some ways that students can interact and share with grandparents or older neighbors and friends. If the situation presents itself, perhaps an intergenerational project could become a class project for the year. The close proximity of a nursing home or care center for the elderly certainly presents some more obvious opportunities to share and become involved with older people, but there are other alternatives:

    — Have members of the class write and send a monthly letter to their own grandparent(s).
    — Establish a relationship by mail with residents of a nursing home in your city. Send student pictures, cards, and letters on a regular basis. Send tapes of the class singing holiday songs. If the home has access to a video recorder, make videotaped messages and musical programs for the residents. It would be nice if the residents could respond personally, but remind students that some may not be able to do so.
    — Identify special older neighbors with whom students could establish individual relationships. These friends could be invited to school to see classroom programs, have cookies and "tea" during a writer's showcase program, or just be honored guests for a portion of the day. Hold a special Invite-a-Friend Day, when the students invite their older friends to have lunch with them in the school cafeteria.

Connections

Karen Ackerman is the author of the Caldecott Award-winning title *Song and Dance Man* (Knopf, 1988). Her other titles include *Flannery Row: An Alphabet Rhyme*, illustrated by Karen Ann Weinhaus (Atlantic/Joy Street, 1986); *Moveable Mabeline*, illustrated by Linda Allen (Philomel, 1990); and *Araminta's Paint Box*, illustrated by Betsy Lewin (Atheneum, 1990). Ackerman writes poetry and is also a playwright. She lives in Cincinnati, Ohio.

Adler, David A. *A Picture Book of Abraham Lincoln*. Illustrated by John Wallner and Alexandra Wallner. Holiday, 1989. (Biography)
This book provides simple facts about Lincoln's childhood, his young adulthood, his presidency, the Civil War, and his death.

- Use the dates at the back of the book to create a timeline.

- Mention the fact that Abraham Lincoln is honored by having his image on the U.S. one cent coin. Discuss why students feel Lincoln was chosen to be honored on the penny.

- Coin designs are seldom changed or new denominations minted, but the U.S. Postal Service regularly selects new images for postage stamps. Discuss the merits of topics or individuals honored by U.S. postage stamps. Select your own choice for someone to be honored or an event to be commemorated and submit data and a rationale to support your choice. Specific criteria for events or people to be honored on a postage stamp can be obtained from:
    Citizens Stamp Advisory Committee
    U.S. Postal Service Headquarters
    475 l'Enfant Plaza Southwest
    Washington, DC 20260-6753

The data and rationale for convincing the postal service to honor a specific person or event should be sent to the committee, who will make recommendations to the postmaster general, who will make the final determination.

Adler, David A. *A Picture Book of Benjamin Franklin*. Illustrated by John Wallner and Alexandra Wallner. Holiday, 1990. (Biography)
Factual information is given about Franklin's life and achievements as an inventor, scientist, writer, and statesman.

- Make a timeline of Franklin's life using information given in the text and in the date chart at the end of the book.

- Make a list of all the things invented or begun by Benjamin Franklin. Search other sources and biographies for additional information.

- Make a list of famous people who would have known Benjamin Franklin. With a timeline show when their lives would have overlapped. Developing a sense of perspective with regard to historical events and the lives of historical figures helps students understand the total history of a place or person.

Ahlberg, Allan. *The Black Cat*. Illustrated by André Amstutz. Greenwillow, 1990; *The Pet Shop*. Illustrated by André Amstutz. Greenwillow, 1990. (Junior novels)
These are stories about skeletons—Funnybones. In one story a black cat wants to use the skeleton's sled, and in the other a noisy skeleton dog is traded for another pet.

- Discuss the superstitions that revolve around black cats, ladders, the number **13**, and so on. Read Lila Perl's *Blue Monday and Friday the Thirteenth: The Stories Behind the Days of the Week* (Clarion, 1986).

- Research breeds of cats and determine which ones could be "black cats." Make a chart identifying and giving information about black cats.

Connections

Allan Ahlberg and Janet Ahlberg have collaborated on several books. Janet Ahlberg created the illustrations for Allan's first book, *Funnybones* (Greenwillow, 1981). That book is set in a dark house and dark cellar and has a lot of skeletons. Allan Ahlberg and Janet Ahlberg have written many other books, including *The Jolly Postman*. The Ahlbergs live in England. For more information about them see *Bookpeople: A First Album* (Teacher Ideas Press, 1990).

Ahlberg, Janet, and Allan Ahlberg. *The Jolly Postman or Other People's Letters*. Little, Brown, 1986. (Picture book)
The story line is a simple one. The jolly postman sets out on his bicycle to deliver letters to people along his route. The first letter is addressed to "Mr. and Mrs. Bear, Three Bears Cottage, The Woods." An envelope holds the actual letter written to the Bears. It is an apology from Goldilocks along with an invitation to Baby Bear to attend a birthday party where "ther will be 3 kinds of ice cream and a majishun." Other letters are delivered to the Wicked Witch at the Gingerbread Bungalow; Mr. V. Bigg at Beanstalk Gardens; Cinderella at Half Kingdom Road; B. B. Wolf, Esq., c/o Grandma's Cottage; and finally a birthday greeting to Goldilocks at Banbury Cross. With that final delivery the jolly postman goes "home for the evening—for tea!"

- Create letters of your own for favorite fairy tale characters. What would the troll write to the biggest billy goat gruff, Rumpelstiltskin to the queen, the fisherman's wife to the fish, the cat to Dick Whittington, the Pied Piper to the mayor of Hamlin?

Connections

Those readers who know well the fairy tales on which the letters in *The Jolly Postman* are based will more fully enjoy the humor. Prior to sharing *The Jolly Postman*, encourage students to read the following tales: "The Three Bears," "Hansel and Gretel," "Cinderella," "The Three Little Pigs," "Jack and the Beanstalk," and "Little Red Riding Hood." After wide reading of fairy tales, especially those of the Grimm brothers and Charles Perrault, read aloud *The Jolly Postman*. Share the book with a large group by using transparencies or enlargements of the letters and postcards. These will provide a model and motivation for the development of creative presentations of letters written by other folklore characters.

- Use this book to illustrate the various perspectives from which a story or incident might be viewed. After reading any novel or story, identify one of the characters in the story that might tell the story from a different point of view. Discuss how that character might view events in a different way than the character now telling the story. Write a letter or a diary entry describing a specific incident from the alternate character's point of view.

Alexander, Sally Hobart. *Sarah's Surprise*. Illustrated by Jill Kastner. Macmillan, 1990. (Picture book)
An outing to gather mussels turns into a fearful climb for Sarah as she climbs over wet rocks and around deep crevasses. When Sarah's mother sprains her ankle, Sarah finds that she can overcome her fears to get the necessary help for her mother.

- In this situation Sarah proves to herself that she can do what needs to be done. In some ways this story is like *Katy Did It* by Victoria Boutis (Greenwillow, 1982). Read that book and discuss the similarities.

- Identify other stories that deal with the same main thesis or emotions. For example, in Carol Carrick's *The Foundling* (Clarion, 1977), Christopher must overcome his grief for Bodger, his pet that was killed several weeks before. The story of Bodger's death is told in *The Accident*, by Carol Carrick (Clarion, 1976). Christopher comes to terms with his grief before he can accept a new puppy. Other stories that might fit this category include books dealing with the emotions revolving around a new baby in the house, such as Ezra Jack Keats's *Peter's Chair* (HarperCollins, 1967).

Alexander, Sue. *Muriel and the Scary Dragon*. Illustrated by Chris L. Demarest. Little, 1985. (Picture book)
Famous Muriel is the best tightrope walker in the world. She is asked to help rid the kingdom of a fire-breathing dragon. Muriel has an unusual way of taking care of the dragon.

- Develop conceptual skills by creating a model of the scary dragon. Make a long cardboard dragon and cut it into sections. Put a handle on the back of each section so that it can be held. Use the dragon to help dramatize the story.

Alexander, Sue. *World Famous Muriel and the Magic Mystery*. Illustrated by Marla Frazee. Crowell, 1990. (Picture book)

One morning Muriel receives a note on her doorstep. The note announces the magic show to be put on by "the Great Hokus Pokus." During the show the Great Hokus Pokus makes animals appear and disappear and then *he* disappears. Muriel and Professor M. C. Ballyhoo do not think the magician's disappearance is part of the show. The professor asks Muriel to help find the Great Hokus Pokus. She and the professor have several misadventures before they find him.

- The Great Hokus Pokus goes to the library to search out some magic books so that he can find out how to do some tricks. Visit your school or public library and locate some books on magic. Learn a magic trick and perform it for your friends.

- After several students have learned a magic trick, hold a Magic Day and invite another class, parents, or special friends.

- Ask a local magician to visit the class and show some simple tricks to the class.

Connections

Sue Alexander is a good friend of Newbery Award-winning author Sid Fleischman. In fact, she dedicated this book about Muriel to him. Fleischman once made his living as a magician. In another book by Alexander, *Witch, Goblin, and Ghost's Book of Things to Do* (Pantheon, 1982), Fleischman created a magic trick especially for Goblin to perform in the book. Goblin says he has been taught the magic trick by "Mr. Mysterious." On the poster in the book, Mr. Mysterious looks a lot like the real Sid Fleischman. Use this connection to motivate more reading, especially of other books by Alexander, and to find out the type of books Fleischman writes. For more information about author Sue Alexander see *Bookpeople: A First Album* (Teacher Ideas Press, 1990), and for more information about Fleischman see *Bookpeople: A Second Album* (Teacher Ideas Press, 1990).

Allen, Pamela. *Hidden Treasure*. Illustrated by Pamela Allen. Putnam, 1986. (Picture book)

While two brothers are fishing they snag a chest that they suppose is filled with treasure. One brother pushes the other overboard and keeps the treasure for himself. He then must take precautions that no one finds and takes the treasure from him. Even though he is not shown opening the chest, he drags the "treasure" to a high mountain, where he spends all of his time burrowing deep into the mountain to create a cavern. He hides the chest in the cavern and protects the entrance with a boulder and a rock fortress. Alone on the mountain he is obsessed with protecting his treasure. Only on the last page do we see the brother who had been pushed overboard. He evidently made it to shore, married, and raised a family. He is shown in a cozy room, sitting on a sofa, reading to what appears to be his grandchildren. The unwritten question is: "Who has the greatest treasure?"

- Before reading the story brainstorm a list of things that would be considered treasures.

- After reading the story discuss the question of which brother had the most valuable treasure. Did the treasure chest hold any actual "treasure," and of what use was it to the brother who had it? After the discussion brainstorm another list of things that would be considered treasures. Have student's ideas changed?

- Read books about real treasures that have been uncovered. An excellent source is *Sunken Treasure* by Gail Gibbons (Crowell, 1988). The book details the efforts, over a 20-year time span, to recover the treasures that went down with *Nuestra Señora de Atocha*, a ship on its way back to Spain from South America in 1622. The final pages of the book highlight the details surrounding the sinking of other ships that went down with treasures. Included is information about the *Mary Rose*, an English warship that sank in 1545 off the coast of England; the *Vasa*, a Swedish warship that capsized in Stockholm's harbor in 1628; the *Whydah*, a pirate ship that ran aground off Cape Cod, Massachusetts, in 1717; and the *Titanic*, a luxury liner that struck an iceberg off the coast of Nova Scotia in 1912. More information about the *Titanic* can be located in *The Titanic: Lost and Found* by Judy Donnelly (Random, 1987) and *Exploring the Titanic* by Robert D. Ballard (Scholastic, 1988).

Allen, Pamela. *I Wish I Had a Pirate Suit*. Illustrated by Pamela Allen. Viking, 1990. (Picture book) Make-believe pirate adventures bring together a small boy and his swashbuckling older brother.

- Read other pirate stories, such as Pat Hutchins's *One-Eyed Jake*, illustrated by Pat Hutchins (Greenwillow, 1979), or Margaret Mahy's *Sailor Jack and the Twenty Orphans*, illustrated by Robert Bartlet (Watts, 1970).

- Read poems about pirates. Mildred Plew Meigs's "The Pirate Don Durk of Dowdee" can be found in *The Arbuthnot Anthology of Children's Literature*, edited by May Hill Arbuthnot et al., 3d ed. (Scott, Foresman, 1971), and Robert Louis Stevenson's "Pirate Story" in *A Child's Garden of Verses*, illustrated by Tasha Tudor (Walck, 1947). Stevenson's *A Child's Garden of Verses* is available in several illustrated versions.

- Not all pirates were scoundrels as one might believe from the way pirates are usually portrayed. Some pirates attempted to right the injustices of society by setting up free colonies. Investigate the history of several pirates who became national heroes or patriots. Sir Henry Morgan became commander of English forces in Jamaica. Jean Laffite helped American forces defend New Orleans in the War of 1812. Others who committed acts of piracy include Sir Francis Drake, William Dampier, Captain Jack "Calico Jack" Rackham, Bartholomew "Black Bart" Roberts, Captain Kidd, Edward "Blackbeard" Teach, Stede Bonnet, Captain Greavs, Anne Bonney, and Mary Read.

Connections

T. J. and the Pirate Who Wouldn't Go Home by Carol Gorman (Scholastic, 1990) is a contemporary story about T. J., a sixth-grader, and his Uncle Ainsley, who use a time machine to bring Captain Billy from out of the past and into the twentieth century. Captain Billy really enjoys TV game shows and Big Macs but he also keeps on burglarizing stores and pickpocketing people, actions not out of character for pirates. T. J. and his uncle decide that Captain Billy must go back. The problem is that Captain Billy doesn't want to return. During the reading of the first chapter ask listeners to note phrases that describe Captain Billy. Do not share the cover of the book. Ask listeners to draw their images of Captain Billy. The larger the drawings the more interest they will generate when they are displayed. After the pictures are created, reread the first chapter and compare the details in the book with those in the pictures of the captain. Then look at the cover of *T. J. and the Pirate Who Wouldn't Go Home* (Scholastic Apple edition). Do you think the cover illustrator read the book? Why or why not? Some of the pirate stories and poems can be enjoyed by very young students and older students as well. Ask an older class in your school to read *T. J. and the Pirate Who Wouldn't Go Home*, to draw pictures of pirates, and to display them near your students' classroom. Use the pictures as a springboard for sharing Allen's and Hutchins's pirate stories.

Baker, Keith. *Who Is the Beast?* Illustrated by Keith Baker. Harcourt, 1990. (Picture book)
Jungle animals flee from a mysterious beast. Each one tells of a terrifying feature of the beast. A huge tiger hears their cries and becomes alarmed. Eventually he discovers that *he* is the beast that they are running away from. Tiger attempts to show the other animals that they are all beasts and can be friends.

- Compare Baker's book to the mix-up in *Who's in Rabbit's House* by Verna Aardema (Dial, 1977).

- Make an alphabet riddle book of beasts. Illustrate each animal on a full page and then add a preceding page giving a description of the animal. Each description should contain two or more attributes of the animal.

- Read other animal riddle books. Jan Garten's *An Alphabet Tale* (Random, 1964) uses an alphabet format, and Beatrice Schenk de Regniers's *It Does Not Say Meow and Other Animal Riddles* (Dial, 1972) showcases more familiar animals with illustrations by Paul Galdone.

- Discuss phrases using common characteristics of animals: stubborn as a mule, mad as a hornet, quacks like a duck, big as an elephant, laughs like a hyena, eats like a pig, swims like a fish, busy as a bee, and sly as a fox. Interview parents and add to the list of sayings that refer to animals.

- Use the phrase list developed in the preceding activity to help solve the riddles in *Q Is for Duck: An Alphabet Guessing Name* by Mary Elting and Michael Folsom, illustrated by Jack Kent (Houghton, 1980).

Balian, Lorna. *Wilbur's Space Machine*. Illustrated by Lorna Balian. Holiday, 1990. (Picture book)
Wilbur and Olive have a comfortable little house in their valley until neighbors begin to move in and one of them has a pesky little boy. To solve their problem Wilbur invents a "space" machine. The space machine is not what one might think. This space machine puts "space" into balloons. Eventually the balloons are tied onto every corner of Wilbur and Olive's home and lift it aloft. Somehow, high in the sky, their pesky little neighbor has managed to sail aloft with them. They solve the problem by attaching him to some of the balloons and sending him aloft by himself.

- Over a period of time the space around Wilbur and Olive's home gets more and more congested. That element of the story line could be compared to the story line in Virginia Lee Burton's *The Little House* (Houghton, 1939). Compare and contrast the story grammar in these tales to determine the similarities and to identify the variant endings.

- Discuss the multiple meaning of the word *space* as used in the term *space machine*. Then help students develop additional vocabulary by encouraging them to brainstorm another list of words that have the same spelling but have two entirely different meanings, such as *watch, rose*, and *bat*.

- Let partners choose a word from the brainstormed list. Each set of partners should illustrate each of the two meanings of the word. For example, the word *rose* could be illustrated with a drawing of the flower, and the illustration for the other definition (of the verb *to rise*) could show something rising above a surface, such as a magician's assistant rising above a bed.

Connections

Lorna Balian began writing to help support her family of six children. The ideas for her stories usually come from her own life. Her children first used the term *aminal*; later the word became the title for *The Aminal* (Abingdon, 1972). An 82-year-old neighbor and her duck Willy gave Balian the idea for *Sometimes It's Turkey, Sometimes It's Feathers* (Abingdon, 1973). And the cat in *Amelia's Nine Lives* (Abingdon, 1986) was a cat in the Balian household. Balian creates many of her illustrations in watercolor or pen and ink. She and her husband, John Balian, live in Hartford, Wisconsin.

Bang, Molly. *The Paper Crane*. Illustrated by Molly Bang. Morrow, 1985. (Picture book)
   A new highway that bypasses an established restaurant causes a decline in customers and puts the restaurant on the verge of closing. One day a stranger comes, orders a meal, and in payment of the meal folds a paper crane. The paper crane comes to life and attracts multitudes of new customers to the restaurant. When the restaurant is once more firmly established, the stranger returns, plays the flute for the dancing crane, and rides away with the crane into the sky.

* Locate and use directions to fold a paper crane (or another object). Use the subject headings "Paper Folding and Crafts" and "Origami" in your library media center's catalog. One source of information about folding paper cranes is *The Art of Chinese Paper Folding for Young and Old* by Maying Soong (Harcourt, 1948).

* Compare the magic in Bang's book to that in other books where an object or plaything comes to life:

   Hearn, Michael Patrick. *The Porcelain Cat*. Illustrated by Leo Dillon and Diane Dillon. Little, 1987.

   Lionni, Leo. *Let's Make Rabbits*. Illustrated by Leo Lionni. Pantheon, 1982.

   Steig, William. *The Amazing Bone*. Illustrated by William Steig. Farrar, 1976.

   Williams, Margery. *The Velveteen Rabbit: Or How Toys Become Real*. Illustrated by David Jorgensen. Knopf, 1985. (Many other editions with illustrations by other artists are available of this classic first published in 1922.)

* A legend surrounding Japanese beliefs regarding the paper crane is told in Eleanor Coerr's *Sadako and the Thousand Paper Cranes*, illustrated by Ronald Himler (Putnam, 1977) (see entry on pp. 124-25).

Connections

Molly Garrett Bang uses at least three names in her writing: Molly Bang, Garrett Bang, and Molly Garrett Bang. She began writing when editors told her no one wrote the way she illustrated. She was told her work was too scary and too much in the style of the Japanese. So she wrote scary stories she could illustrate. In 1973 *The Goblins Giggle and Other Stories* was published by Scribner. She also collected folktales that she had heard and read while in Japan and published them in *Men from the Village Deep in the Mountain and Other Japanese Folk Tales* (Macmillan, 1977). She created the wordless Caldecott Honor Book *The Grey Lady and the Strawberry Snatcher*

(Four Winds, 1980) and *Wiley and the Hairy Man* (Macmillan, 1976). *Wiley and the Hairy Man* is a "conjure" tale from the American South. More recently Bang has written *Ten, Nine, Eight* (Greenwillow, 1983) and *Dawn* (Morrow, 1983), a version of "the Crane Wife."

Molly Bang was born December 29, 1943, in Princeton, New Jersey, and grew up in Baltimore, Maryland. Her father, Frederik Bang, was a research physician, and her mother, Betsy Garrett Bang, is a medical researcher who also translated and authored several books that Molly Bang has illustrated. Molly Bang lives in Woods Hole on Cape Cod in Massachusetts with her husband, Richard Campbell, and her daughter, Monika.

Banks, Kate. *Big, Bigger, Biggest Adventure*. Illustrated by Paul Yalowitz. Knopf, 1990. (Picture book)

This is an account of three brothers, Peter, Louis, and Henry, who go down valleys, up mountains, under dark clouds, get wet, and are late. The story is a vehicle for using comparative adjectives: big, bigger, biggest; tall, taller, tallest; and so on.

- Use this story to introduce comparative adjectives.

- Discuss using the -*er* suffix when two things or objects are being compared and using the -*est* suffix when three or more things or objects are being compared.

- Play the "comparing, comparing game." The game is a round robin exercise where each person in the group makes a comparison statement. If the first person uses a comparative statement using an -*er* adjective, the next person must use an -*est* comparative adjective correctly. In addition, no one can use an adjective root word that has already been used. Once someone has used *bigger* or *biggest*, neither word can be used again. The object is to repeat this game often enough so that eventually the round-robin is successfully completed around the entire room. This is a great game to use during those few minutes before recess or lunch.

Connections

Kate Banks was born in Maine. At the beginning of her writing career she worked as an assistant editor for children's books at a New York publishing house. One of her first books was *Alphabet Soup*, illustrated by Peter Sis (Knopf, 1988). Kate Banks lives in Rome, Italy.

Barton, Byron. *Bones, Bones, Dinosaur Bones*. Illustrated by Byron Barton. HarperCollins, 1990. (Picture book)

Six paleontologists search for dinosaur bones. When they find some, the bones are wrapped, loaded, and trucked to a natural history museum, where a Tyrannosaurus rex skeleton is reassembled.

- Use this book as an introduction to paleontology.

- Continue the focus on a scientific study of dinosaurs by reading Aliki's *Digging Up Dinosaurs* (Crowell, 1981; 1988). Aliki's title is also a Reading Rainbow featured book.

- Barton's book shows candy-colored dinosaurs in bold silhouettes outlined in black. The dinosaurs that are featured include Apatosaurus, Parasaurolophus, Gallimimus, Stegosaurus, Thicodontosaurus, Tyrannosaurus rex, Ankylosaurus, and Triceratops. Investigate these dinosaurs and have students share the information they find by making information charts about each.

- Read Barton's *Dinosaurs, Dinosaurs* (Crowell, 1989).

- Develop students' ability to conceptualize by having them make a scale model of a favorite dinosaur using a wire frame and papier-mâché.

Connections

Byron Theodore Vartanian Barton is the first generation of his Armenian family to have been born in America. He was born on September 8, 1930, in Rhode Island but grew up in Los Angeles. In the 1950s after he had served in the army and finished art school, he moved to New York. He worked at CBS, where he designed short films for titles and promotions. Some of his friends and his wife (they divorced after three years) were working with children's books. Barton also became interested and now works on children's books most of his time. Among his favorite children's books is *Wind in the Willows* by Kenneth Grahame (many versions are available), and one of his favorite illustrators is the late Lois Lenski. Use this information to stimulate interest in his other books and in the books of Grahame and Lenski.

Bellamy, David. *How Green Are You?* Illustrated by Penny Dann. Clarkson N. Potter, 1991. (Information book)
This book introduces whales and tells how they can help us save the environment. It encourages young people to learn what they can do to make the world "green."

- Use the information in the book to start a compost pile at your school and at home.

- Make a bird feeder, "a simple bird table," to keep the birds fed during the winter.

- On the back pages of the book are addresses of organizations that are working to save the environment. Write to the organizations for more information about how you and your class can help save the environment.

- Write an action plan proposal for your class. Submit your action plan to the administrators of your school for approval and support. Correlate the listing of more than 100 ways to help. *Save the Earth* by Betty Miles (Knopf, 1974; 1991) may be of some assistance.

Birdseye, Tom. *Airmail to the Moon.* Illustrated by Stephen Gammell. Holiday, 1988. (Picture book)
Ora Mae Cotton and her family live in Crabapple Orchard (in the Appalachians). Ora Mae has lost a tooth and thinks she left it under her pillow, but when she awakens in the morning the tooth is not there and it appears the tooth fairy has not come either. Ora Mae accuses almost everyone of taking her tooth. But the ending is predictable as Ora Mae thrusts her hand deep into her pocket.

- Use this book as a great read-aloud on the day someone loses his or her first tooth.

- Correlate with a focus on the books of Cynthia Rylant (see *Bookpeople: A First Album* [Teacher Ideas Press, 1990]), who writes about her experiences growing up in the Appalachians. Stephen Gammell also illustrated one of those books, *The Relatives Came* (Bradbury, 1985). Use this opportunity to locate the Appalachian area on a map of the United States and discuss how Rylant's life experiences relate to the material in her books.

- Focus on the illustrated books of Stephen Gammell. The following is a list of some of the books he has illustrated.

Books Illustrated by Stephen Gammell

And Then the Mouse... by Malcolm Hall (Four Winds, 1980)

The Best Way to Ripton by Maggie S. Davis (Holiday, 1982)

Come a Tide by George Ella Lyon (Orchard, 1990)

Git Along, Old Scudder by Stephen Gammell (Lothrop, 1983)

Halloween Poems compiled by Myra Cohn Livingston (Holiday, 1989)

A Net to Catch the Wind by Margaret Greaves (HarperCollins, 1979)

The Old Banjo by Dennis Haseley (Macmillan, 1983)

Once Upon MacDonald's Farm by Stephen Gammell (Four Winds, 1981)

Song and Dance Man by Karen Ackerman (Knopf, 1988)

The Story of Mr. and Mrs. Vinegar by Stephen Gammell (Lothrop, 1982)

Terrible Things: An Allegory of the Holocaust by Eve Bunting (HarperCollins, 1980; Jewish, 1989)

Thunder at Gettysburg by Patricia Lee Gauch (Putnam, 1975; 1990)

Where the Buffaloes Begin by Olaf Baker (Warne, 1981)

Will's Mammoth by Rafé Martin (Putnam, 1989)

Wing-a-Ding by Lyn Littlefield Hoopes (Joy Street, 1990)

Connections

Tom Birdseye knows about teeth being lost. He has been a kindergarten teacher in Sandpoint, Idaho. He lives with his family—a wife and daughter—in Sagle, Idaho. His writing is varied and addresses many topics. His first book, *I'm Going to Be Famous* (Holiday, 1986), was a humorous novel about Arlo Moore's desire to be the banana-eating record holder. *Airmail to the Moon* was his second book. In 1990 Holiday published two books by Birdseye. *Tucker* is an adventure novel, and *A Song of Stars*, illustrated by Ju-Hong Chen, is a traditional love story that is the basis for Chi Hsi, the Festival of the Milky Way in China, and Tanabata, the Weaving Loom Festival in Japan. Both the Festival of the Milky Way and the Weaving Loom Festival honor the annual reunion of the herdsman and the princess weaver. Birdseye's 1991 title *Waiting for Baby* (Holiday) was illustrated by Loreen Leedy.

Blos, Joan. *Old Henry*. Illustrated by Stephen Gammell. Morrow, 1987. (Picture book)
    Henry rents an old house in much need of repair. His neighbors are outraged when he fixes nothing. Their actions drive him out and then they find that they miss him.

- Use this book to motivate a discussion about how we treat other people and how we can look for the positive traits in other people.

- Compare the story line with that in Betsy Byars's *After the Goat Man* (Viking, 1974).

Connections

Joan Blos was born December 9, 1928, in New York City, where she grew up. For many years she taught children's literature classes to people who planned to teach. She then became a teacher who sometimes wrote. Now she is a writer who sometimes teaches. Her first novel, *A Gathering of Days: A New England Girl's Journal, 1830-32* (Scribner, 1979), was given the Newbery Award. Blos and her psychoanalyst husband live in Ann Arbor, Michigan; they have two children.

Bodsworth, Nan. *Monkey Business*. Illustrated by Nan Bodsworth. Dial, 1986. (Picture book)
Dorothy's aunt is overly concerned that Dorothy will contract some germs or danger at the zoo and cautions her about touching everything. Dorothy's imagination brings her into closer touch with the animals.

- The illustrations that indicate the scenes where Dorothy's aunt is in control show large realistic animals on an antiseptic white background; the scenes where Dorothy's imagination is in control are illustrated with brightly colored animals and Dorothy's imaginary involvement. Use the illustrations as a model for indicating point of view. Create an innovative text based on a classroom incident. On one page give a statement as students might have perceived the situation, and on the following page make a statement on the same incident from an adult's point of view. Then illustrate the statements making sure the colors and illustrations depict a difference.

Boyd, Lizi. *Sam Is My Half Brother*. Illustrated by Lizi Boyd. Viking, 1990. (Picture book)
Hessie spends the summer with her dad and stepmother and their new baby, Sam. Hessie needs some time to adjust to a half brother getting some of the attention.

- Make a family tree; include branches for various types of family situations. The child's name could go on the trunk of the tree and parent branches could sprout from there.

- Build vocabulary and understanding of alternative family situations by discussing the terms *half brother/sister, step brother/sister/mother/father, foster brother/sister/mother/father, natural or birth mother/father, family of choice*, etc.

Brett, Jan. *The First Dog*. Illustrated by Jan Brett. Harcourt, 1988. (Picture book)
Kim, a cave boy, and Paleowolf live in the Ice Age. Together they conquer hunger and help one another. Paleowolf becomes the first "dog."

- Develop a perspective of historical events by making a timeline to demonstrate the number of years ago that the Ice Age existed.

- Infer what might happen to Kim and the wolf during the next year.

- Research the existence of humans during this period of time. Did wolves exist? Could this story be real? Why or why not?

Brett, Jan. *Goldilocks and the Three Bears*. Illustrated by Jan Brett. Putnam, 1987. (Picture book)
This is a fresh new retelling of a popular fairy tale.

- Focus on the borders that foreshadow the story action on the following pages. Discuss the technique of foreshadowing in writing and how events in real life are often foreshadowed by other events that occur.
- Discuss what the elaborate illustrations tell about the lifestyle of the bear and the things they like to do. Make a list of inferences you can make about the bears.

Connections

Norwell, Massachusetts, is the home of Jan Brett, illustrator of *The Owl and the Pussycat* (Putnam, 1991), *The Mitten* (Putnam, 1990), *The Wild Christmas Reindeer* (Putnam, 1990), *Berlioz the Bear* (Putnam, 1991), and *Annie and the Wild Animals* (Harcourt, 1985). Brett often travels with her husband, a member of the Boston Symphony Orchestra, to countries all over the world. Her illustrations include Norwegian sleighs, Japanese gardens, and costumes from many countries and localities. Her illustrations for *The Owl and the Pussycat* are from the Caribbean. In the summer the Bretts move to a cabin in the Berkshire Mountains, where they enjoy music, the birds, and wild animals.

Brown, Margaret Wise. *Big Red Barn*. Illustrated by Felicia Bond. HarperCollins, 1989. (Picture book)

This rhythmic text mentions 13 different animals and "an old scarecrow leaning on his hoe." All lived together in the big red barn. The story follows the animals through a day's activities on the farm.

- Make a list of the 13 animals in the story, and to practice research skills, locate specific facts and details about them.
- The animals in the book are all farm animals. Make lists of 13 animals that fit into other categories: zoo animals, nocturnal animals, daytime animals, feathered animals, animals from Africa, animals from India, animals with four feet, animals with wings. Compare the lists to determine if any of the animals named are included on more than one list. Brainstorm more categories of animals and then list animals in those categories. Discuss the types of activities that animals in each of these categories might engage in during a typical day.

Connections

Margaret Wise Brown is said to have been the first author to make the writing of picture books an art. A great lover of animals and collector of stray dogs and cats, she often featured animals in the classic tales she wrote for young readers. She was born in Brooklyn, New York, in 1910 and died at the age of 42 while traveling in France. Many of her stories are being republished with new illustrations. Susan Jeffers created new illustrations for Brown's *Baby Animals* (Random, 1989). *Baby Animals* was first published in 1941. One of Brown's most popular books is *Goodnight Moon* (HarperCollins, 1947). A pop-up book based on that book, *The Goodnight Moon Room*, was published in 1984 by HarperCollins. Using the pseudonym of Golden MacDonald, Margaret Wise Brown wrote *The Little Island* (Doubleday, 1946). Leonard Weisgard created the illustrations for that edition and won a Caldecott Award for them. Earlier Brown had written *The Runaway Bunny* (HarperCollins, 1942; 1970).

Browne, Jane. *Sing Me a Story: Action Songs to Sing and Play*. Crown, 1991. (Picture book)
This book contains 13 songs, words and music, to share with young children. Each relates to a nursery rhyme or fairy tale—from "Sing a Song of Sixpence" to "Sleeping Beauty."

- Read the stories or rhymes that inspired each of the songs in this book. Share and sing the songs. Let the children tape their voices singing the songs and put the tape in a listening center.

- Fifty-six Mother Goose rhymes are set to music in *Songs from Mother Goose: With the Traditional Melody for Each*, compiled by Nancy Larrick and illustrated by Robin Spowart (HarperCollins, 1989). Larrick has included endnotes giving more information about Mother Goose and suggestions for actions or adaptations for some of the rhymes. Share and enjoy the songs and the Mother Goose rhymes.

Connections

A musician, Jane Browne teaches music and directs a preschool group in her home. It was her work with preschoolers that inspired the collection of songs to accompany nursery tales. She is married to British author and illustrator Anthony Browne. Their two children, Joseph and Ellen, are among the nine youngsters pictured in the book.

Buckley, Rich. *The Greedy Python*. Illustrated by Eric Carle. Picture, 1985. (Picture book)

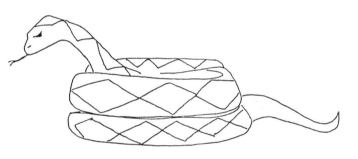

The greedy python gulps down every animal he meets. During one binge he eats 10 animals, each one larger than the one before it—from mouse to elephant. The animals create such havoc inside the python that he has to cough them all out, leaving him hungrier than before. Then he sees his own tail, grabs it, swallows hard, and disappears.

- Instead of the python seeing his tail, imagine that he visits your classroom and eats one object belonging to each person in your class. The object should be one that is easily identifiable with a specific person. For example, if one child wears a special style eyeglasses, that might be the object of his that the python would swallow. Another child, who likes to read about turtles, might have her small turtle-shaped eraser swallowed by the python. Make a larger-than-life picture of the python and inside place your illustrations of the objects eaten by the python.

- Read about pythons. Do they swallow things whole? What characteristics do they have that Buckley uses in his writing and that Carle depicts in his illustrations for the story.

Bulla, Clyde Robert. *The Chalk Box Kid*. Illustrated by Thomas B. Allen. Random, 1987. (Junior novel)
Nine-year-old Gregory's house does not have room for a garden, but he succeeds in creating a surprising and very different garden in an unusual place.

- Draw a chalk garden of your own, using chalk and construction paper.

- Many people who do not have room for a garden create patio gardens or window box gardens. Investigate the possibilities and plan a garden that could be planted in a small space. Marc Brown's *Your First Garden Book* (Little, 1981) gives some suggestions for planting a garden and caring for it.

Bunting, Eve. *The Wall.* Illustrated by Ronald Himler. Clarion, 1990. (Picture book)
A boy and his father travel a great distance to visit the Vietnam Veterans Memorial in Washington, D.C. They search for the name of the boy's grandfather, who died in Vietnam.

- Use the factual information about the Vietnam Memorial given in the book to begin a list of significant events that occurred during the Vietnam War. Use the list to construct a timeline of the events.

- Ask students to interview their families to create a list of family members who have served in the armed forces. Ask that they obtain some basic information about the family member's participation. Make a composite list of veterans (living or dead) from any war or conflict that children want to inscribe on their wall of honor.

- Read another book about the Vietnam wall, *A Wall of Names: The Story of the Vietnam Veterans Memorial* by Judy Donnelly (Random, 1991, A Step into Reading book: Step 4).

Bunting, Eve. *The Wednesday Surprise.* Illustrated by Donald Carrick. Clarion, 1989. (Picture book)
Grandma watches Anna every Wednesday night, and on those nights they read together. On Anna's dad's birthday Anna has a surprise for him. When the time comes, Anna brings out a bag of books and Anna's grandmother selects one to read to her son—Grandma has learned to read.

- Discuss the reasons some adults might not know how to read: did not go to school, could not learn to read as a child, etc. Continue by discussing programs in the community that might help someone who wants to learn to read.

- Discuss the concept that English may be a second language for many who have emigrated to the United States and that the use of English may be something they have to learn. Invite into the classroom people from the community who use English as a second language. Ask them to discuss how they adapted to using English and what adjustments they have had to make.

Connections

Eve Bunting emigrated to the United States from Ireland. She and her family settled in California. When her children were grown she began to write books for children. Although she didn't have to change languages when she moved to the United States, she sometimes gets homesick for Ireland and writes about her native country. Other authors, such as Uri Shulevitz, had to learn English in order to write. Shulevitz won the 1969 Caldecott Medal for his illustrations for *The Fool of the World and the Flying Machine* by Arthur Ransome (Farrar, 1968). But later, when Shulevitz began to write as well as illustrate, he created many other books, including *Toddlecreek Post Office* (Farrar, 1990). Isaac B. Singer, noted author of adult and children's stories, came to the United States from Poland in 1935 and always wrote his stories first in Yiddish. He died in a Miami nursing home July 25, 1991. More information about Bunting can be located in *Bookpeople: A First Album* (Teacher Ideas Press, 1990), and for information about Isaac Singer, use the Weston Woods filmstrip/cassette *Meet the Newbery Author: Isaac Bashevis Singer.* Singer explains some of his writing procedures and discusses the origins of *Zlateh the Goat,* a story often included in anthologies.

Burningham, John. *John Patrick Norman McHennessy—the boy who was always late*. Crown, 1987. (Picture book)

Burningham aptly foreshadows the subject of this episode tale by placing on the book's cover a schoolmaster in a black robe giving a young student a menacing glare. The endpapers also help to foreshadow what is to come—they are filled with the scrawled phrase "I must not tell lies about crocodiles and I must not lose my gloves." Each time John Patrick Norman McHennessy sets off along the road to learn he is confronted by an unusual situation that causes him to be late for school. The schoolmaster does not believe him and imposes a punishment of writing or saying a phrase out loud a number of times. John Patrick Norman McHennessy is first confronted by a crocodile, then a lion; on the third day he is swept off a bridge by a tidal wave. Finally he sets off along the road to learn, nothing happens, and he arrives at school on time; but when he arrives he finds his schoolmaster being held from the rafters by a big hairy gorilla. But John Patrick does not believe what he sees because, " 'There are no such things as great big hairy gorillas in the roofs around here, Sir.' And John Patrick Norman McHennessy set off along the road to learn."

Many story maps suggest that once a situation or problem is set up, there are three preliminary attempts to resolve the problem followed by a fourth attempt that results in a resolution. This story illustrates that story pattern in both text and illustration. Burningham introduces each episode with an image of John Patrick against a background of color and light. The confrontation is shown in a luminous double-page spread. But once John Patrick reaches the school, the white space begins to close in around him. The final page in each episode has John Patrick isolated in his punishment and completely surrounded by white space. The final section, which turns the tables on the schoolmaster, ends with John Patrick exiting into a glowing sunrise.

- To give students practice in organizing and writing logical paragraphs, follow the pattern of the story and create another situation that will delay John Patrick Norman McHennessy's arrival at school. Use the illustrative pattern established by Burningham and illustrate the text you have created. Each episode will begin "John Patrick Norman McHennessy set off along the road to learn. On the way ...," and the episode will conclude with John Patrick giving his teacher an explanation for why he is late for school and the teacher assigning a punishment. The final phrase of each episode will begin, "So John Patrick Norman McHennessy stayed in late and...."

- To add the new episodes to Burningham's book, purchase a paperback copy of the title, split the pages apart, three-hole punch the cover and the pages, and rejoin the pages with plastic or metal rings. As new episodes are created in the Burningham style, insert them between the episode where the boy is swept away by a tidal wave and the concluding episode.

Connections

John Burningham has twice won the prestigious Kate Greenaway Medal (Great Britain's equivalent of the United States' Caldecott Medal). Burningham likes to show relationships between adults and children in his books. Some of his most popular books are *Come Away from the Water, Shirley* (Crowell, 1977) and *Mr. Gumpy's Motor Car* (Macmillan, 1975). He is married to Helen Oxenbury, who also creates children's books. Their two oldest children, Lucy and Bill, are grown. Their third child, Emily, is a preteenager. They live in Hampstead, London, where they collect antiques, rebuild old houses, play tennis, and write and illustrate books. They spend some of their time each year at their house in the hills of southwest France.

Byars, Betsy. *Hooray for the Golly Sisters!* Illustrated by Sue Truesdell. HarperCollins, 1990. (Picture book)

May-May and Rose are two zany sisters who are constantly involved in outrageous adventures with some elements of mystery.

- The first book about these two women is *The Golly Sisters Go West* by Betsy Byars (HarperCollins, 1985). Discuss details of the time period and identify the facts that Byars includes in the two books.

- Both books about May-May and Rose are set in the pioneer days. Other books of similar readability and set in the same approximate time period can be used to build a larger base of information about the period. Read some of the following books about pioneers and then discuss the pioneer days.

Pioneers

Brenner, Barbara. *Wagon Wheels*. Illustrated by Don Bolognese. HarperCollins, 1978.

Hooks, William H. *Pioneer Cat*. Illustrated by Charles Robinson. Random, 1988.

Sandin, Joan. *The Long Way Westward*. HarperCollins, 1989.

Whelan, Gloria. *Next Spring an Oriole*. Illustrated by Pamela Johnson. Random, 1987.

Calmenson, Stephanie. *The Principal's New Clothes*. Illustrated by Denise Brunkus. Scholastic, 1989. (Picture book)

The principal, Mr. Bundy, "the sharpest dresser in town," is scammed by a pair of con artists in the same fashion that the emperor was flimflammed in Andersen's classic "The Emperor's New Clothes."

- Students will enjoy this book infinitely more if they are well acquainted with the classic Andersen tale. Read several of the editions that feature Andersen's story and some information about Andersen. After students are quite familiar with the traditional tale, share Calmenson's wacky adaptation. Versions of Andersen's tale have been illustrated by Erik Blegvad (Harcourt, 1959), Virginia Lee Burton (Houghton, 1949), Jack Kent (Four Winds, 1977), Anne F. Rockwell (Crowell, 1982), Janet Stevens (Holiday, 1985), and Nadine Bernard Wescott (Little, 1984).

- Use Calmenson's story as an example of a modernized version of a classic tale. Pair it with Emberley's *Ruby*, a modern-day version of "Little Red Riding Hood" (see entry on p. 132). Anthony Browne illustrated an updated version of *Hansel and Gretel* by Wilhelm Grimm and Jacob Grimm (Knopf, 1981). After reading a classic version of either "Little Red Riding Hood" or "Hansel and Gretel," identify the details the writers had to change to make the story more contemporary.

Connections

After being an elementary school teacher and a children's book editor, Stephanie Calmenson became a full-time writer. She was born in Brooklyn, New York, and now lives in New York City. Calmenson has collaborated with Joanna Cole in compiling *The Beginning Reader's Treasury: Ready ... Set ... Read!* (Doubleday, 1988). She also wrote *What Am I?: Very First Riddles* (HarperCollins, 1989). That book, which presents catchy rhyming riddles (the answers are everyday objects), would be a perfect lead-in to Beatrice Schenk de Regniers's simple animal riddle book *It Does Not Say Meow and Other Animal Riddle Rhymes* (Clarion, 1972). Another of Calmenson's books is a counting book, *Dinner at the Panda Palace*

(HarperCollins, 1991). A famished elephant arrives for dinner along with two carsick lions, three harried pigs, four primping peacocks, and a number of other animals, until all 10 tables are taken at the Panda Palace—but everyone is welcome and there's always room for one more.

Carle, Eric. *Papa, Please Get the Moon for Me.* Illustrated by Eric Carle. Picture, 1986. (Picture book)

Monica wishes to play with the moon, so her papa sets out to get it for her. He carries a ladder (shown on a foldout page) and stretches it up to the moon. Once Monica begins to play with the moon she sees it grow smaller and go back to the sky; the next night the sliver of a moon appears in the sky and begins to grow larger and larger until it is a full moon.

- Introduce the concept of the phases of the moon. Make sequential pictures showing those phases.

- Read another book that shows the phases of the moon, *Bear Shadow* by Frank Asch (Prentice, 1985).

Carle, Eric. *The Tiny Seed.* Illustrated by Eric Carle. Picture, 1987.

A tiny seed survives through four seasons while other seeds die. The tiny seed grows into a tall, beautiful flower until autumn, when the seeds are blown into the wind again.

- Carle often uses tissue paper to create collages. Create a tissue paper flower using a collage technique similar to the process used by Carle:

  —Cut or tear the tissue paper into the desired shapes.
  —Arrange the shapes on a paper background; the tissue paper shapes could be overlapped to create different effects.
  —Dilute glue (one part white glue to one part water) and use the glue to brush over the tissue paper shapes. Allow the glue to dry and affix the pieces to the background.

Connections

Eric Carle was born June 25, 1929, in Syracuse, New York, but spent most of his growing-up years in Germany. He returned to the United States in 1952. One of his most popular books is *The Very Hungry Caterpillar* (Crowell, 1969). In many of his illustrations he hides the names or initials of his two children, Cirsten and Rolf. His dogs and cats also appear in his books. Carle's books often include foldout pages and flaps that reveal hidden surprises. His books are wonderful examples to promote the creation of unique illustrations in student-published books. Carle currently lives in North Hampton, Massachusetts. For more information see *An Author a Month (for Pennies)* (Libraries Unlimited, 1988).

Carlidge, Michelle. *Mouse House*. Illustrated by Michelle Carlidge. Dutton, 1990. (Picture book)
Tiny mice dwell behind movable doors and flaps, in human-type houses, in a teapot, in a book bag, and in a cookie box. Keen eyes will be needed to enjoy the pictures.

- Investigate information about real mice. What do they eat? Where do they live? Make an information chart about mice.

- Read another book about a mouse in the house, Nancy Van Laan's *A Mouse in My House*, illustrated by Marjorie Priceman (Knopf, 1990). Did Van Laan use any actual facts about mice in her book? Make a list of the things Van Laan probably knew about mice when she wrote her book.

Carlstrom, Nancy White. *Grandpappy*. Illustrated by Laurel Molk. Little, 1990. (Picture book)
With his grandpappy Nate watches a heron, finds a four-leaf clover, walks by the seashore, shops for supplies, and listens when his grandpappy says, "Be a light, Nate, a light in a dark place."

- List four things you do with your grandfather (or grandmother or someone else special).

- Compare Nate's grandpappy with your grandfather (or grandmother or someone else special). How are the two people similar and how are they different?

Carris, Joan. *The Greatest Idea Ever*. Illustrated by Carol Newsom. Lippincott, 1990. (Novel)
For several years the Howard family lived in England. In this fourth book about the Howard boys, Gus Howard finds life in the small town of Hampshire, Ohio, quite dull. So he sets out to create some interest. He manages to turn the tables on tattletale Nanny Vincent when he figures out a way to make her sit on her own plate of spaghetti. He sets up a business at school to earn enough money to keep his new puppy. But Gus's shenanigans manage to get him in trouble until he realizes that he needs just one more good idea—an idea to keep him out of trouble.

- Nanny Vincent was a tattletale. Explain how you would deal with a tattletale without becoming one yourself or without losing your own sense of honesty and morals.

- Carris has written three other books about the Howard boys: *When the Boys Ran the House* (Harper, 1982), *Pets, Vets, and Marty Howard* (Harper, 1984), and *Hedgehogs in the Closet* (Lippincott, 1988). After reading at least one other book about the Howard boys, identify details and information that show how the boys changed from one book to another. Write a paper that explains the changes; support inferences with details from the books.

Carris, Joan. *Hedgehogs in the Closet*. Illustrated by Carol Newsom. Lippincott, 1988. (Novel)
Nick Howard does not want to move to England for two years. But when he realizes that his father's work is going to take the rest of the family there, Nick agrees to try it for four months.

- Much information about the differences in language and life in England is presented through this fictionalized account. Use the information to focus on similarities and differences among other English-speaking countries.

- Hedgehogs provide interesting "pets" for the Howard household. Collect information and make a list of facts about the hedgehog. Be sure to find out their natural habitat, what they eat, etc.

- Make a list of the advantages, if any, of having a hedgehog in the house.

- Compare the experiences of the family in this book with the experiences the family has with the pig in Carris's *Just a Little Ham* (Little, 1989) (see next entry).

Carris, Joan. *Just a Little Ham*. Illustrated by Dora Leder. Little, 1989. (Novel)
A typical family adopts a pig as a family pet. Pandors, the pig, proves to the family that pigs are clean and full of personality. But, when the pig grows older he becomes clever and rebellious.

- Compare this pig to Wilbur in E. B. White's *Charlotte's Web* (HarperCollins, 1974).

- Find information about pigs. List the pros and cons of keeping a pig as a pet.

Connections

Joan Carris explains one of the main reasons she writes, besides loving to write: "I think that my readers and I share a love of many things. Through our shared love for animals, for chocolate cake, chili dogs, and pizza, for amusement parks and fireworks and cartoons...." Carris's career began in Iowa, where she taught high school English in Nevada and Des Moines. A "glut of English teachers" left her with no place to go so she plunked her typewriter on the family's dining room table and began to educate young people through her writing. She met her future husband at Iowa State University and married him soon after graduation. They have three children—Mindy, Leigh Ann, and Brad—all three grown and on their own. Like the Howards, Joan Carris's family lived in England for a time. When the Carrises moved back to the States, they settled in New Jersey but later moved to a suburb of Washington, D.C., where they had to teach their cat a new "meow"—one with a southern accent.

Carson, Jo. *Pulling My Leg*. Illustrated by Julie Downing. Orchard, 1990. (Picture book)
Uncle Tom teases his red-haired, freckle-faced niece about pulling her loose tooth with his "ex-trac-tion" tools: a screwdriver, a hammer, and pliers.

- This book is sure to stimulate the telling of stories about how teeth have been lost. Readers can develop the ability to logically organize information by organizing and sharing the story of how one of their teeth came out.

- Read another story that focuses on the idea of a lost tooth, Tom Birdseye's *Airmail to the Moon* (see entry on pp. 113-14).

Caseley, Judith. *Apple Pie and Onions*. Illustrated by Judith Caseley. Greenwillow, 1987. (Picture book)
Rebecca loves her grandmother and the stories she tells, but one day something goes wrong. Grandma understands and she knows just what to do.

- Compare and contrast Rebecca's experience with that of Bizzy Bones in *Bizzy Bones and Moosemouse* by Jacqueline Briggs Martin (Lothrop, 1986).

Chorao, Kay. *The Child's Storybook*. Illustrated by Kay Chorao. Dutton, 1987. (Collected traditional tales)
This is a "read-to-me" collection of several classics, including "Jack and the Beanstalk," "Hansel and Gretel," "The Ugly Duckling," "The Wonderful Teakettle," "The Lion and the Hare," and "The Pied Piper."

- Use the table of contents of this book to focus on the skill of locating stories by using a table of contents.

- Find other versions of the stories in this book and compare and contrast the versions.

Connections

Ann McKay Sproat Chorao has been drawing since she was a preschooler growing up in Indianapolis, Indiana. Most of her elementary years were spent in Cleveland, Ohio, where she continued to be interested in writing, drawing, and painting. She attended college in Norton, Massachusetts, and art school in London, where she met her husband. Since her first book, *The Repair of Uncle Toe* (Farrar, 1972) was published, she has illustrated many books by other authors, including Barbara Williams's story of a young turtle's "toothache," *Albert's Toothache*. For many years the Choraos have lived in New York City and have spent summers in Canada. They have three grown sons: Jamie, Peter, and Ian.

Cobb, Vicki. *Writing It Down*. Illustrated by Marylin Hafner. Lippincott, 1989. (Information)
 This picture-filled book describes the various processes used to make paper, ballpoint pens, pencils, and crayons.

- Page 11 describes making writing paper from toilet paper. Gather the materials that are needed for this project and put them in a "paper-making center." Make an enlargement of page 11 and post it so that the instructions can be followed in the center.

- The inconvenience of the fountain pen is cited as one of the reasons the ballpoint pen came to be. Set up a writing station with various types of pens: feather pens, fountain pens that need to be dipped in ink, fountain pens with ink cartridges, inexpensive ballpoint pens, and more expensive ballpoint pens. Label each pen with a letter of the alphabet. At the center allow children to explore and use each type of pen. After students have had an opportunity to experiment with each type, they should record their preferences on an "I prefer" chart.

Name	Pen preference	Reason for preference

- Make a bar chart showing student preferences for each pen. How did the pens compare?

- Pencils come in all shapes and sizes. Ask children to bring in, for example, their biggest, smallest, brightest, longest, shortest, and most used pencils for a display. Brainstorm other categories for the pencil display. Once the pencils are brought in, use them to form other categories and groupings: red pencils, chewed pencils, or whatever is appropriate. Use the pencils in a display about pencils and how they are made. Children can make charts of related information—"What I Can Do with a Pencil," "The Long and the Short of It," and so on.

- Put all of the writing tools mentioned in the book in a writing center along with card stock for book covers and materials that can be used to bind the pages together. As books are created and "published," put them in the center to be read and shared.

Coerr, Eleanor. *Sadako and the Thousand Paper Cranes*. Illustrated by Ronald Himler. Putnam, 1977. (Picture book)
 When the atom bomb was dropped on Hiroshima, Sadako was there. Ten years later Sadako finds that she has leukemia. But the Japanese have a legend about cranes and Sadako begins to make a thousand cranes before she dies.

- Make a paper crane. Directions can be found in *The Art of Chinese Paper Folding for Young and Old* by Maying Soong (Harcourt, 1948). If that book is not available, locate books that may have directions for folding a paper crane. Use the subject headings "Paper Folding and Crafts" and "Origami" in your library media center's catalog.

- Calculate the mathematical answers to the following questions:

  - How many years has it been since the atom bomb was dropped on Hiroshima (1945)?
  - Sadako was able to make 644 cranes. How many more cranes must her classmates make in order to have 1,000 paper cranes?
  - If your class wanted to make 1,000 paper cranes, how many would each person have to make?
  - If your class were to make the rest of the paper cranes for Sadako, how many would each person have to make?

Connections

Eleanor Coerr has written many books, each based on a historical fact, including *The Big Balloon Race*, illustrated by Carolyn Croll (HarperCollins, 1981), and *The Josephina Quilt Story*, illustrated by Bruce Degan (HarperCollins, 1986). Her book *Lady with a Torch* (HarperCollins, 1986) tells the story of how the French sculptor Frédéric Auguste Bartholdi planned and built the Statue of Liberty. Read any of Coerr's books that are available and discuss the historical period in which each of the books is set. Coerr is a native of Saskatchewan, Canada, and has lived in many countries, including Japan, the Philippines, Taiwan, and Ecuador. She now lives in Monterey, California.

Cole, Joanna. *Don't Tell the Whole World*. Illustrated by Kate Duke. HarperCollins, 1990. (Picture book)
Farmer John's wife, Emma, tells everything she knows. She cannot keep a secret. One day John uncovers a money box in his field. Knowing that his wife will tell everyone, he stages three other incredible incidents so that when she tells about the money she will also tell about the fish growing in the tree, etc., and the other people will not believe her.

- List the events in this story that could and could not have logically occurred.

- Farmer John was able to fool Emma because she observed factual events and then made inferences about the situation. However, the inferences were not correct. Discuss the facts in this story and the inferences that were made about the facts. For example, the fish were in the tree, and because they were in the tree Emma inferred that they grew in the tree. In fact, Farmer John put them in the tree.

- Read another story by Joanna Cole, *It's Too Noisy* (Crowell, 1989). This book is also illustrated by Kate Duke. Compare and contrast this story with *Don't Tell the Whole World*. Were there any inferences made in *It's Too Noisy* that changed the course of the story?

Cole, Joanna. *It's Too Noisy*. Illustrated by Kate Duke. Crowell, 1989. (Picture book)
This Jewish tale recounts how a farmer attempts to get some peace and quiet in a very noisy cottage.

- Compare to the story grammar in Margot Zemach's *It Could Always Be Worse* (Farrar, 1976).

- Compare to the somewhat opposite story line in *Always Room for One More* by Sorche Nic Leodhas, illustrated by Nonny Hogrogian (Holt, 1966).

Cook, Scott, reteller. *The Gingerbread Boy*. Illustrated by Scott Cook. Knopf, 1987. (Picture book)
This classic tale is illustrated with unique, expressive paintings that depict the gingerbread boy as a roly-poly, bread-like cookie. But he still gets eaten by the fox in the end.

- Compare this retelling with other versions of "The Gingerbread Boy."

- Change the ending of the story: What if the fox doesn't eat the gingerbread boy? What will happen next?

- Change the setting for the story. Rewrite the story as if it happened on your birthday, on Christmas, or on Valentine's Day. What details could you include that would change the setting?

Cooney, Barbara. *Hattie and the Wild Waves*. Illustrated by Barbara Cooney. Viking, 1990. (Picture book)
An unusual, inquisitive child determines the course of her own future. Set in the comfort of an affluent Brooklyn society at the turn of the century, this is the third of Cooney's biographies in picture book form. Cooney's mother is the model for the protagonist. The family comes to America from Germany. The three children in the family are given music lessons and the girls are taught to do needlework. But, Hattie, the youngest child, cares only about drawing and spends her time scribbling and drawing. In the summer the family moves to a house beside the ocean and Hattie continues to dream and paint. As the years pass she announces her decision: "I am going to be an artist."

- Compare Hattie and her determination with the determination of Tommy in Tomie dePaola's *The Art Lesson* (see entry on pp. 128-29).

- Compare Hattie with the grown-up Miss Rumphius in Cooney's *Miss Rumphius* (Viking, 1982).

Connections

Barbara Cooney and her twin brother were born in 1917 in Brooklyn, New York. Her father was a stockbroker and her mother an artist. The family, which included two younger brothers, lived on Long Island but spent summers in Maine. As far back as she can remember Barbara Cooney loved to draw. She includes in her illustrations images from her childhood and her travels. The illustrations for *Miss Rumphius* include favorites from her life: an embroidered shawl, a favorite armchair, a picture of her grandson, and sites from many of the New England areas where she has lived much of her life. Cooney now lives in Massachusetts and South Bristol, Maine. For more information see *Bookpeople: A First Album* (Teacher Ideas Press, 1990).

Czernecki, Stefan, and Timothy Rhodes. *Nina's Treasures*. Illustrated by Stefan Czernecki and Timothy Rhodes. Sterling, 1990. (Picture book)
Nina the hen manages to rescue her owner from starvation by laying a clutch of marvelous painted eggs.

- The illustrations have the decorative style of Ukrainian folk art. Compare these illustrations with those in Jan Brett's *Goldilocks and the Three Bears* (Putnam, 1987). Brett's illustrations also have the decorative style of Ukrainian folk art.

- Create some wonderfully painted eggs and display them. *My First Activity Book* by Angela Wilkes (Knopf, 1989), pages 6-9, will provide some basic ideas that will help youngsters begin to make "Fancy Eggs" and "A Nestful of Eggs."

- Read a story that includes beautifully decorated eggs as one of the elements in the story. Read *The Talking Eggs: A Folktale from the American South* by Robert D. San Souci, illustrated by Jerry Pinkney (Dial, 1989).

Degan, Bruce. *Jamberry*. Illustrated by Bruce Degan. HarperCollins, 1983. (Picture book)
This is a book of joyful rhymes that feature real berries and berries with rhythmic names.

- To develop the ability to identify specific points of information, list all the names of the berries used in the verses. Check (√) those that are real berries and put an o by those that are not real.

√ blueberry	o pawberry	o clackberry	√ cloudberry
o hatberry	o quickberry	√ raspberry	o boomberry
o shoeberry	o quackberry	o razzamatazzberry	o zoomberry
o canoeberry	√ blackberry	o brassberry	
o hayberry	o trainberry	o moonberry	
√ strawberry	o trackberry	o starberry	

- Degan uses the names of five real berries in his verses: blackberry, cloudberry, raspberry, blueberry, and strawberry. Look up *cloudberry* in a dictionary. List adjectives that describe the cloudberry. Use the descriptive chart (see appendix A, p. 190) to record adjectives that describe the other berries. The words can focus on how the berries look, or if enough berries are available to have a tasting party, use the chart to record words that describe the berries' taste.

- Brainstorm a list of other berries that exist. Possibilities include cranberries, mulberries, and gooseberries. Write descriptions for those berries that would distinguish them from the other berries.

Connections

Bruce Degan never rode a school bus to his Brooklyn, New York, elementary school, but he became very well acquainted with school buses when he began to illustrate Joanna Cole's Magic School Bus series. The image of Ms. Frizzle that he draws in the Magic School Bus series is based on his 10th grade geometry teacher, a blond woman with frizzy hair. Ms. Frizzle is shown with red hair and is dressed in clothes that indicate some of her next classroom escapades. Before becoming a full-time illustrator Degan was a high school art teacher. He began creating children's books in 1970. He works in an upstairs studio in his family's Newtown, Connecticut, home where he enjoys watching birds and listening to books on tape while he paints. Bruce Degan's wife, Chris, collaborated with him to create the illustrations for Aileen Fisher's *When It Comes to Bugs* (HarperCollins, 1986). Chris created the black scratchboard art and Bruce created the color overlays. The Degans have two sons, Benjamin and Alexander.

Delacre, Lulu. *Nathan's Fishing Trip*. Illustrated by Lulu Delacre. Scholastic, 1988. (Picture book)
 A mouse, Nicholas Alexander, takes an elephant, Nathan, on his first fishing trip. Several misadventures occur but they do catch a rainbow trout—though neither angler has the heart to eat it.

- Investigate types of trout. Write about each type of trout in such a way as to distinguish one type from the other.

- Invite a parent or grandparent who fishes to share information about fishing with the group.

Delton, Judy. *My Mom Made Me Go to Camp*. Illustrated by Lisa McCue. Delacorte, 1990. (Picture book)
 Afraid to leave home and go to summer camp, this young boy finds unexpected delight in catching a fish and learning to swim.

- Set up the classroom as a "day camp" and go to camp one day. Learn new crafts, new physical skills, and camp songs. Use each of the opportunities to locate books that give directions for crafts and physical exercises and music books that include popular camp songs. Follow the directions in the books to create the activities for Camp Day.

- Write about new experiences at camp.

dePaola, Tomie. *The Art Lesson*. Illustrated by Tomie dePaola. Putnam, 1989. (Picture book)
This book, which is available in big book format from Trumpet, is a biographical story exploring dePaola's early days in school and his emergence as an artist and writer.

- The final page shows dePaola sitting at his drawing desk with illustrations from many of his books tacked on the bulletin board above his desk. Identify the illustrations and the books represented.

- In *The Art Lesson* dePaola tells of hiding under the covers of his bed and drawing pictures on his sheets. He tells of the same experience in poetic form in a poem that begins, "It was my secret place...." In 1986 the poem was included in *Once Upon a Time ... Celebrating the Magic of Children's Books in Honor of the Twentieth Anniversary of READING IS*

FUNDAMENTAL (Putnam). Later the poem was included in *Tomie dePaola's Book of Poems* (Putnam, 1988). Use these two selections to emphasize the concept that information or experiences can be communicated in various forms. Follow up this dialogue by reading a story poem and a collaborative narrative about the same event. Possible topics include Paul Revere's ride, Johnny Appleseed's life, and the arrival of Columbus in America.

Connections

Tomie dePaola has created more than 200 books for young readers. Among his most popular are those about Strega Nona: *Strega Nona* (Prentice, 1975), *Big Anthony and the Magic Ring* (Harcourt, 1979), *Merry Christmas, Strega Nona* (Harcourt, 1986), and *Strega Nona's Magic Lessons* (Harcourt, 1982). Another favorite title by dePaola is *Helga's Dowry: A Troll Love Story* (Harcourt, 1977). He has told two tales about the origin of state flowers: *The Legend of the Bluebonnet: An Old Tale of Texas* (Putnam, 1983) and *The Legend of the Indian Paintbrush* (Putnam, 1988). From the time he could hold a pencil, Tomie dePaola was drawing, but it wasn't until he was 31 that he sold his first illustrations to a publisher (Coward-McCann for a science book, *Sound*, by Lisa Miller). The next year, 1966, Bobbs-Merrill published *The Wonderful Dragon of Timlin*, a book dePaola both wrote and illustrated. Now, in addition to creating his own books, he is creative director of Whitebird Books, a new imprint of Putnam. DePaola currently lives in New London, New Hampshire. For more information about Tomie dePaola see *An Author a Month (for Pennies)* (Libraries Unlimited, 1988).

---

de Regniers, Beatrice Schenk, et al. *Sing a Song of Popcorn*. Illustrated by 10 Caldecott artists. Scholastic, 1988. (Poetry collection)

First published in 1969 by Scholastic as a little red paperback book, *Poems Children Will Sit Still For*, this collection was intended for teachers to read aloud to their students. Now revised and updated with the art of 10 Caldecott Award-winning artists, the book is both a child's book and a read-aloud volume for teachers to share with their students.

- The book is divided into nine thematic units: fun with rhymes, weather, spooky poems, story poems, animals, people, nonsense poems, haiku, and poems about seeing, feeling, and thinking. Integrate poems from these sections into curriculum focuses.

- Utilize the art of each artist to stimulate expressive art activities in the classroom using the same or similar techniques. The following is a list of the art media used by each of the illustrators for his or her section of the book.

Marcia Brown—Watercolor

Leo Dillon and Diane Dillon—Pastels with glazes of watercolor

Richard Egielski—Watercolor and pencil

Trina Schart Hyman—India ink with acrylic and gouache on bainbridge board

Arnold Lobel—Watercolor with ink and pencil

Maurice Sendak—Gouache and watercolor with sepia ink

Marc Simont—Watercolor and charcoal

Margot Zemach—Watercolor

- Focus on each of the illustrators in an author/illustrator focus unit. Material on seven of the artists and their books can be located in the following publications from Libraries Unlimited:

Marcia Brown — *An Author a Month (for Pennies)*, pp. 1-15

Leo Dillon and Diane Dillon — *Bookpeople: A First Album*, pp. 65-68

Trina Schart Hyman — *Bookpeople: A First Album*, pp. 101-5

Arnold Lobel — *An Author a Month (for Pennies)*, pp. 151-70

Maurice Sendak — *My Bag of Book Tricks*, pp. 55, 177-79, 241-46

Margot Zemach — *An Author a Month (for Pennies)*, pp. 171-87

Dragonwagon, Crescent. *Home Place*. Illustrated by Jerry Pinkney. Macmillan, 1990. (Picture book)
This great pictorial history of home and family is illustrated with both African-American and white families. A girl and her parents discover an abandoned homesite in the woods. The story brings to life the family who lived and worked in the home as well as the family who discovered it.

- Interview people in your neighborhood, visit the public library, and investigate people who lived in your home through reference sources such as city directories and phone books. Write a short history of your "homeplace."

- As a long-range project, research and share information about communities within your city or town and about people significant in the history of your community.

Connections

Crescent Dragonwagon is the author of many books: *Alligator Arrived with Apples: A Potluck Alphabet Feast*, illustrated by Jose Aruego and Ariane Dewey (Macmillan, 1987); *Always, Always*, illustrated by Arieh Zeldich (Macmillan, 1984); *Diana, Maybe*, illustrated by Deborah Kogan Ray (Macmillan, 1987); *Half a Moon and One Whole Star*, illustrated by Jerry Pinkney (Macmillan, 1986); *Jemima Remembers*, illustrated by Troy Howell (Macmillan, 1984). Dragonwagon is the daughter of renowned children's book editor and children's author Charlotte Zolotow. Dragonwagon and her husband operate a quaint bed and breakfast in Eureka Springs, Arkansas.

Dubanevich, Arlene. *Pigs in Hiding*. Four Winds, 1983.
Speech balloons are used throughout this hilarious story about games involving nearly 50 pink pigs. A household of pigs play hide-and-seek.

- Use the balloon speech to develop an awareness of the use of quotation marks. Rewrite the dialogue in the book by putting the words in the balloons in quotation marks and indicating who is being quoted.

- Demonstrate how to draw a cartoon-type pig as in the book. Ask students to follow the oral instructions to create pig pictures that include at least four pigs doing something together — at church, at a picnic, in the park, at a parade, at a play, or at the pool. Then ask that the directions be written so that others might learn to draw pigs.

- Create a pig bookmark and then write the directions so that your classmates can create a similar one.

- Read another book that has an animal tricking another with food. One might be Keiko Kasza's *The Wolf's Chicken Stew* (see entry on p. 143).

Dunbar, Joyce. *Ten Little Mice*. Illustrated by Maria Majewska. Harcourt, 1990. (Picture book)
Ten little mice, one-by-one, scurry home to their nest.

- Compare and contrast to *Nine Ducks Nine* by Sarah Hayes (see entry on p. 49).

- Give learners the opportunity to organize and retell. Make 10 little mice and retell the counting story, making innovations in the text as the retellings evolve.

- Tell the story of "20 little mice" or of "10 little kittens."

Dunrea, Olivier. *Eppie M. Says....* Illustrated by Olivier Dunrea. Macmillan, 1990. (Picture book)
Eppie M. "knows just about everything there is to know," according to her younger brother, Ben. Ben tries to give everything she says a try, even staying awake to see if the Man-in-the-Moon really does watch all night.

- Compare Ben and Eppie M.'s relationship to the relationship of the siblings in *Much Bigger Than Martin* by Steven Kellogg (Dial, 1976), *The Pain and the Great One* by Judy Blume (Bradbury, 1984; Dell, 1986), or *Worse Than Willy* by James Stevenson (Greenwillow, 1984).

Ehlert, Lois. *Color Farm*. Illustrated by Lois Ehlert. HarperCollins, 1990. (Picture book)
Bright graphics, geometric shapes, and die-cut pages form the images of farm animals in this book. The animals include a rooster, duck, chicken, dog, goose, sheep, cat, cow, and pig. The shapes used include a square, hexagon, circle, heart, diamond, rectangle, oval, and triangle.

- Give learners the opportunity to develop their own perceptual abilities. Use card stock with shapes cut out of the center. Put the template over another sheet of paper and ask students to trace around the inner edge of the shape on their template. When you remove the template an outlined shape should be visible on the sheet of paper. Use the shape outline as the beginning of an animal drawing. When the drawings have been completed, display the menagerie.

Ehlert, Lois. *Growing Vegetable Soup*. Illustrated by Lois Ehlert. Harcourt, 1987.
Boldly colored vegetables—tomatoes, potatoes, corn, cabbage, and others—are shown as a father and a child plant. When the vegetables are ripe, they are gathered and cooked into a delicious vegetable soup.

- Brainstorm a list of all the vegetables the children can think of. Discuss the difference between fruits and vegetables.

- Use the list generated in the preceding activity to categorize and chart the number of green vegetables, red vegetables, orange vegetables, and so on.

- Determine if the vegetables on the list grow on a vine, a bush, or underground. Categorize the vegetables into groups. Determine other ways to categorize them.

- Write recipes for vegetable soup and put them in a cookbook.

- Bring vegetables, wash them, cut them up, and make vegetable soup. Or use the recipe on the dust jacket or back cover of the book. Double or triple the recipe to feed the size group you have.

- Plant and grow some of your own vegetables. Radishes can be grown in a flowerpot, and lettuce, which is rather quick to grow, can be harvested in a few weeks. Or visit a neighbor's vegetable garden or a neighborhood supermarket's produce section.

- Grow bean sprouts. Use mung beans, string beans, or alfalfa seeds. Wash and soak the beans or seeds. Drain them and put them into screw-top jars with holes punched in the lids. Every day rinse and drain the seeds or beans. Sprouts will be ready to eat in about five days.

- Put one jar of seeds in a cool, dark cupboard. Compare the growth of those seeds with the ones kept in the light. Discuss the need for plants to have sunlight to grow.

Connections

In 1980 Lois Ehlert's illustrations for *Color Zoo* (HarperCollins, 1979) earned a Caldecott Honor Award. She has also created *Feathers for Lunch* (Harcourt, 1990) and *Fish Eyes: A Book You Can Count On* (Harcourt, 1990) and has illustrated *Chicka Chicka Boom Boom* by Bill Martin, Jr., and John Archambault (Simon, 1989) and *THUMP, THUMP, Rat-a-Tat-Tat* (HarperCollins, 1989). Her illustrations are most often boldly colored shapes set against a contrasting bold background. Ehlert was born and raised in Beaver Dam, Wisconsin. She attended the Layton School of Art. Her illustrations for *Fish Eyes: A Book You Can Count On* earned her a citation naming the book a *New York Times* Best Illustrated Book of the Year. Ehlert now lives in Milwaukee.

Emberley, Michael. *Ruby*. Illustrated by Michael Emberley. Little, 1990. (Picture book)
Ruby, the mouse, survives the clutches of the crafty cat during a treacherous trip to Granny's house through the Boston city streets. *Ruby* gives a contemporary and citified twist to the "Red Riding Hood" story.

- Before reading *Ruby* make sure children are thoroughly familiar with versions of the traditional "Little Red Riding Hood" story. Included in those that are most popular are:

Little Red Riding Hood

de Regniers, Beatrice Schenk. *Red Riding Hood: Retold in Verse for Boys and Girls to Read Themselves*. Illustrated by Edward Gorey. Atheneum, 1972. (Available as a Weston Woods filmstrip/cassette.)

Hogrogian, Nonny, illustrator. *The Renowned History of Little Red Riding Hood*. Crowell, 1967.

Hyman, Trina Schart. *Little Red Riding Hood*. Illustrated by Trina Schart Hyman. Holiday, 1983.

Marshall, James. *Red Riding Hood*. Illustrated by James Marshall. Dial, 1987.

- Identify the major motifs and elements from "Little Red Riding Hood" that Michael Emberley used for *Ruby*.

- Make a map showing the route Ruby took through the city streets.

Esbensen, Barbara Juster. *Words with Wrinkled Knees*. Illustrated by John Stadler. Crowell, 1986. (Poetry)
In this book are poems of a hippopotamus (a waddling word), a snake (a hissing word), and an owl (a moonstruck word). Other poems feature a whining mosquito, a squat frog, a serene whale, a fur-covered bat, a sticky spider, a roaring lion, a shy giraffe, a springing kangaroo, a feathered hummingbird, a bristling porcupine, a vertical seahorse, a black crow, a shadowing wolf, a loose-footed camel, a leggy centipede, a best-dressed penguin, and an "out-of-print" dinosaur.

- Read and savor these unique poems focusing on the characteristics and "feel" of the words that name animals.

- If you wish to read descriptive poems about animals, read Eric Carle's *Animals, Animals* (Philomel, 1989). Laura Whipple selected the poems, but it is Carle's collages that make this collection a perfect blend of poetry and art. Use a wide range of poetry collections that include poems about animals. Select a particularly favorite poem and illustrate it. Learn it by heart and recite it to the class.

Field, Rachel. *A Road Might Lead to Anywhere*. Illustrated by Gilles Laroche. Little, 1990. (Poetry/picture book)
Field's poem takes readers to faraway places, and Laroche's illustrations aptly show the bustling shops in Mexico and scenes along the Maine coastline.

- Let the road take you somewhere special that you would enjoy; create a diorama of that special place.

- Find other poems by Rachel Field. Use a poetry index (*Granger's Index to Poetry* or *Brewton's Index to Children's Poetry*) in your school or public library. Find a poem you like and read it to your friends.

Flournoy, Valerie. *The Patchwork Quilt*. Illustrated by Jerry Pinkney. Dial, 1985. (Picture book)
Tanya helps her grandmother make a beautiful quilt that contains many "scraps" of the family's life.

- Make a classroom quilt. The quilt can be made of individual blocks created by individual children or by the family of each child participating. Combine the blocks into a quilt. Integrate the making of the quilt with math skills by encouraging the children to measure and plan the structure of the quilt. If younger children are making the quilt, it may be advantageous to ask a volunteer to actually sew the quilt together. Older children could handstitch the quilt together.

- Compile a booklet in which each "chapter" explains the significance of one block. Where did the material come from? What significance did the block have for the person donating it? Edit and revise the writings and publish them in a "quilt" book.

- Coordinate with a reading of *The Keeping Quilt* by Patricia Polacco (Simon, 1988).

Fox, Mem. *Shoes from Grandpa*. Illustrated by Patricia Mullins. Orchard, 1989. (Picture book)
This is a cumulative story about the shoes Jessie gets from her grandpa. Several other relatives attempt to add an item of clothing for Jessie to wear with the shoes from Grandpa. But she'd rather have jeans.

- Discuss the idea of a cumulative story. Share other examples, such as "The House That Jack Built," "The Old Woman and the Pig," or Nonny Hogrogian's *One Fine Day* (Macmillan, 1971).

- Read other books by Mem Fox.

Connections

Merrion "Mem" Frances Partridge Fox was born March 5, 1946, in Melbourne, Australia. She grew up in the African country of Rhodesia (now called Zimbabwe), where her parents were missionaries. Eventually Mem Fox became a teacher and started storytelling in her native Australia. In a college writing class she wrote the first draft of *Possum Magic*. It is now one of Australia's best-selling books. Fox lives in Adelaide, South Australia. For more information about Fox see *Bookpeople: A Multicultural Album* (Teacher Ideas Press, 1992).

Freedman, Russell. *Lincoln: A Photobiography*. Clarion, 1987. (Biography)

This book covers Lincoln's life from his boyhood, to his law career, to his courtship of Mary Todd, and his years as president. Emphasis is on his presidential years (1861-1865), including the Civil War period.

- Correlate with activities for Jim Murphy's *The Boys' War: Confederate and Union Soldiers Talk About the Civil War* (Clarion, 1990), a photograph-filled account drawn from actual letters and diaries of boys under the age of 16 who fought in the Civil War. A collection of anecdotes about Lincoln, *True Stories About Abraham Lincoln* by Ruth Belov Gross (Lothrop, 1990), would also be useful during the introduction of Lincoln.

- Use the book to introduce a focus unit on the Civil War or a wide-reading unit using historical fiction books set during the Civil War.

Books Set During the Civil War

Beatty, Patricia, and Phillip Robbins. *Eben Tyne, Powdermonkey*. Morrow, 1990.

Beatty, Patricia. *Turn Homeward, Hannalee*. Morrow, 1984.

Blos, Joan. *A Gathering of Days: A New England Girl's Journal, 1830-32*. Scribner, 1979.

De Angeli, Marguerite. *Thee, Hannah!* Doubleday, 1949.

Fox, Paula. *The Slave Dancer*. Illustrated by Eros Keith. Bradbury, 1973.

Fritz, Jean. *Brady*. Illustrated by Lynd Ward. Coward, 1960.

Gauch, Patricia Lee. *Thunder at Gettysburg*. Illustrated by Stephen Gammell. Putnam, 1975; 1990.

Haugaard, Erik. *Orphans of the Wind*. Illustrated by Milton Johnson. Houghton, 1966.

Hickman, Janet. *Zoar Blue*. Macmillan, 1978.

Hunt, Irene. *Across Five Aprils*. Follett, 1964.

Keith, Harold. *Rifles for Watie*. Crowell, 1957.

Monjo, F. N. *The Drinking Gourd*. Illustrated by Fred Brenner. Harper, 1970.

Perez, N. A. *The Slopes of War*. Houghton, 1984.

Steele, William O. *The Perilous Road*. Illustrated by Paul Galdone. Harcourt, 1958.

Connections

Russell Freedman tells of the time an opponent of Abraham Lincoln's called him "two-faced." Lincoln is said to have responded with, "I'll leave it to my audience, if I had a face other than this one, do you think I'd wear this one?" The need to discuss biography is evident in another story Freedman relates. He tells of a letter he received: "Dear Mr. Freedman, I read your biography of Abraham Lincoln. I liked it. Did you take the pictures yourself?" Freedman feels that his storytelling helps to evoke pictures and to create realistic scenes that will help pull readers into the story. He is able to point out small personal details such as the fact that Lincoln greeted visitors with "howdy," that Lincoln called his wife "Mother," and that he mended his spectacles with string. Freedman conducts much primary research before writing a new book. He traveled to China in 1990 in anticipation of a possible book on China, and for one about the Mandans he visited an Indian reservation at Fort Berthold in North Dakota. For his books about Lincoln and Eleanor Roosevelt he examined diaries, letters, photographs, and scores of other documents and artifacts surrounding his subjects. More information about Russell Freedman can be located in *Bookpeople: A Second Album* (Teacher Ideas Press, 1990).

Galbraith, Kathryn O. *Laura Charlotte*. Philomel, 1990. (Picture book)

Laura Charlotte loves her ragged stuffed elephant that has been handed down from her grandmother to her mother to her. As Laura hugs her elephant, the story of the toy's origin is told to her. The story tells of the love given to the elephant over the years and explains how the elephant's name was given to her because her mother had loved the name (and elephant) so much.

- Ask students to interview their parents to determine how their names were chosen and to organize the information into individual reports. They might include in their reports some information about their namesakes.

- The elephant was a favored object for Laura. Discuss other books in which an object has special significance for one of the characters in the book. One book to read is *Bizzy Bones and Uncle Ezra* by Jacqueline Briggs Martin (Lothrop, 1984). Make a list of the books and characters and discuss.

- Investigate the origin of a special piece of furniture in your house, or some other item owned by your family. Organize the information and present it in writing.

- Read Jane Yolen's *Sky Dogs* (see entry on p. 170).

Connections

Discuss given names as opposed to surnames (family names). Use a name book, like those commonly used by expectant parents for naming their baby, to find out the meaning and origin of each student's name. Make a name poster highlighting information about each name and the student to whom it belongs. Does the name fit the person's appearance, personality, and status in life?

Garland, Michael. *My Cousin Katie*. Illustrated by Michael Garland. Crowell, 1989. (Picture book)
    Katie's city cousin is coming to visit her on the farm and she is excited. The book contains wonderful photograph-like illustrations of many different farm animals.

- Compare Katie's cousin's city life with Katie's life in the country.

- Compare *My Cousin Katie* with "City Mouse, Country Mouse" in terms of lifestyle contrasts.

- Discuss what you think your life would be like if you lived in a different setting.

- Use this book to focus on the concept of setting within a book. Discuss how the author and illustrator depict a setting. What words or parts of the illustrations help you to know that Katie lived in the country and her cousin in the city.

Gauch, Patricia Lee. *Christina Katerina and the Great Bear Train*. Illustrated by Elise Primavera. Putnam, 1990. (Picture book)
Christina Katerina wishes to avoid the homecoming of her new baby sister, so she takes her seven stuffed bears on a shoe-box train ride across town.

- Explore the theme of a new baby in the house by reading some of the following stories:

New Baby

Browne, Anthony. *Changes*. Illustrated by Anthony Browne. Knopf, 1990.

Greenfield, Eloise. *She Come Bringing Me That Little Baby Girl*. Illustrated by John Steptoe. Lippincott, 1974.

Hutchins, Pat. *The Very Worst Monster*. Illustrated by Pat Hutchins. Greenwillow, 1985.

Keats, Ezra Jack. *Peter's Chair*. Illustrated by Ezra Jack Keats. HarperCollins, 1967.

- Have children bring their favorite stuffed bears to school and instruct them as follows: Make a shoe-box train of your own. Display each favorite bear, reading its favorite book, in a shoe box. Make a shoe-box engine and a shoe-box caboose.

- It's fun to make things and to play imaginative games. Use Angela Wilkes's *My First Activity Book* (Knopf, 1989) and *My First Science Book* (Knopf, 1990) to motivate some hands-on activities that will promote investigation and imaginative play.

George, William T., and Lindsay Barrett George. *Beaver at Long Pond*. Illustrated by Lindsay Barrett George. Greenwillow, 1988. (Information book)
This book is filled with facts about the life of the beaver and its nocturnal routines.

- Research and list other nocturnal animals.

- Read about other nocturnal animals and list the common behaviors exhibited by the majority of them. See Joanna Cole's *Large as Life Animals*, illustrated by Kenneth Lily (Knopf, 1985).

- Develop perceptual skills by choosing a nocturnal animal and making a scale model of that animal.

Geraghty, Paul. *Look Out, Patrick!* Illustrated by Paul Geraghty. Macmillan, 1990. (Picture book)
During his walk Patrick observes flowers and song-filled birds, but he seems oblivious to the dangers around him.

- Different animals hide on each page. Test your visual acuity by searching for the hidden animals; then make some hidden animal pictures of your own.

Gibbons, Gail. *Beacons of Light: Lighthouses*. Morrow, 1990. (Picture book)

This book details the origins, purposes, and locations of lighthouses on the shores of the United States and provides informational background for fictional accounts of keeping a lighthouse. See *Keep the Lights Burning, Abbie* by Peter Roop and Connie Roop (Carolrhoda, 1985).

- Investigate to determine if there are any functioning lighthouses in the nation's waters today.

- Locate historic and current lighthouses on a map of the United States.

- Make a scale model of an actual lighthouse. Use balsa wood or cardboard. Make the lighthouse to scale, if possible.

Connections

The first lighthouse in America was erected by the Province of Massachusetts in 1716 on Little Brewster Island at the entrance to Boston Harbor. The lighthouse was authorized by an act of Congress on July 23, 1715, and the light was first lit on September 14, 1716. Use this information to stimulate student research into lighthouses.

Gibbons, Gail. *Monarch Butterfly*. Illustrated by Gail Gibbons. Holiday, 1989. (Information picture book)

The life cycle of the monarch butterfly, its body parts, and its migration patterns are explained.

- Introduce a butterfly/insect unit with this book.

- Use Cecilia Fitzsimons's *My First Butterflies: A Pop-Up Field Guide* (HarperCollins, 1985) as a model for creating a butterfly notebook.

Connections

Gail Gibbons has been writing children's books since 1975. Before writing her books she investigates the topic firsthand. For example, when she wrote *Deadline! From News to Newspaper* (Crowell, 1987), she visited many newspaper offices and shops and talked to dozens of people who work to put out a newspaper each day or week. Before writing *The Pottery Place* (Harcourt, 1987), she investigated several pottery workshops near her home. Her real-life experiences driving a truck while she and her husband, Kent Ancliffe, were building their house resulted in *Trucks* (Crowell, 1981). Observing the plentiful butterflies on the 300 acres surrounding their Corinth, Vermont, home helped her with her book *Monarch Butterfly*. More information about Gibbons can be located in *Bookpeople: A Second Album* (Teacher Ideas Press, 1990).

Giganti, Paul, Jr. *How Many Snails?* Illustrated by Donald Crews. Greenwillow, 1988. (Picture book)
This is more than a counting book; each page holds special illustrative details.

- Look for specific details on each page: spots on the dogs, stripes on the snails, icing on the cupcakes. Count and recount items on each of the pages.

- Create your own counting books (see chapter 3).

Greene, Carol. *Laura Ingalls Wilder*. Illustrated by Steve Dobson. Rookie Reader series. Children's, 1990. (Biography)
Filled with photographs of the Ingalls and Wilder families, this Rookie Reader biography capsulates information about the author of the Little House books.

- Use the listing of dates in the book to create a timeline.

- Introduce Laura by sharing some interesting information about her life. Then booktalk the books she wrote about her life.

- Introduce other books of biography.

- American School Publishers has available a filmstrip/cassette, *Meet the Newbery Author: Laura Ingalls Wilder*.

Grimm, Jacob, and Wilhelm Grimm. *Hansel and Gretel*. Illustrated by Susan Jeffers. Dial, 1986. (Picture book)
This traditional retelling shows intricate details of a forest full of life.

- Deep in the heart of the book is a two-page spread showing Hansel and Gretel lost in a very large, dark forest. Compare with the only other two-page spread in the book: a brightly colored gingerbread house. How does the darkness and lightness affect our perception of the danger in each situation?

- Note the evolution of the "witch" character. At first she is portrayed as a grandmotherly person but later is shown with red eyes and green teeth. How did Jeffers's illustrations contribute to the story?

- Take note of the wildlife within the forest. Why do you think Jeffers took care to include the wildlife in the story?

- Compare this book with other versions of "Hansel and Gretel." Locate the versions by using the author listing Grimm, Wilhelm and Jacob Grimm or Grimm brothers in the public or school library media center's catalog.

Grimm, Jacob, and Wilhelm Grimm. *Twelve Dancing Princesses*. Retold by Betsy Byars. Illustrated by K. Y. Craft. Morrow, 1989. (Picture book)
This classic fairy tale details the actions taken by a handsome prince to solve the mystery of 12 princesses and their tattered slippers.

- Compare this retelling to the retelling by Anne Carter, *The Twelve Dancing Princesses*, illustrated by Anne Dalton (Lippincott, 1989).

Hadithi, Mwenye. *Lazy Lion*. Illustrated by Adrienne Kennaway. Little, 1990. (Picture book)
King Lion orders his subjects to build him a house. The animals—white ants, weaver birds, aardvarks, a honey badger, and a crocodile—try to do as the king has asked, but they succeed only in building a house that *they* might live in. To this day Lion has not found a house.

- Read Verna Aardema's *Who's in Rabbit's House?*, illustrated by Leo Dillon and Diane Dillon (Dial, 1977). Compare the confusion over descriptions that the animals in this story have with the misconceptions that the animals in *Lazy Lion* have when they start to build Lion's house.

- Each of the animals in Hadithi's story seems to have an egocentric viewpoint, that is, able to see images only from its own perspective. Compare the egocentric behavior of these animals with the fish in Leo Lionni's *Fish Is Fish* (Pantheon, 1970).

Hammer, Charles. *Wrong-Way Ragsdale*. Farrar, 1987. (Novel)
This survival story tells of 13-year-old Emment, who flies himself and his bratty little sister 300 miles away to the Ozarks in an old plane.

- Read aloud a segment of the story as an example of a first-person narrative.

Harshman, Marc. *Snow Company*. Illustrated by Leslie W. Bowman. Cobblehill, 1990. (Picture book)
Teddy's house is suddenly filled with unexpected guests when a blizzard stops all travel. Warm and friendly events are portrayed in gentle illustrations.

- Compare the story grammar with that of Beatrice Schenk de Regniers's *The Snow Party* (Lothrop, 1989). Note that de Regniers's book was first published with illustrations by Reiner Zimnik by Pantheon in 1959. The Lothrop edition features new illustrations by Bernice Myers. If both editions of the de Regniers's book are available, evaluate the effect of Zimnik's and Myers's illustrations on the text.

- Leslie W. Bowman's illustrations mimic the style of the illustrations executed in color by Stephen Gammell. Discuss Bowman's and Gammell's illustrations. See the entry on pages 113-14 for Birdseye's *Airmail to the Moon* for a list of books illustrated by Gammell.

Hennessy, B. G. *School Days*. Illustrated by Tracey Campbell Pearson. Viking, 1990. (Picture book)
An eventful day at school is recorded in line drawings and watercolors.

- Record a day in your school life through diary entries and pictures.

- Find other books about school life. Read one of Harry Allard's books about Miss Nelson or one of Patricia Reilly Giff's books about the Polk Street School Kids.

Hoban, Tana. *Look! Look! Look!* Illustrated by Tana Hoban. Greenwillow, 1988. (Picture book)
The photographs in this book are exposed first through a small cutout square. After attempting to identify the object through this small cutout, turn the page and uncover the entire photograph.

- To develop the ability to organize and present information, create a class book. Cut out pictures from magazines that depict single objects. Cut around the object and glue to a piece of paper. Cut out a small square in the center of another piece of paper. Place the piece of paper with the cutout square in front of the object's photo to create a photo riddle as Hoban did. Combine students' riddles to create a class book. Be sure to add a title page and a cover with title and author.

- Extend the experience by using Hoban's *Look Again* (Macmillan, 1971).

Hoopes, Lyn Littlefield. *Wing-a-Ding*. Illustrated by Stephen Gammell. Joy Street, 1990. (Picture book)
Efforts by Jack's friends to rescue Jack's toy (a wing-a-ding), which is stuck in a tree, fail. Finally, the wing-a-ding just flies out of the tree.

- Compare Gammell's illustrations in *Wing-a-Ding* with his illustrations for other books. What are the common characteristics of his style? For a list of books illustrated by Gammell, see entry for Birdseye's *Airmail to the Moon* on pages 113-14.

- Rescuing a toy is a theme common to this book and to Jane Hissey's *Old Bear* (Philomel, 1986). Compare and contrast the two stories.

Hopkins, Lee Bennett. *Happy Birthday*. Illustrated by Hilary Knight. Simon, 1991.
This book contains poems to celebrate everyone's birthday. Knight's energy-filled illustrations depict a birthday party, from the writing of invitations to the festivities to the writing of thank-you notes.

- Share a poem each day a child celebrates a birthday.

- Correlate the idea of writing invitations and thank-you notes with Loreen Leedy's *Messages in the Mailbox: How to Write a Letter* (see entry on pages 145-46).

- Read Patricia Polacco's *Some Birthday!* (Simon, 1991). Patricia's family seems to have forgotten her birthday. Her dad suggests a trip to one of the scariest places on earth, the home of the Clay Pit Bottoms Monster. Some birthday!

- Write or tell about a special birthday you have had, or a birthday celebration you wish you had had.

Howe, James. *Hot Fudge*. Illustrated by Leslie Morrill. Morrow, 1990. (Junior novel)
Hot Fudge introduces the Harold and Chester animal characters popular in Howe's novels for intermediate readers: *Howliday Inn* (Macmillan, 1982; Avon, 1987) and *The Celery Stalks at Midnight* (Macmillan, 1983; Avon, 1984). Harold relates a day's events and reveals his love of chocolate and his sense of duty and responsibility.

- Use as a read-aloud to introduce longer novels. Discuss characters.

- Read another title with these characters: *Scared Silly: A Halloween Treat* by James Howe, illustrated by Leslie Morrill (Morrow, 1989).

- Because the book contains a caution about feeding chocolate to dogs, investigate what kinds of food a dog should be fed.

- Make the chocolate fudge from the recipe in the book.

- James Howe is a lover of chocolate and so is Robert Kimmel Smith, author of *Chocolate Fever* (Dell, 1986; Putnam, 1989). Make a bar graph illustrating the number of students in the classroom who consider themselves chocoholics and to those who don't. Be sure to define *chocoholic* before taking the survey.

- Write letters to favorite authors and illustrators or to community personalities to determine which are chocoholics. Be sure to include the class definition of a chocoholic and enclose a self-addressed stamped postcard for their response. Most authors and illustrators can be reached through their current publisher. Addresses for many authors are included in the appendixes of the Author a Month series, the Bookpeople albums, and *Adventures with Social Studies (Through Literature)* — all published by Libraries Unlimited/Teacher Ideas Press. Addresses for community personalities are available in city telephone books or directories, which can usually be found in the reference department at the public library.

Howe, John. *Jack and the Beanstalk*. Illustrated by John Howe. Little, 1989. (Picture book)
This is a retelling of a classic fairy tale.

- To help students visualize the size of the characters, make life-size stand-up cutouts of Jack and the giant.

- Compare Howe's version with other versions of "Jack and the Beanstalk."

Hurwitz, Johanna. *Russell Sprouts*. Illustrated by Lillian Hoban. Morrow, 1987. (Junior novel)
Russell, a first-grader, dresses in his tiger pajamas so that he can be a tiger for Halloween. His friends cannot suspect that he is wearing his pajamas. The last chapter tells of his science project. He chooses a potato that is supposed to sprout. He wishes he had chosen beans when it seems that the potato is never going to sprout. Finally, during school vacation the potato sprouts, but as Russell is getting ready to take it to school, his sister drops it on the floor and ruins it. But digging in the dirt Russell finds some tiny little potatoes that he does take to school. After the show-and-tell activity, Russell's mother cooks the potatoes and they eat them.

- Plant beans and potatoes and observe the time it takes for them to sprout and grow. Measure and chart the growth daily.

- Use your creativity to make a Halloween costume from something you have around the house.

Hutchins, Pat. *What Game Shall We Play?* Illustrated by Pat Hutchins. Greenwillow, 1990. (Picture book)
Duck and Frog don't know what game to play, so they set out to find Fox. But he doesn't know what to play either. So they try to find Mouse. Finally it is Owl who gives them a logical answer.

- The seven animals from Hutchins's earlier book *The Surprise Party* (Macmillan, 1969; 1986) return in this sequel. Compare Hutchins's depiction of the seven animals in the earlier title to the animals in this title. How has her art technique changed or evolved?

- In *The Surprise Party* the animals are searching for a party. In this new tale the animals are trying to find a game to play. What else could the animals want to find or do? Make a list.

- Make puppets for each of the seven animals, retell the stories, and create new stories about the animals.

Hyde, Dayton O. *Island of the Loons*. Atheneum, 1985. (Novel)
When a storm forces Jimmy to stay on the island and he finds himself in a position to save an escaped convict, he himself becomes a prisoner. The two manage to survive for more than a year.

- Make a map of the area showing the locations of the action.

- Create a bird and plant identification guide for Jimmy and Burkey. Research to make sure your information is accurate.

Ivimey, John W. *The Complete Story of the Three Blind Mice*. Illustrated by Victoria Chess. Joy Street, 1990. (Picture book)
Music is included in this complete story behind the rhyme.

- Sing the song.

- Correlate with a reading of Jim Aylesworth's *The Complete Hickory Dickory Dock* (Atheneum, 1990). Use the two books as models of an elaboration on a story. Play with some other rhymes and make up stories to such rhymes as "Humpty Dumpty," "Tom, Tom, the Piper's Son," "Georgie Porgie Pudding and Pie," and other favorites.

Johnston, Tony. *The Soup Bone*. Illustrated by Margot Tomes. Harcourt, 1990. (Picture book)
A little old lady in search of a soup bone finds a skeleton that decides to become a permanent part of her household.

- Compare and contrast to the story line in Paul Galdone's *The Teeny Tiny Woman: A Ghost Story* (Clarion, 1984) or Jane O'Connor's *The Teeny Tiny Woman*, illustrated by Tomie dePaola (Random, 1986).

Johnston, Tony. *Yonder*. Illustrated by Lloyd Bloom. Dial, 1988. (Picture book)
A newly married couple move to a forested area and with the birth of each child plant a plum tree. As the family grows so does the community around their home. By the time the children are grown, so are the plum trees—and Grandpa dies. The last page shows the beginning of a new cycle.

- Write about a family tradition in your home.

- Extend the concept of communities and their history of growth. Read Virginia Lee Burton's *The Little House* (Houghton, 1939) and Blair Lent's *Bayberry Bluff* (Houghton, 1987).

- Research the historical origins of your town or community.

Connections

Tony Johnston did not particularly like the name her parents, David and Ruth Taylor, gave her at birth so she changed her name to "Tony." She liked the alliterative sound it created with her last name, Taylor. In 1966 she married Roger Johnston, and although her name was no longer alliterative, she did not change it again. The Johnstons moved to Mexico City, where they lived for 15 years. In the late 1980s they returned to her home state of California and now live in San Marino, California. More information about Tony Johnston can be located in *An Author a Month (for Nickels)* (Teacher Ideas Press, 1990).

Jonas, Ann. *Reflections*. Illustrated by Ann Jonas. Greenwillow, 1987. (Picture book)
After reading the story read back through the book starting at the end.

- See if you can reverse a favorite story and return to the beginning from the end.

Josephs, Anna Catherine. *Mountain Boy*. Illustrated by Bill Ersland. Raintree, 1985. (Junior novel)
Union soldiers escape from a Confederate prison in South Carolina and come to Tommy Zachary's home in North Carolina to ask him to lead them across the Blue Ridge Mountains of Tennessee. This is the story of that journey.

- Use a map of the United States to locate the places mentioned in the text.

- Research and list some historical events contemporary with the events in this book. For example, who was president of the United States? How many states were part of the Union at the time? Who were some famous people of the period? What was going on in your own state at that time?

- Read other books set during the Civil War (see index).

Kandoian, Ellen. *Maybe She Forgot*. Illustrated by Ellen Kandoian. Cobblehill, 1990. (Picture book)
Jesse waits to be picked up after ballet lessons, but her mom has been delayed by traffic problems.

- The illustrations aptly portray the dilemmas Jesse's mother is facing, but what about Jesse's concerns? Illustrate some of the things you think might be going through Jesse's mind.

- Read another story that focuses on a similar experience, *Waiting for Mama* by Beatrice Schenk de Regniers, illustrated by Victoria deLarrea (Clarion, 1984).

Kasza, Keiko. *The Wolf's Chicken Stew*. Illustrated by Keiko Kasza. Putnam, 1989. (Picture book)
A wolf schemes to fatten up a chicken so that she will be nice and plump for his chicken stew. He leaves "100 scrumptious doughnuts" at her doorstep hoping that she will eat them and get nice and fat. He also leaves "100 scrumptious pancakes" and a "100-pound scrumptious cake." Finally he goes to confront her at her door and finds a skinny-looking hen in an apron. He is surprised to find 100 grateful chicks who smother him with kisses in thanks for all the food. The hen invites him in and cooks him a nice dinner. When he leaves he muses that he just might go home and bake those cute chicks "100 scrumptious cookies."

- Bake 100 scrumptious cookies and take them to a nursing home to distribute.

- Use this book as part of your school's focus on the 100th day of school mathematics activities (see chapter 3).

- Compare and contrast the wolf character with the wolf in other stories, such as "Little Red Riding Hood" and "The Three Little Pigs." Discuss the image of the wolf as portrayed in folk stories.

Connections

Keiko Kasza was born in Hiroshima-ken, Japan, on December 23, 1951. She grew up and attended school in Japan but came to the United States to attend California State University at Northridge. She was a graphic artist but decided to work on books when she saw some of the work of Leo Lionni. She has written and illustrated several other books, including *The Pig's Picnic* (Putnam, 1988), *When the Elephant Walks* (Putnam, 1990), and *Coco's Mother* (Putnam, 1992). Kasza is featured in *An Author a Month (for Dimes)* (Teacher Ideas Press, 1993).

Keller, Holly. *Henry's Happy Birthday*. Illustrated by Holly Keller. Greenwillow, 1990. (Picture book)

Everything is going wrong at Henry's birthday party. He even wishes that the birthday was somebody else's. But the party improves and the birthday is enjoyed.

- Use your creativity to make an invitation to a special event at your school or home.

Kinsey-Warnock, Natalie. *The Wild Horses of Sweetbriar*. Illustrated by Ted Rand. Cobblehill, 1990. (Picture book)

The storyteller remembers a year she spent as a young girl on an island off the coast of Nantucket. She worried that the wild horses living on the island would die during the long harsh winter.

- This book could introduce Marguerite Henry's novel *Misty of Chincoteague* (Rand, 1947). Henry's book is a classic tale of Misty, a descendant of Spanish horses that struggled ashore after a shipwreck near Assateague Island. *Stormy, Misty's Foal* (Rand, 1963) continues Misty's story.

Connections

Assateague and Chincoteague are islands located off the coasts of Maryland and Virginia. The descendants of horses that survived the shipwreck still live on these islands. Every July the residents of the islands hold Pony Penning Day, during which ponies are penned up and auctioned for the benefit of the volunteer fire department. More information about the islands and Pony Penning Days was published in *National Geographic Traveler* (Summer 1985) in an article, "All the Pretty Little Ponies: Chincoteague's Roundup" by K. M. Kostyal, and in Jack Denton Scott's book *Island of the Wild Horses* (Putnam, 1978).

Kuhlin, Susan. *Going to My Ballet Class*. Illustrated by Susan Kuhlin. Bradbury, 1989. (Picture book)

This nonfiction title is illustrated with photographs of "real" children. The book explains the rationale for dancers' hairstyles, clothing, etc. It also introduces ballet steps and gives general information for the reader unacquainted with ballet as an art form.

- The first-person narrative of the book will provide a model for student narratives about activities they experience.

- The book refers to the Joffrey ballet class; investigate the origins of the Joffrey Ballet and other well-known performing companies.

- Invite ballet students to visit the classroom to demonstrate basic ballet steps. Be sure to include some male dancers if possible.

- Maria Tallchief was the first Native American to become a prima ballerina in a ballet company. Find out what contributions she made to ballet and to her Native-American community.

Lauber, Patricia. *Seeds Pop•Stick•Glide*. Illustrated by Jerome Wexler. Crown, 1981; 1991. (Information)
This book, in discussing many aspects of the plant kingdom, makes a distinction between those seeds that are dispersed by animals and people and those that travel by wind or water or are self-scattered.

- Locate details and demonstrate the ability to organize information by making an information chart showing ways seeds travel.

- Categorize seeds that travel by wind, water, etc. Make a pictorial graph.

- Follow a seed from germination to mature plant stage. Show the stages in a series of sequential drawings.

Lauber, Patricia. *What's Hatching Out of That Egg?* Illustrated by photographs. Crown, 1979; 1991. (Information)
Much information is provided about specific eggs and the animals that hatch out of them. Many different eggs are featured, including the eggs of the ostrich, python, bullfrog, and monarch butterfly.

- Make an egg identification chart summarizing the information presented in the book.

- Correlate with the information given in four titles in Knopf's Eyewitness books: *Insect* by Laurence Mound (Knopf, 1990), *Reptile* by Colin McCarthy (Knopf, 1991), *Fish* by Steve Parker (Knopf, 1990), and *Bird* by David Burnie (Knopf, 1988).

Leedy, Loreen. *The Bunny Play*. Illustrated by Loreen Leedy. Holiday, 1988. (Information picture book)
This text with illustrations guides children through all steps of producing a play, from selection of material through final performance. The text is written for children.

- Use the suggestions to produce a play from a traditional tale.

- The bunnies in this book produce a musical play of "Little Red Riding Hood." Compare and contrast their version to narrative versions of the "Little Red Riding Hood" tale. Locate editions by using the catalog in your school or public library.

Leedy, Loreen. *Messages in the Mailbox: How to Write a Letter*. Illustrated by Loreen Leedy. Holiday, 1991. (Picture book)
Leedy has a magical way to get young readers interested in topics they might otherwise avoid. When students finish reading this book they will want to write letters: friendly letters, invitations, thank-you notes, get-well letters, and many other types of correspondence. But probably of most interest will be the instructions on writing shape and puzzle letters and on writing with invisible ink.

- Focus on writing letters by teaming Leedy's book with Gail Gibbons's *The Post Office Book: Mail and How It Moves* (HarperCollins, 1982) and Vera B. Williams and Jennifer Williams's *Stringbean's Trip to the Shining Sea* (Greenwillow, 1988) (see Williams's entry on p. 167). Encourage students to write and send letters to people with whom they would like to correspond. Write to grandparents, pen pals from a class across town or in another state, friends who have moved away, favorite authors, etc.

Connections

Loreen Leedy has written many books about things to do and make. In *A Dragon Christmas* (Holiday, 1988), Dragon shows how to make decorations, cards, and tasty treats. *The Dragon Halloween Party* (Holiday, 1986) shares activities for Halloween. Creating a newspaper is highlighted in *The Furry News: How to Make a Newspaper* (Holiday, 1990). And in *The Great Trash Bash* (Holiday, 1991), the residents of the town find ways to get rid of trash and change their habits so that their town will not have trash problems in the future. Loreen Leedy lives in Winter Park, Florida.

Lester, Alison. *Imagine*. Illustrated by Alison Lester. Houghton, 1990. (Picture book)
Imagine simply by turning pages going to different places and seeing animals from those places—the jungle, ocean, countryside, and African plains.

- Search for the wildlife listed in the borders of the pages. The lists place animals in categories; verify the accuracy of the lists.

Lobel, Anita. *Alison's Zinnia*. Illustrated by Anita Lobel. Greenwillow, 1990. (Picture book)
This ABC book with an unusual focus shows beautifully realistic flowers on each page. The panel at the bottom of each page depicts Alison in an action (verb). It is one of the few books that illustrates the meaning of a verb—"Alison acquired an Amaryllis for Beryl. Beryl bought a Begonia for Crystal." The connecting pattern brings the text full circle with "Zena zeroed in on a Zinnia for Alison."

- Make an information chart, such as one you might find on the back of a seed packet, for each of the flowers depicted in Lobel's book. Investigate the information to be included. Most seed packets include the plant's final height, its growing zone, the season it blooms, the best location in which to plant it, its light and water needs, etc.

- Write an innovation on the text. Perhaps you could use children's names and animals. "Amy arrested an Armadillo and took it to Bob. Bob brought a Bear with him and gave it to Carl. Carl caught a Cat and...." Think of other categories you might wish to use with the same pattern.

Connections

Anita Lobel was born Anita Kempler in Cracow, Poland. She came to the United States and eventually studied art at Pratt Institute, where she met Arnold Lobel. They were married in 1955 and became the parents of two children, Adrianne and Adam. Anita is an actress and singer who originally used her art to work with set design. Through the encouragement of Arnold she began to illustrate books for children. They collaborated on earlier works. One of the most popular collaborations was *On Market Street* (Lothrop, 1981). Arnold wrote the rhythmic prose and Anita provided the ingenious paintings. Anita Lobel lived for many years in Brooklyn, but since Arnold's death she has lived in New York City and Florida.

Lowry, Lois. *Rabble Starkey*. Houghton, 1987. (Novel)

Rabble is different in looks—she has ginger-colored hair and green eyes—and she is different in behavior. She and her mother move into a garage apartment to care for the family of Rabble's best friend while the mother is in the hospital (for months). Rabble finds herself with a new set of obstacles to overcome when she discovers she has to deal with a four-year-old and a "real" family.

- This book is set in an Appalachian town; correlate with Cynthia Rylant's book of poems *Waiting to Waltz: A Childhood* (Macmillan, 1984) about life in Beaver, West Virginia.

- Use as part of a focus on various family structures. Read other books and categorize the family arrangements as represented in each of the books. Graph or chart the findings. How representative are the depictions of family structures in books of literature as compared to those structures as represented by students in a regular classroom?

Lyon, George Ella. *Basket*. Illustrated by Mary Szilagyi. Orchard, 1990. (Picture book)

A little girl tells of her grandmother's lost "little white oak basket, left from the farm," which disappeared in a move. Over the years whenever anything is missing, Grandmother thinks that it must be in the basket. After Grandmother dies, the basket is found; although it contains only one spool of thread, it has held many, many memories.

- Correlate activities for this book with activities for Sharon Bell Mathis's *The Hundred Penny Box*, illustrated by Leo Dillon and Diane Dillon (Viking, 1975) (see index).

- Put a "memories basket" in the classroom and encourage students to place in it objects that represent memories for them. At a later time use the objects to motivate experience stories or sharing times.

Macaulay, David. *Black and White*. Illustrated by David Macaulay. Houghton, 1990. (Picture book; Caldecott Award, 1991)

Four interrelated stories move from episode to episode in opposite corners of each page. Commuters create objects out of newspapers while they wait patiently for the train. A lost herd of black-and-white Holstein cows create "udder chaos." A young boy returns to his parents, and a robber and a dog play integral roles in another saga.

- Write the story portrayed in each of the four-panel sequences.

- Note the characters that are part of more than one story. Discuss why these are important.

- Cut words and letters from newspapers to make your own sentences and messages.

- Read some information about Macaulay's friend Chris Van Allsburg. Information about him is provided in *An Author a Month (for Pennies)* (Libraries Unlimited, 1988). Then look at the stories in Macaulay's book once more. Are there hidden references to Van Allsburg?

Maestro, Betsy. *Snow Day*. Illustrated by Giulio Maestro. Scholastic, 1989. (Picture book)

This informative book details the task of digging out a town after a snowstorm. Brightly colored illustrations bring to life the drawings of trucks and snow equipment.

- Compare and contrast with Virginia Lee Burton's *Katy and the Big Snow* (Houghton, 1943). Maestro's *Snow Day* shows machines currently used for snow removal, whereas Burton's *Katy and the Big Snow* provides a direct contrast from five decades earlier.

Mahy, Margaret. *The Great White Man-Eating Shark*. Illustrated by Jonathan Allen. Dial, 1989. (Picture book)

Norvin, a boy who looks a lot like a shark, wants to be alone when he goes swimming in the cove, so he pretends to be a shark and scares all the other swimmers away. Later, a female shark scares him away from the water.

- Compare with the tricky animals in Patricia McKissack's *Monkey-Monkey's Trick: Based on an African Folk Tale*, illustrated by Paul Meisel (Random, 1988).

- Discuss the themes of greed and trickery. Identify other books with these same themes.

Markmann, Erika. *Grow It! An Indoor/Outdoor Gardening Guide for Kids*. Illustrated by Gisela Konemund. Random, 1991. (Information)

This book provides detailed information about choosing and caring for plants, from watering to getting rid of plant pests to wintering the plants.

- Using the plant illustrations on pages 40 and 41 as a guide, choose at least five plants that have one common characteristic, such as purple blooms, variegated leaves, or solid green foliage. List the plant names and their common characteristic.

- Choose one of the plants on page 40 or 41. Investigate the plant and make a chart showing information about it: appearance of seed or bulb, length of germination period, height of mature plant, growing time, etc.

- The addresses of 20 seed companies are listed on page 43 of Markmann's book. Write a letter to one of the companies requesting a catalog for the classroom. When the catalog arrives, search for seeds or plants that will grow in your area. Order seeds and create a flowerbox or a flower garden for your school or home.

- Choose a flower that might be a special one for a friend or someone in your family because of its name, its shape, or its color. For example, my mother's name is Helen. A natural flower to grow for her is helenium, which means "Helen's flower." My grandmother loves the color purple, so any flower of that color would be appropriate.

Marshak, Samuel. *Hail to Mail*. Translated by Richard Pevear. Illustrated by Vladimir Radunsky. Holt, 1990. (Picture book)

John Peck travels the world and is followed by a letter that finally catches up with him in New York.

- Read other stories about mail and how it travels. Gail Gibbons's *The Post Office Book: Mail and How It Moves* (HarperCollins, 1982) presents another perspective of a letter's travels.

Martin, Jacqueline Briggs. *Good Times on Grandfather Mountain*. Illustrated by Susan Gaber. Orchard, 1992.

Old Washburn is a whittler who believes in dealing with a situation as it is dealt him. When the cow jumps the fence he converts the milk bucket into a drum. When the chickens leave the homestead, he understands their getting tired of sitting on eggs all day, and when grasshoppers eat his beans, he whittles the beanpoles into tub-thumpers. Similarly, when the raccoons eat the corn, he makes the corncobs into whistles. When a storm blows down his cabin, he uses the wood to make a fancy fiddle, and when his neighbors hear the music he is making, they come running to the party—and build him a new house.

- Tub-thumpers, whistles, and fiddles made from wood, corncobs, or beanpoles, all contribute to the making of music. Discuss other musical instruments that could be made and played. A portion of the 25-minute, 16mm film *Gene Deitch: The Picture Book Animated* (Weston Woods, 1977) discusses Deitch's research in Prague, Czechoslovakia, and his attempts to locate authentic musical instruments to use in conjunction with animating Gail E. Haley's *A Story, A Story* (Atheneum, 1970). In the segment, they create wooden instruments from planks, paddles, etc. The ideas might be utilized in combination with the ideas from Martin's book to create musical instruments that could be used to create a rhythm band. Practice the music and take the music to a nursing home or to another classroom, or invite parents or others in the school community to come in and enjoy a "concert" given with the instruments.

- Old Washburn is an optimist. Compare Old Washburn and his outlook on life with the title character in Jim Aylesworth's *Shenadoah Noah*, illustrated by Glen Rounds (Holt, 1985).

- If possible, locate a whittler in your area and invite him or her to discuss whittling with readers at your school.

Martin, Rafé. *Foolish Rabbit's Big Mistake*. Illustrated by Ed Young. Putnam, 1985. (Picture book)
   In one of the oldest versions of "Henny Penny," "Chicken Little," or "The Sky Is Falling," Rabbit asks, "What if the earth broke up?" Three rabbits, several bears, an elephant, a snake, and a lion are all involved in the scare when an apple is heard hitting the ground and the sound is thought to be "the earth breaking up." It is the lion who saves the day by helping the animals muster the courage to face the situation.

- Compare and contrast to several versions of "Henny Penny" or "Chicken Little." Familiar editions include "Chicken Licken" by P. C. Asbjørnsen in *Tomie dePaola's Favorite Nursery Tales* (Putnam, 1986); "Henny-Penny" in *The Three Bears & 15 Other Stories*, selected and illustrated by Anne Rockwell (Crowell, 1975; Trophy, 1984); *Henny Penny*, retold and illustrated by Paul Galdone (Clarion, 1968); *The Story of Chicken Licken*, illustrated by Jan Ormerod (Lothrop, 1986); and Steven Kellogg's modern adaptation, *Chicken Little* (Morrow, 1985).

- Write another story using the chain reaction pattern.

- Compare the lion's role in this story with the role Swimmy plays in Leo Lionni's *Swimmy* (Pantheon, 1963). Discuss how the lion is portrayed in each of the stories.

Marzollo, Jean. *Pretend You're a Cat*. Illustrated by Jerry Pinkney. Dial, 1990. (Picture book)
   Rhyming verses ask readers to "purr like a cat," "scratch like a dog," "snort like a pig," etc.

- Integrate with a unit focusing on animals.

- Write your own version of this story, substituting animals from Africa, Australia, or other specific locations. Make sure the animal's sounds represent accurate information.

Mayer, Mercer. *There's Something in My Attic*. Illustrated by Mercer Mayer. Dial, 1988. (Picture book)
   After moving from the city to a farm, a young girl discovers the attic and the noises in it.

- Create your own vision of a "nightmare" that might be found in your attic. Draw or paint a picture of your nightmare.

- After discussing the word *garret*, read the title poem from Lenore Blegvad's *The Parrot in the Garret and Other Rhymes About Dwellings*, illustrated by Erik Blegvad (Atheneum, 1982).

- Cut a piece of paper into the triangular shape of an attic (garret) and then illustrate the inside of the attic. Use watercolor, collage, or any other artistic technique that will coordinate with other aspects of literature appreciation.

- Share another experience of finding out what is in an attic by reading Karen Ackerman's *Song and Dance Man*, illustrated by Stephen Gammell (Knopf, 1988).

- Correlate with other "monster" hiding books such as James Howe's *There's a Monster Under My Bed*, illustrated by David Rose (Macmillan, 1990).

- Compare and contrast the experience with "something" in the attic with Elisabeth's experiences of finding something in the cellar in *Spiders in the Fruit Cellar* by Barbara M. Joosse, illustrated by Kay Chorao (Knopf, 1983).

McDonald, Megan. *Is This a House for Hermit Crab?* Illustrated by S. D. Schindler. Orchard, 1990. (Picture book)
When Hermit the crab outgrows his old house, he attempts to find a new one before the pricklepien fish finds him. After rejecting several objects that he finds along the shore, he finally finds a house that is just right for him. Soft pastels give the appearance of chalk-drawn illustrations.

- Relate to information about crabs and to Eric Carle's *A House for Hermit Crab* (Picture, 1988) and the classic information book about hermit crabs *Pagoo* by Holling C. Holling, illustrated by L. W. Holling (Houghton, 1957).

McKenna, Colleen O'Shaughnessy. *Too Many Murphys*. Illustrated by Colleen O'Shaughnessy McKenna. Scholastic, 1988.
Collette is the oldest child in her family, a family that she feels is too large. Before Christmas she wishes to be an only child. Her parents grant her wish for one day. She loves having the attention of her parents all to herself, but when her parents plan to begin the Christmas decorating with just the three of them, Collette knows that much of the fun will be missing if her siblings are not there. Collette insists that the others be brought home so that the decorating can be shared.

- Write about what your life would be like as an only child. Or if you are an only child, what would your life be like as the oldest in a large family?

- Discuss holiday traditions at your house.

McKissack, Patricia C. *Mirandy and Brother Wind*. Illustrated by Jerry Pinkney. Knopf, 1988. (Picture book)
Mirandy must capture Brother Wind in order to win the cakewalk.

- Make your own decorated papier-mâché cake as the prize for a cakewalk.

- Describe the powers of a conjure woman.

- Discuss the phrase "dancing with the wind." Then discuss other phrases and their figurative and literal meanings. The books of Fred Gwynne are naturals to share here. Read Gwynne's *A Chocolate Moose for Dinner* (Simon, 1976; 1987), *The King Who Rained* (Simon, 1970; 1987), *The Sixteen-Hand Horse* (Simon, 1987), and *A Little Pigeon Toad* (Simon, 1988).

Miller, Ned. *Emmett's Snowball*. Illustrated by Susan Guevaro. Holt, 1990. (Picture book)
With the help of friends, Emmett builds a giant snow boulder. When the boulder rolls down main street, there is a great commotion.

- Compare the commotion caused by the boulder with the commotion caused by Big Anthony in *Strega Nona* by Tomie dePaola (Prentice, 1975).

- Build something with a group of friends. Describe how you had to work together. Provide step-by-step instructions for other groups.

Most, Bernard. *The Cow That Went Oink*. Illustrated by Bernard Most. Harcourt, 1990. (Picture book)

There was once a cow that went "oink," and she was terribly unhappy until she met a pig that went "moo." They teach each other and become the only animals on the farm who can make two sounds.

- Make a list of things you can do and could teach to someone else.

- Make a poster advertising your willingness to teach someone else how to do something. If you feel you do not know how to do something special, read a book to learn a magic trick, figure out how to make a paper airplane, etc.

Most, Bernard. *Four & Twenty Dinosaurs*. Illustrated by Bernard Most. HarperCollins, 1990. (Picture book)

This is a simple collection of nursery rhyme parodies that transform familiar nursery rhymes into verses about dinosaurs. Verses parodied include Jack and Jill went up the hill; Peter Piper; Rain on the green grass; Hark! Hark! The dogs do bark; Pat-a-cake; Needles and Pins; London Bridge; Diddle, diddle, dumpling; "Bow-wow," say the dogs; Little Miss Muffet; Go to bed late; Hush-a-bye, baby; Little Jack Horner; Here we go round the mulberry bush; One, two, three, four, and five; Old Mother Hubbard; Hey diddle, diddle; Cobbler, cobbler, mend my shoe; Mary had a little lamb; Three little kittens; There was an old woman who lived in a shoe; The man in the moon; and Sing a song of sixpence.

- Choose your own theme and write parodies of favorite nursery rhymes.

- Most did not change the text of all the nursery rhymes, but instead used the illustrations to change the tone or interpretation of the rhymes. Using a theme such as space or farm animals, give a new interpretation to a favorite nursery rhyme by illustrating it in a new and innovative manner.

Connections

Do not assume that older readers are familiar with nursery rhymes. Some children have never read them, and others will have forgotten them. Prior to using writing or art activities with Most's book, build or activate readers' prior knowledge by asking them to read nursery rhymes. Favorite collections that are excellent sources for nursery rhymes include:

- Briggs, Raymond. *The Mother Goose Treasury*. Coward, 1966.

- dePaola, Tomie. *Tomie dePaola's Mother Goose*. Putnam, 1985.

- Lobel, Arnold. *The Random House Book of Mother Goose*. Random House, 1986.

- Tudor, Tasha. *Mother Goose*. Walck, 1944.

Myers, Bernice. *It Happens to Everyone*. Illustrated by Bernice Myers. Lothrop, 1990. (Picture book)

Anxieties of the first day of school are told in alternating views: that of the teacher and that of the student.

- Tell about another incident from two points of view. Another example of this type of tale is Judy Blume's *The Pain and the Great One* (Bradbury, 1984). The story gives accounts of several incidents from the viewpoints of a brother and sister.

- First day of school jitters is also the focus of Robert Quackenbush's *I Don't Want to Go, I Don't Know How to Act* (Lippincott, 1983).

- Older students might enjoy reminiscing about their "first day of school." Bring in photographs and include them in a display, "First Days of School Remembered." You may want to display the photographs without identifying the subject. Number the photographs and attempt to match them with the correct students.

- Use photocopies of the original student photos for "wanted posters" that students will write concerning their first year or two at school. For example, "Wanted, an unidentified fugitive, for sitting at the edge of the group and sucking his thumb. If you should encounter this thumb-sucker, do not attempt to apprehend him but call 398-2830. At the time of the offense Brian was 3 feet 6 inches tall, with brown hair and blue eyes. Now he would be 5 feet 1 inch tall, with dark brown hair and blue eyes." Other offenses might include not taking a nap, wanting only to read, crying every morning at the school door, or simply being *too* cute.

Netzel, Shirley. *The Jacket I Wear in the Snow*. Illustrated by Nancy Winslow Parker. Greenwillow, 1989. (Picture book)
This is a cumulative story of a girl's preparation for playing in the snow.

- Make felt pieces and retell the story using a feltboard.

- Write innovations on the text: "This is the suit I wear to the beach," "This is the food I fix for dinner," etc.

Numeroff, Laura Joffe. *If You Give a Mouse a Cookie*. Illustrated by Felicia Bond. Scholastic, 1985. (Picture book)
This circular chain story begins with what would happen if you give a mouse a cookie and ends with the mouse wanting another cookie.

- Brainstorm a list of animals that you might give some food. Then use the list to begin innovations on the text: If you give a _____ a _____ .... Continue with the tale in the same pattern used in Numeroff's story.

- Correlate with a reading of another tale by Numeroff, *If You Give a Moose a Muffin*, illustrated by Felicia Bond (HarperCollins, 1991).

Ockenga, Starr, and Eileen Doolittle. *A Book of Days: Then and Now*. Houghton, 1990. (Information)
This keepsake-type book, which is designed to be a permanent record of special family days and photographs, includes a family tree.

- Design an original family scrapbook and gradually add family stories, photocopies of photographs of the story subjects, accounts of family traditions, traditional holiday customs, and so on. Ask older family members to help fill in a family tree.

- Write a story about an event in your family's history; a good model is Deborah Kogan Ray's *My Daddy Was a Soldier: A World War II Story* (Holiday, 1990).

O'Keefe, Susan Heyboer. *One Hungry Monster*. Illustrated by Lynn Munsinger. Little, 1989. (Picture book)
A young boy attempts to control the naughty but lovable monsters in his own house. As the numbers in the counting book get larger, so does the craziness of the monsters. Both the Arabic and spelled-out numerals are used in these crazy and fun verses.

- Following a recipe, bake and enjoy some apple muffins like the "apple muffin the monsters never got."

- Make a list of all the food the monsters get into and categorize it. Are there overlapping characteristics that would put some of the foods into more than one category?

- Write a story about the 10 monsters when they return the next time. Will they get the apple muffin? Will they fail to find another type of food the next time?

Old MacDonald Had a Farm. Illustrated by Nancy Hellen. Orchard, 1990. (Picture book)
This is an old song with an inventive presentation. Cutout pages reveal a cow behind a pile of sacks, a round pig behind a barrel, and a fluffy sheep behind a sheaf of wheat. The complete song appears at the end of the book.

- Sing the song.

- Make illustrations for the other stanzas of the song.

- Read other illustrated versions of the song. After readers are thoroughly familiar with the more traditional versions, try reading some of the zany innovations. Traditional retellings include versions illustrated by Lorinda Bryan Cauley (Putnam, 1989), David Frankland (Merrill, 1980), Tracey Campbell Pearson (Dial, 1984), Glen Rounds (Holiday, 1989), and Robert M. Quackenbush (Lippincott, 1972). Zany versions to try include Judi Barrett's *Old MacDonald Had an Apartment House*, illustrated by Ron Barrett (Atheneum, 1969) and Stephen Gammell's *Once upon MacDonald's Farm*, illustrated by Gammell (Four Winds, 1981).

Oppenheim, Joanne. *"Not Now!" Said the Cow*. Illustrated by Chris Demarest. Bantam, 1990. (Picture book)
This is an easy-to-read variant of the traditional "Little Red Hen" story.

- Before reading Oppenheim's title, use versions of "Little Red Hen" for critical reading activities.

  - Read Paul Galdone's *The Little Red Hen* (Clarion, 1973). Discuss the characters (hen, cat, dog, mouse) and the sequence of events, including the statements "Not I" and "I will."
  - Reread Galdone's story and invite student participation in the responses to the hen's questions.
  - Read Linda McQueen's version of the same story, *The Little Red Hen* (Scholastic, 1985). Discuss the characters (hen, goose, cat, dog) and the sequence of events, including the statements "Not I" and "I Will."
  - Compare the characters and story grammar in McQueen's version to the story grammar in Galdone's version.
  - Make a chart of the story characters and their contributions and actions in McQueen's story.
  - Read "The Little Red Hen" by Joseph Jacobs in *Tomie dePaola's Nursery Tales* (Putnam, 1986). Continue the comparison activities by referring to the Galdone and McQueen versions. The characters in Jacobs's tale include a hen, a pig, a cat, and a duck.
  - Summarize what has been learned about "The Little Red Hen." The characters are a hen and three other animals, which can vary from one version to another. Hen wants others to help plant, care for, harvest, and grind wheat. Others will not help. Hen uses grain to bake cake or bread. Others volunteer to help eat the cake or bread. Hen eats it alone (or with her chicks).
  - If available read Tony Palazzo's *The Little Red Hen* (Doubleday, 1958). In Palazzo's story there is a hen and four other characters (pig, cat, dog, duck) and the hen bakes cookies instead of cake or bread. Compare those story details with the details in the stories previously read. Is the story grammar (basic story plot) the same?

- Connect prose and poetry by reading the poem "The Goose, the Dog and the Little Red Hen" (see appendix A, p. 191). Compare the poem with prose versions. The basic story is the same but this version has just two characters, a frog and a mouse, in addition to the hen.

- Read Oppenheim's story *"Not Now!" Said the Cow*.

- Create a class retelling of "The Little Red Hen" story. Decide on the characters and what they will make (pizza). Follow the story grammar. Print the story and make into a booklet with each child illustrating a portion with black-and-white drawings. Duplicate so that each child will have a copy to color as desired.

Parker, Steve. *Mammals*. Illustrated by Jane Burton and Dave King. Knopf, 1989. (Information)
Photographs and text examine the development, feeding habits, and protective behavior of mammals and their physical adaptation to their environment.

- Introduce a unit on mammals with this book.

- Select an interesting mammal and make an informational chart about that animal. This can be a group or partner activity.

Paulsen, Gary. *The Voyage of the Frog*. Orchard, 1989. (Novel)
David takes on the obligation of scattering his uncle's ashes on the sea that they both loved. Once on the bay a violent storm threatens to capsize the sailboat, the *Frog*.

- Keep a log that David might have written during his days on the *Frog*.

- Introduce readers to the idea of an epilogue. Write an epilogue for this story.

- Have students create a model of the *Frog*.

Paxton, Tom. *Engelbert the Elephant*. Illustrated by Steven Kellogg. Morrow, 1990. (Picture book)
Thanks to some imaginative mice, Engelbert unexpectedly receives an invitation to the royal ball. This rhythmic ballad is perfectly complemented by Kellogg's detailed illustrations.

- After enjoying the book for its story, look again and note all of Kellogg's ingenious illustrative details that extend the story.

- Do you think Engelbert will go to the ball next year? Explain.

- Enjoy other stories illustrated by Steven Kellogg. Use the catalog in your school or public library to locate books illustrated by Kellogg.

Peet, Bill. *Cock-a-Doodle Dudley*. Illustrated by Bill Peet. Houghton, 1990. (Picture book)
Every morning Dudley wakes up the barnyard inhabitants, and everyone loves him except Gunther, the grouchy gander. Gunther believes that Dudley is making the sun shine and he doesn't like it, so he sets out to "peck him to a frazzle."

- This situation is similar to some interaction that takes place among children in school. Discuss situations that might occur when a new student comes to school or when someone is different from the others. Compare these situations with Dudley and Gunther's relationship.

- Make puppets of the barnyard animals in this story and then retell the story using the puppets.

- After retelling the story once or twice, rework it and change some of the episodes. Use thinking skills to determine if the book will end differently if some of the things that happen change.

Polacco, Patricia. *Babushka's Doll*. Illustrated by Patricia Polacco. Simon, 1990. (Picture book)
Natasha demands that her grandmother drop her work whenever Natasha wants something. One day when Grandmother (Babushka) leaves, Natasha decides to play with Babushka's doll. The doll springs to life and makes demands on Natasha, who becomes completely exhausted and learns her lesson.

- When Natasha plays with Grandmother's doll she gets unexpected results. Compare the happenings in this story to what happens when Big Anthony messes around with Strega Nona's spaghetti pot in *Strega Nona* by Tomie dePaola (Prentice, 1975).

- Read other stories about dolls and their relationship with those who play with them.

Dolls and Those Who Play with Them

Ackerman, Karen. *Moveable Mabeline*. Illustrated by Linda Allen. Philomel, 1990. (Junior novel)

Francis, Frank. *Natasha's New Doll*. Illustrated by Frank Francis. O'Hara, 1971.

Griffith, Helen V. *Caitlin's Holiday*. Illustrated by Susan Condie Lamb. Greenwillow, 1990. (Novel)

Kroll, Steven. *The Hand-Me-Down Doll*. Illustrated by Evaline Ness. Holiday, 1983.

McGinley, Phyllis. *The Most Wonderful Doll in the World*. Illustrated by Helen Stone. Lippincott, 1950; Scholastic, 1990.

Tudor, Tasha. *The Doll's Christmas*. Illustrated by Tasha Tudor. Oxford, 1950.

Waddell, Martin. *The Hidden House*. Illustrated by Angela Barrett. Philomel, 1990.

Zolotow, Charlotte. *William's Doll*. Illustrated by William Pène du Bois. HarperCollins, 1972.

Prelutsky, Jack. *Beneath a Blue Umbrella*. Illustrated by Garth Williams. Greenwillow, 1990. (Poetry)
These short humorous rhymes of adventure and fun in strange and unusual places feature a variety of characters, both human and animal.

- Use a map to locate the places mentioned in the rhymes.

- Read a poem—one a day.

Ray, Deborah Kogan. *Stargazing Stars*. Illustrated by Deborah Kogan Ray. Crown, 1991. (Picture book)
A little girl and her mother go outside with a warm blanket to sit under the sky to watch for a shower of shooting stars. The art was created with transparent watercolor and watercolor pencil.

- In an endnote in the book, Ray says, "A shooting star is a meteor burning as it enters the earth's atmosphere. The amount of meteor activity varies during the year. The Perseid meteor shower is the brightest star shower to watch. It peaks around August 12 and is best seen very late at night." Locate additional information about shooting stars and meteors. Share the information in chart or report form.

- Draw a picture of you and some special adult doing something you enjoyed.

- Coordinate with a fictionalized account of an actual meteor landing as retold by Patricia Polacco in *Meteor!* (Putnam, 1987).

Rayner, Mary. *Mrs. Pig's Bulk Buy*. Macmillan, 1981. (Picture book)

Mrs. Pig's children like to put ketchup on everything they eat, so Mrs. Pig buys a large supply of it. She feeds them ketchup soup and ketchup sandwiches and puts ketchup on their cereal. Soon they wish they could eat their food "plain." But the story does explain why pigs are pink.

- Make a list of foods that students like to eat with ketchup. Put the foods into types or categories.

- Use crayons to draw a picture of a favorite meal. Put ketchup on everything by making a red tempera paint wash (one part paint to one or two parts water) and brushing the red paint wash over the entire picture.

- Make ketchup sandwiches to eat with soup—serve samples. Write the "recipes" for these and other concoctions.

- Fingerpaint with red fingerpaint to make "ketchup" designs.

- Compare and contrast the story grammar of this story with *Bread and Jam for Frances* by Russell Hoban, illustrated by Lillian Hoban (HarperCollins, 1965).

Reader's Digest Children's World Atlas. Reader's Digest, 1991. (Reference)

This atlas contains 61 maps, 300 illustrations, essential geographical facts, and information about language, religion, climate, agriculture, etc.

- After introducing the atlas, put it in an investigation center, and as book authors or settings are discussed or specific regions studied, put location cards in the center with suggestions for locating or finding the regions on the maps. Encourage students to add questions or location cards to the center.

Rice, Eve. *Peter's Pockets*. Illustrated by Nancy Winslow Parker. Greenwillow, 1989. (Picture book)

A new pair of pants without pockets causes problems for a young boy.

- Note the unique use of animal illustrations throughout the book.

- The book is basically one about the emotional relationship between a boy and his uncle. Discuss the family ties that make a person an uncle or an aunt. Write: I have an uncle named _____ and he ... or: I have an aunt named _____ and she.... Continue the statement by telling about a special memory you have of your aunt or uncle.

Rosen, Michael. *Freckly Feet and Itchy Knees*. Illustrated by S. Sweeten. Doubleday, 1990. (Picture book)

Zany poems focus on the wonders and peculiarities of noses, hands, feet, eyes, knees, and "all kinds of bellies."

- Introduce the senses of smell, feel, and sight.

- Try writing your own poems about someone who "looks just like that."

Rosen, Michael, reteller. *We're Going on a Bear Hunt*. Illustrated by Helen Oxenbury. McElderry, 1990. (Picture book)

A family sets out to go on a bear hunt in this story full of repetition and cumulative action. The story goes full circle as the family finally finds the bears, only to make a hasty retreat.

- Read the story over and over and enjoy choral-reading the story. As readers become more familiar with the story, add hand and body actions to accompany the reading.

- Extend the understanding of this story by sharing other versions. One similar tale is told by Margaret Siewert and Kathleen Savage in *Bear Hunt*, illustrated by Leonard W. Shortall (Prentice, 1976).

- As a class project, make up your own verses for this story and illustrate the verses.

Ruckman, Ivy. *No Way Out*. HarperCollins, 1988. (Novel)
A flash flood interrupts a nature hike along Zion Narrows by the Virgin River in Utah. What was to be an outdoor experience filled with pleasant memories turns in minutes into a fight for survival.

- Use the newspaper article and the Zion Narrows map from the book to introduce the story and to locate the area on a larger map.

- Correlate with a wide-reading focus on other books of survival.

Ruckman, Ivy. *This Is Your Captain Speaking*. Walker, 1987. (Novel)
Tom Palmer is not too interested in high school athletics, so he spends time at the nursing home where his mother works. As his relationship with Roger begins to grow so does his maturity.

- Debate the topic of euthanasia.

- How do Tom and his personality change from the beginning of the story to the end of the story?

Rylant, Cynthia. *Night in the Country*. Illustrated by Mary Szilagyi. Bradbury, 1986. (Picture book)
This is a book of sounds—sounds in the night in the country: squeaks of the house, patter of rabbits in the yard, an apple falling to the ground, and other sounds that precede the coming of the day. Vivid colors are blended into the dark of the night.

- List the five senses: hearing, sight, taste, touch, smell. Identify the sense that is appealed to in this book—hearing. Make a list of things that might have been seen, tasted, felt, or smelled in conjunction with these sounds.

- Make a hearing book for your classroom, or home. Make similar books for the other senses.

- Make a companion book focusing on night sounds in the city.

Sachar, Louis. *There's a Boy in the Girl's Bathroom*. Knopf, 1987. (Novel)
Bradley Chalkers is disliked by almost everyone at school. Even the teachers feel he has a serious behavior problem. His private world is inhabited by his miniature animal collection. Bradley's life changes when a new student, Jeff, arrives from Washington, D.C., and the new school counselor, Carla Davis, begins to notice Bradley.

- Introduce the role of the school counselor with this book.

- Invite your school counselor into your classroom to discuss her or his role in the school.

Schroeder, Alan. *Ragtime Tumpie*. Illustrated by Bernie Fuchs. Little, 1989. (Novel)
This is a fictional account of the childhood of the entertainer Josephine Baker. Amidst the poverty and lively street life of St. Louis in the early 1900s, Tumpie, a young African-American girl, longs to find an opportunity to dance. The illustrations bring to life St. Louis during that period.

- Read in conjunction with a focus on the civil rights movement.

- Investigate the origins of jazz and its influence on music today.

- Connect with Tomie dePaola's *Bonjour, Mr. Satie* (see entry on pp. 92-93). Josephine Baker is one of the visitors to Gertrude Stein's salon.

Scieszka, Jon. *The Frog Prince Continued*. Illustrated by Steve Johnson. Viking, 1991. (Picture book)

After the princess kisses the frog he turns into a prince and they supposedly live happily ever after. But Scieszka tells us the rest of the story. All the princess does is nag, and the prince often slips down to the pond to flick his tongue at a fly. He decides that things would be better if he were a plain old frog, so he goes into the deep dark woods in search of a witch willing to take time off from her fairy tale to help him out.

- Elaborate on another favorite tale by telling what happens after the traditional ending. For example, where are Hansel and Gretel and their dad right now? How old is Red Riding Hood and what is she doing? What has happened to the third little pig in "The Three Little Pigs"? Two other books that might be used as examples of an elaboration on a classic tale are John W. Ivimey's *The Complete Story of the Three Blind Mice* (see entry on pp. 141-42) and Jim Aylesworth's *The Complete Hickory Dickory Dock* (Atheneum, 1990).

Scieszka, Jon. *The True Story of the Three Little Pigs by A. Wolf*. Illustrated by Lane Smith. Viking, 1989. (Picture book)

This is A. Wolf's story of how unfortunate circumstances brought about the demise of two of the three little pigs. After all, he just needed a cup of sugar and he hadn't expected a fit of sneezing. Could he help it?

- This is a traditional tale retold from the point of view of the villain or at least from the point of view of the character always thought to be the villain. Retell other familiar tales from the point of view of the traditional villain. First make a list of classic tales and the character in each from whose perspective the tale is generally told. Then go back through the list and identify another major character who could tell the story:

Story title	Perspective	Another Character
"The Three Billy Goats Gruff"	billy goats	troll
"Little Red Riding Hood"	Red Riding Hood	wolf
"Jack and the Beanstalk"	Jack	giant
"There Was an Old Woman Who Lived in a Shoe"	woman	children
"The Gingerbread Boy"	gingerbread	fox

Keep in mind that the perspective need not be that of the character who is telling the story, but can be the view from which the story is being told by the storyteller.

Selznick, Brian. *The Houdini Box*. Illustrated by Brian Selznick. Knopf, 1991. (Junior novel)

Victor tries to imitate the tricks he has heard that Houdini performed. Eventually, Victor meets his idol and begs him to explain some of the mysteries. The mysterious locked box soon becomes the focus—perhaps the secrets to the most famous tricks ever performed are contained in this box.

- A fictional book that contains some facts and information about the real Houdini. In an author's note at the end of the book, Selznick explains that he changed the place (from Detroit to New York) but not the date of Houdini's death. He thought he had made up the "Houdini box," but then he found a 1974 newspaper article that details a search for a box supposedly left behind by Houdini. Research the life of Ehrich Weiss, who later became known as the magician Harry Houdini, and make a list of the facts Selznick included in his book that are actually facts about the real Houdini. For example, did Houdini escape from an iron milk can in less than 20 seconds? Did Houdini hold his breath for more than 5,000 seconds while escaping from a crate dropped into the ocean? Could Houdini walk through brick walls?

- Make a list of four facts about a famous person you have studied. Then incorporate those facts into a fictional story about that person.

Shelby, Anne. *Potluck*. Illustrated by Irene Trivas. Orchard, 1991. (Picture book)
Alpha and Betty invite all their friends to an alphabetical foods party. Acton brings asparagus soup and Zeke and Zelda bring a zucchini casserole.

- Play a memory game similar to the game sometimes called "packing my trunk." That game usually begins with a phrase similar to "I went to Australia and took an apple" and continues with "I went to Australia and took an apple, then I traveled to Bulgaria and took a ball...."

- Make a new list of foods that begin with the same letter as the name of each child in the classroom. Each child could make up a lunch menu including only foods that begin with that child's name. For example, Jane might suggest juice, jelly sandwiches, grilled jackfish (a local name for various fishes, especially the northern pike), jackfruit (an East Indian fruit related to the mulberry family, like the breadfruit), and jambalaya (a Creole dish made of spicy rice and seafood or meat—shrimp, oysters, crab, ham, chicken, sausage, etc.—with green peppers, onions, and tomatoes). Suzanne might list sandwiches, stew, string beans, sardines, sauerkraut, and strawberry shortcake.

Shulevitz, Uri. *Toddlecreek Post Office*. Illustrated by Uri Shulevitz. Farrar, 1990. (Picture book)
Toddlecreek's post office serves as a combination community center, library, shelter, and repair shop, but it has little official business. It isn't long before the postal inspector decides that the post office should be closed. A gentle way of life vanishes.

- When this change occurs it seems that part of the town will die. In another story, *Bayberry Bluff* by Blair Lent (Houghton, 1987), the gentle, idyllic town also changes, but this time into a bustling center of activity. Compare life in Toddlecreek with life in Bayberry Bluff. Compare predictions for life in each town 10 years from now.

Shute, Linda. *Clever Tom and the Leprechaun*. Illustrated by Linda Shute. Morrow, 1988. (Picture book)
Tom Fitzpatrick and the leprechaun attempt to outwit each other. In the end the leprechaun is the more ingenious.

- Discuss the legend of the leprechaun. Use the notes at the end of the book as one information source.

- Locate other books about leprechauns and identify traits of leprechauns that appear in the book. Some suggested titles follow.

Leprechauns

Balian, Lorna. *Leprechauns Never Lie*. Illustrated by Lorna Balian. Abingdon, 1980.

Calhoun, Mary. *The Hungry Leprechaun*. Illustrated by Roger Antoine Duvoisin. Harper-Collins, 1962.

Kennedy, Richard. *The Leprechaun's Story*. Illustrated by Marcia Sewall. Dutton, 1979.

McDermott, Gerald. *Tim O'Toole and the Wee Folk*. Illustrated by Gerald McDermott. Viking, 1990.

Singer, Marilyn. *Twenty Ways to Lose Your Best Friend*. Illustrated by Jeffrey Lindberg. Harper, 1990. (Junior novel)
In this story of friendship and broken friendship Emma and Sandy make several lists.

- Describe the qualities your best friend would have.

- Make a list titled "Twenty Ways to Make a Friend" or "Twenty Ways to Keep a Friend."

Skurzynski, Gloria. *Dangerous Ground*. Bradbury, 1989. (Novel)

For a number of years, while her parents work in the Texas oil fields, 11-year-old Angela has lived with her 78-year-old great aunt in Wyoming. Now Angela is going back to her parents. Aunt Hil and Angela embark on a final trip to Yellowstone National Park. Along the way Aunt Hil acts disoriented and increasingly confused. Is her condition a result of the strain of the impending separation, Alzheimer's disease, or old age?

- The setting in this book could be used as a focus when the Western states are studied in social studies.

- Find out more about Yellowstone National Park. Make a list of the facts about the park that Skurzynski includes in her fictional book.

- What is Alzheimer's disease? Discuss.

Slepian, Jan, and Ann Seidler. *The Hungry Thing Returns*. Illustrated by Richard E. Martin. Scholastic, 1990. (Picture book)

The Hungry Thing and his daughter come to school, and only the children understand what they want to eat.

- Read the book and invite listener participation as the rhyming pattern is repeated.

- Draw a picture of the food that The Hungry Thing wants to eat.

- Draw a picture of what you think The Hungry Thing's wife would look like. Describe her in words.

- Brainstorm a list of real food and then play with the list to change the real words into nonsense words as The Hungry Thing would say them.

- Make a school lunch menu using words for food that The Hungry Thing would recognize.

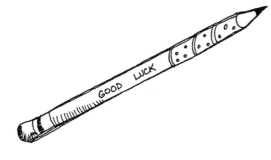

Stanley, Diane. *The Good-Luck Pencil*. Illustrated by Bruce Degan. Macmillan, 1986. (Picture book)

Mary Ann has forgotten to complete her math homework and her pencil has disappeared. She uses a pencil she finds to finish her homework and gets a perfect grade. Her assignment is to write about her family and to "make it interesting." Mary Ann writes a family fantasy and her fantasies begin to become true.

- Write a fantasy story about your family.

- Read other stories about magic pencils or drawing instruments, such as the books in the following list, and then write your own story of a magical drawing experience.

Magical Drawings

Alexander, Martha. *Blackboard Bear*. Dial, 1969.

Bang, Molly Garrett. *Tye May and the Magic Brush*. Greenwillow, 1981.

Browne, Anthony. *Bear Hunt*. Atheneum, 1979.

Demi. *Liang and the Magic Paint Brush*. Holt, 1980.

Gackenbach, Dick. *Mag, the Magnificent*. Clarion, 1985.

Stevenson, James. *No Friends*. Illustrated by James Stevenson. Greenwillow, 1986. (Picture book)
A boy and girl move into a new neighborhood and worry about making new friends. Grandpa relates a story from his childhood, a story about an experience in a new neighborhood.

- Use the balloon speech to help script the story as a drama presentation. The balloon speech can also be used to illustrate how quotation marks would have been used if the text had been written in conventional form without the bubbles.

- Help children find their positive attributes by creating a "name mobile" (see appendix A, p. 193).

Swann, Brian. *A Basket Full of White Eggs*. Illustrated by Ponder Goembel. Orchard, 1988. (Riddle book)
These proverbs in riddle form are from many countries, including Italy, Saudi Arabia, and the Philippines. The answers to the riddles are revealed in the paintings on the same page.

- Discuss the clues on each page that are helpful in solving the riddle.

- Find or create an original riddle and illustrate the riddle, giving the answer in the illustration.

- Display the riddle pages on a bulletin board and eventually combine them into a riddle book.

Thurber, James. *Many Moons*. Illustrated by Marc Simont. Harcourt, 1990. (Picture book)
The king's attempts to allow the ailing Princess Lenore to own the moon are frustrated. But the problem is solved by the princess herself, but only when the wise court jester asks her. The original edition of this book with illustrations by Louis Slobodkin was awarded the Caldecott Medal in 1944.

- Compare/contrast the illustrations by Slobodkin with Simont's watercolor illustrations.

- Determine if you can which type of moon the little girl wishes to have. Names of various moons in specific months have been gathered from various sources, including astronomical calendars, weather articles, and information from government sources.

  January: Old Moon, Moon After Yule, Wolf Moon, Winter Moon, Deep Snow Moon

  February: Snow Moon, Hunger Moon, Wolf Moon, Trapper's Moon, Crust of Snow Moon

  March: Sap Moon, Crow Moon, Lenten Moon, Fish Moon, Worm Moon, Snowshoe Breaking Moon

  April: Grass Moon, Egg Moon, Sprouting Grass Moon, Pink Moon, Planter's Moon, Maple Sugar Moon

  May: Planting Moon, Milk Moon, Mother's Moon, Flower Moon, Budding Plant Moon

  June: Rose Moon, Flower Moon, Strawberry Moon, Stockman's Moon

  July: Thunder Moon, Hay Moon, Buck Moon, Summer Moon, Midsummer Moon

  August: Green Corn Moon, Grain Moon, Sturgeon Moon, Harvest Moon

  September: Harvest Moon, Fruit Moon, Fall Moon, Wild Rice Moon

  October: Hunter's Moon, Dying Grass Moon, Harvest Moon, Falling Leaves Moon

  November: Frosty Moon, Beaver Moon, Hunter's Moon, Freezing Moon

  December: Long Night Moon, Moon Before Yule, Cold Moon, Christmas Moon, Descending Cold Moon

  Each of the moons has some story behind it. For example, Native Americans called the February moon Hunger Moon because of the sparsity of animals and food available for hunting or gathering during that month. A Harvest Moon is usually a full moon during the harvest season. It is during this time that the moon offers light for the hunter or farmer who works late into the night. Other names indicate human concerns about snow, wolves, and starvation.

- Write a story about how a moon came to have the name it does.
- Focus on the stages of the moon by reading other moon stories.

Moon Stories

Asch, Frank. *Happy Birthday, Moon!* Illustrated by Frank Asch. Prentice, 1982.

Asch, Frank. *Moon Bear*. Illustrated by Frank Asch. Scribner, 1978.

Asch, Frank. *Mooncake*. Illustrated by Frank Asch. Prentice, 1983.

Baylor, Byrd. *Moon Song*. Illustrated by Ronald Himler. Scribner, 1982.

McDermott, Gerald. *Anansi the Spider: A Tale from the Ashanti*. Holt, 1972.

Sleator, William. *The Angry Moon*. Illustrated by Blair Lent. Little, 1970.

Willard, Nancy. *The Nightgown of the Sullen Moon*. Illustrated by David McPhail. Harcourt, 1983.

Van Allsburg, Chris. *Two Bad Ants*. Houghton, 1988. (Picture book)

Two ants leave their colony and find themselves on a dangerous adventure. The illustrations present common everyday objects from the ants' perspective; grains of sugar are as if they are being shown under a microscope.

- Examine under a microscope or powerful magnifying glass some of the objects depicted in the book.
- Discuss the term *epilogue*. Write an epilogue for this story telling about "the two bad ants' " life after they return safely home.

Van Laan, Nancy. *The Big Fat Worm*. Illustrated by Marisabina Russo. Knopf, 1987. (Picture book)

Bird wants to eat Worm, Cat wants to eat Bird, Dog wants to eat Cat, and....

- This predictable text leads to listener participation. Read it aloud and invite participation in the reading.
- Use felt pieces to focus on the characters in the story and to retell the story.
- Read other cumulative tales that have this same pattern. One of the more familiar is "The Old Woman and Her Pig." Two versions that are often available are Paul Galdone's *The Old Woman and Her Pig* (McGraw, 1960) and "The Old Woman and Her Pig" in *The Old Woman and Her Pig & 10 Other Stories* adapted by Anne Rockwell (Crowell, 1979). The Rockwell title was published in paperback with the title *The Three Sillies & 10 Other Stories to Read Aloud* (Trophy, 1986).
- Write an innovation on these texts. Make a list of animals that have a cumulative connection and then write a story in the pattern of *The Big Fat Worm* and *The Old Woman and Her Pig*.

Van Laan, Nancy. *A Mouse in My House*. Illustrated by Marjorie Priceman. Knopf, 1990.

In a rhyming text, a young boy imagines that he lives in a house with a menagerie. He describes all the animals in the zoo and then announces that "the zoo is ME!" In the book he describes a mouse, cat, dog, snake, bug, fish, ape, bear, pig, and lion.

- Choose another animal and make a verse about that animal in *your* house. Use the pattern of Van Laan's rhymes and repeat the refrains (see appendix A, p. 192):

> A _____(animal)_____ is in my house,
> and it's _____(describe physical features)_____ .
> There's a _____(animal)_____ in my house,
> and it acts like me.
> It _____(describe actions in the house)_____
> as it _____(describe other actions)_____ .
> There's a _____(animal)_____ in my house,
> only I can see.

Van Laan, Nancy. *Rainbow Crow*. Illustrated by Beatriz Vidal. Knopf, 1989. (Picture book)
This Native-American legend from the Lenape tribe in eastern Pennsylvania depicts Crow as the Fire Bearer. Originally the crow had rainbow-colored feathers, but his feathers were blackened and his voice was made hoarse when he got too close to the fire he was bringing to earth to save the Lenape people.

- The crow, also known as Raven, is oftentimes depicted in Native-American legends as haughty, sly, mischievous, and intelligent. Find other Native-American tales that have a crow or raven as a central character. Compare the characteristics of the crow or raven as portrayed in the various stories.

- Collect some information about the Lenape tribe. Sometimes called Leni-Lenape, this tribe is probably better known as the Delawares. Their villages once occupied the whole Delaware River basin. Lenapes near the present site of Philadelphia signed several treaties with William Penn. One of the most famous of their tribe was Tamenend or Tammany, a chief after whom a famous political organization in New York City was named. The Lenapes lived in rectangular, bark-covered houses. They ate wild game and raised corn and other vegetables. They had a tribal chronicle called *Walam Olum*. The *Walam Olum* consisted of picture stories painted on wood that tell the traditions and wanderings of the tribe. Part of the tribe, a band called Munsee, moved to Indiana under pressure from whites. Muncie, Indiana, is named after the Munsee Indians.

Velthuijs, Max. *Elephant and Crocodile*. Translated by Anthea Bell. Illustrated by Max Velthuijs. Farrar, 1990. (Picture book)
Crocodile cannot live without his music, but his neighbor Elephant cannot stand the noise of the constant violin practice. Then Elephant buys a trumpet and Crocodile becomes furious. They finally get together and discuss their love of music over a cup of tea.

- Compare and contrast this situation between Elephant and Crocodile with Sam and Joe's situation in *How Joe the Bear and Sam the Mouse Got Together* by Beatrice Schenk de Regniers (Parents, 1965; rev. ed. Lothrop, 1990).

Venezia, Mike. *Picasso*. Illustrated by Mike Venezia. Children's, 1988. (Picture book)
This book introduces the artist Picasso in large, bold print.

- Use the art reference books to locate some of the artwork of Picasso. Discuss his technique and his art.

- Correlate with a reading of Tomie dePaola's *Bonjour, Mr. Satie*. (Putnam, 1991).

Vernon, Tannis. *Adriana and the Magic Clockwork Train*. Illustrated by Tannis Vernon. Crown, 1990. (Picture book)

Grandmother sends Adriana money to buy a toy for her birthday. After three days of searching, Adriana finds a train that must be cleaned up and painted. While her parents are out and her sitter is downstairs, dolls and little toys help Adriana clean and paint the train. When Adriana goes downstairs to eat dinner, the train crew takes the tiny animals and dolls back home but returns to Adriana's room just in time.

- At the end of Vernon's book Adriana writes a thank-you note to her grandmother. Practice writing thank-you notes of your own. Leedy's book *Messages in the Mailbox: How to Write Letters* gives practical information about writing letters.

- If you can locate an old train, make cleaning and repainting it a class project. If an old train is not available, perhaps another type of toy or keepsake could be restored.

- Read other train stories and poems, such as Donald Crews's *Freight Train* (Greenwillow, 1978), Gail Gibbons's *Trains* (Holiday, 1987), and Diane Siebert's *Train Song*, illustrated by Mike Wimmer (Crowell, 1990).

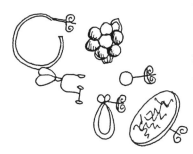

Viorst, Judith. *Earrings!* Illustrated by Nola Langner Malone. Atheneum, 1990. (Picture book)

A redheaded protagonist stomps around expressing all the arguments that she feels her parents will have against the "beautiful, glorious earrings for pierced ears."

- Think about something you have wanted to have or do, and list the arguments your parents might make against it. Then list the arguments you can use to convince your parents that you should be allowed to have or do what you want.

Viorst, Judith. *The Good-Bye Book*. Illustrated by Kay Chorao. Macmillan, 1988. (Picture book)

A little boy is left with a sitter while his parents go out to dinner. The boy makes up excuses and pleas to keep them home.

- Compare to the ploys used by Frances in *Bedtime for Frances* by Russell Hoban, illustrated by Garth Williams (HarperCollins, 1960).

Wahl, Jan. *Tailypo!* Illustrated by Wil Clay. Holt, 1991.

When a strange creature crawls through the walls of a man's home, the man chops off its tail and eats it. The creature comes back looking for its "tailypo."

- Compare and contrast the story grammar and illustrations with Joanne Galdone's *The Tailypo: A Ghost Story*, illustrated by Paul Galdone (Houghton, 1984).

- In Wahl's book, the story is set in Tennessee and is illustrated as an African-American folktale. Locate the state of Tennessee on a map and discuss how Wahl's book is different in cultural background from Galdone's book.

- Visualize the creature and its tailypo. Draw a picture to show what you think the creature would look like.

Wallace, Bill. *Beauty*. Simon, 1988. (Novel)

In addition to dealing with his parents' divorce, 11-year-old Luke must make new friends when he and his mother move to his grandpa's farm. He finds comfort in the companionship of a horse named Beauty.

- Write about a special relationship you have or have had with a pet.

- Locate the states where the story is set: Colorado and Oklahoma.

- Gather information about the states and then discuss how that information compares with the information given in the story.

- Correlate with a reading of *Next-Door Neighbors* by Sarah Ellis (McElderry, 1989) and *Elaine, Mary Lewis, and the Frogs* by Heidi Chang (Crown, 1988).

Wallace, Bill. *Snot Stew*. Illustrated by Lisa McCue. Holiday, 1989. (Novel)
"Is too—Is not—Is too" causes confusion for Kikki and Tony, two barnyard kittens adopted into the house by two children. The kittens find life with humans filled with pleasures and dangers.

- This story is told from the animal's viewpoint. Write an episode of the story from the viewpoint of one of the children.

Ward, Cindy. *Cookie's Week*. Illustrated by Tomie dePaola. Putnam, 1988. (Picture book)
Each day of the week a cat named Cookie manages to find mischief and to create a mess in the house. The book is repetitive and predictable but successfully introduces the sequence of the days of the week.

- Write an innovation on the text. Create a dialogue for a book to be called "Cookie's *Next* Week."

- Create a class book, "Cookie's Year," using each month as a time to explore.

Weiss, Nicki. *Where Does the Brown Bear Go?* Illustrated by Nicki Weiss. Morrow, 1989. (Picture book)
This repetitive book questions where animals go at night. The answer is "home." A predictable book, it is just right for listener participation.

- Enjoy the colored-pencil illustrations. Use pencils to create some drawings of a favorite animal.

- Investigate how animals sleep.

Wiesner, David. *Hurricane*. Illustrated by David Wiesner. Clarion, 1990. (Picture book)
After surviving a hurricane two boys find a felled giant elm tree in their yard. The elm becomes their jungle, pirate ship, and spaceship.

- Learn more about hurricanes by reading Franklyn M. Branley's Let's Read-and-Find-Out Science Book™ *Hurricane Watch*, illustrated by Giulio Maestro (Crowell, 1985).

- A novel that portrays the emotions and aftermath of a severe storm is Ivy Ruckman's *Night of the Twister* (Crowell, 1984). Compare and contrast the events in Ruckman's book with those in Wiesner's book.

Wilkes, Angela. *My First Green Book*. Illustrated with photographs. Random, 1991. (Information book)
The many photographs in this book clarify and enhance the text, which explains several science experiments and science-related activities.

- Conduct the experiments described in the book.

- Keep a "Green Diary" as suggested in the book.

- Carefully check pages 22-23, "Your Garbage," and make a plan that lists at least two things that *you* can do to recycle material.

- Make a wildlife garden.

- Plant a tree.

Williams, Sue. *I Went Walking*. Illustrated by Julie Vivas. Harcourt/Gulliver, 1990. (Picture book)
"I went walking./What did you see?/I saw a brown horse looking at me." During a silly walk around the farmyard, the same pattern introduces the brown horse, a black cat, a red cow, a green frog, a pink pig, and a yellow duck. The animals are drawn realistically, and the little boy who is part of the story becomes increasingly more disheveled as the story proceeds.

- Enjoy the repetitive pattern of this story and compare and contrast it with the story pattern in Beatrice Schenk de Regniers's *Going for a Walk* (HarperCollins, 1982). The book was originally published as *The Little Book* (Walck, 1961). In this book a little girl goes for a walk and meets a cow, a pig, a cat, and a bird. The girl says "hi" to each animal and the animal responds with a "moo," an "oink," or other appropriate sound.

- Compare with the story grammar in *Brown Bear, Brown Bear: What Do You See?* by Bill Martin, Jr., illustrated by Eric Carle (Holt, rev. ed., 1992). In Martin's book children see a brown bear, a red bird, a yellow duck, a blue horse, a green frog, a purple cat, a white dog, a black sheep, and a goldfish.

- Another of Bill Martin, Jr.'s books, *Polar Bear, Polar Bear: What Do You Hear?* illustrated by Eric Carle (Holt, 1991) uses animals and animal sounds in a repetitive pattern.

- With any of the four titles (Williams's, de Regniers's, or the two by Martin) make cutout transparency figures. Retell the stories using the transparency puppets on the overhead.

- Write another story using the pattern of Williams's story. Use different animal and color combinations.

Williams, Ursula Moray. *The Good Little Christmas Tree*. Illustrated by Gillian Tyler. Knopf, 1990. (Picture book)
A Christmas tree in the household of a poor peasant family leaves and goes to the forest to find things with which to decorate itself. On the journey the tree encounters St. Nicholas and returns to the peasant home accompanied by an entourage of angels, animals, and people.

- Compare the story to Hans Christian Andersen's *The Little Fir Tree*.

- Finish the ending of the story. Do the children receive any gifts? If so, what gifts do they receive?

Williams, Vera B. *A Chair for My Mother*. Illustrated by Vera B. Williams. Greenwillow, 1982. (Picture book)
A fire destroys the belongings of a family: Rosa, her mama, and grandmama. The family saves coins in a big jar until there is enough to buy Mother a soft overstuffed chair. A filmstrip/cassette version of this story is available from Weston Woods.

- Look at the borders around each of the illustrations. Note how the images in the borders connect with an element in the story.

- Find a large jar and begin saving pennies for your own goal. Perhaps the class would like to contribute to a food pantry or gather enough money to buy a food basket for a family.

- In *Something Special for Me* (Greenwillow, 1983) Rosa's birthday is approaching. This time she is to be allowed to have the money in the large money jar, which contains her mother's tips as a waitress, to buy anything she wants. After much soul-searching she spends the money on an accordion. Draw a picture of what you would have bought with the money in the jar.

- In *Music, Music for Everyone* (Greenwillow, 1984), the money being saved in the jar is going toward Grandmama's medical expenses, so Rosa sets out to find a way to make some money. Tell how you would make money for the jar and discuss what you would want to save money for. *A Chair for My Mother, Something Special for Me*, and *Music, Music for Everyone* have similar illustrations—watercolors smaller than page size surrounded by a watercolor border, which give the effect of a homemade book. The three books resemble family albums of sort, giving the effect of children's own pictures glued to wrapping paper. Each of the borders reflects the content of the page's illustration. Prepare a bulletin board display to reflect this style. Use a large flower-filled border. In the center feature information about the author and display book jackets from several of her books.

Williams, Vera B. *Cherries and Cherry Pits*. Illustrated by Vera B. Williams. Greenwillow, 1986. (Picture book)
Bidemmi loves to draw and tell stories about what she is drawing. "She always starts with the word THIS." Bidemmi makes her illustrations with a fistful of magic markers. Her imagination tells the story.

- Enjoy writing and drawing by creating your own pictures with magic markers. Then tell the story about what you have drawn. If several students draw pictures and tell stories, combine them into a book.

- Make a poster advertising this very special book.

Williams, Vera B. *"More More More," Said the Baby: Three Love Stories*. Illustrated by Vera B. Williams. Greenwillow, 1990.
Three vignettes show three toddlers with a special grown-up. Bright colors and a soft gentle story convey the message "I love you."

- Ask students to bring a picture of themselves as a toddler. Use photocopies of the pictures to illustrate students' own stories of "love." Discuss the special things that grown-ups did with them when they were toddlers. Write the episodes and create a "More More More" sequel.

- For each of the illustrations create a border that gives a clue to the special happening that is the focus of the written text.

Williams, Vera B., and Jennifer Williams. *Stringbean's Trip to the Shining Sea*. Illustrations by Vera B. Williams and Jennifer Williams. Greenwillow, 1988. (Picture book)
Two young men set off to travel across the country in a pickup. While they are on the trip they send unique and unusual postcards home to their family. The postcards tell the story.

- After reading *Stringbean's Trip to the Shining Sea* prepare some postcards that you should have sent from your last vacation or weekend trip. Be sure to pay particular attention to the design of the stamp and the backside of the postcard.

- Design some special stamps for your postcards.

Williams, Vera B. *Three Days on a River in a Red Canoe*. Illustrated by Vera B. Williams. Greenwillow, 1981.
A mother and her children take a three-day trip down the river in a red canoe. A journal format tells the story of soft gentle companionship and beautiful scenery.

- Set up a tent in the classroom and spend "Three Days on a River in a Red Canoe." Write a diary.

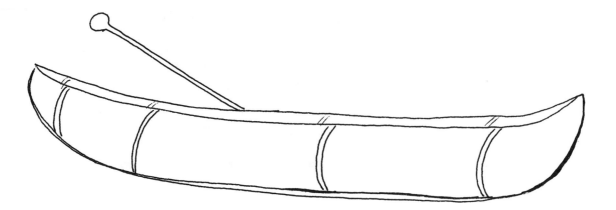

- Make a pop-up scene of you and someone special going down a river in a red canoe (blue canoe, or whatever). If the scene is made in a diorama, the bottom of the stream can be slit open and tabs from a canoe inserted. Fold the tabs so that the canoe is held in the slot. Gently pushing the tabs will move the canoe up or down the stream along the open slot.

Connections

Vera Baker Williams was born on January 18, 1927, in Hollywood, California. She grew up in the New York City area during the Depression. She and her older sister, Naomi, lived in several foster homes, and when they were able to be with their parents it was most often their mother who held the family together. Their father loved to sing and dance.

She met Paul Williams while both were attending Black Mountain College in North Carolina. In the late 1940s they married and lived in a cooperative artists' community in Stony Point, New York. By 1970 Vera and Paul's marriage had ended and Vera moved to Canada, where she lived on a houseboat in the bay at Vancouver, British Columbia, and raised her children—Sarah, Jennifer, and Merce. Those years in Canada included a 500-mile trip on the Yukon River; many of the adventures from this trip were included in *Three Days on a River in a Red Canoe*.

In 1981, as a result of her participation in a women's peace march on the Pentagon, she spent a month in a federal penitentiary in West Virginia. Someday that experience may appear in one of her books.

The illustrations in three of her books, *A Chair for My Mother, Something Special for Me*, and *Music, Music for Everyone*, have similar elements. Watercolor illustrations smaller than the page size are surrounded by watercolor borders, which give the effect of a homemade book—a family album of sorts that suggests a child's own pictures glued to wrapping paper. Each of the borders reflects the content of the page's illustration.

Since leaving Canada in 1978, Vera B. Williams has resided in New York City.

Willis, Val. *The Surprise in the Wardrobe*. Illustrated by John Shelley. Farrar, 1990. (Picture book)
Bobby Bell finds a witch in his wardrobe and takes it to school. The witch manages to change cabbage and stew into french fries and hot dogs. Then bedlam results from a proliferation of frogs.

- The double page spreads are bordered with dozens of tiny, fanciful characters. Discuss the significance of the borders. Then create your own illustration of a zany happening caused by the witch at *your* school. Make a border for your picture.

Wolf, Janet. *Adelaide to Zeke*. Illustrated by Janet Wolf. HarperCollins, 1987. (Picture book)
"A is for Adelaide, who bothered Benny. B is for Benny, who blew bubbles at...." This linear text connects one letter to the next, until the letter **Z** is reached: "Z is for Zeke, who zigzagged home." The last double-page illustration shows Zeke's pet shop, Dr. Dan's doctor's office, and the other animals and people that appear in the story.

- This story has a linear alphabetical story line similar to *Alison's Zinnia* by Anita Lobel (see entry on p. 146). Correlate activities for Lobel's book with those for this book.

- Lobel's book turns the last line of her linear text so that it connects with the first line. How could Wolf's text be rewritten so that her text turns to connect with the beginning?

- Write your own alphabetical linear text.

Wood, Don, and Audrey Wood. *The Little Mouse, the Red Ripe Strawberry, and the Big Hungry Bear*. Illustrated by Don Wood. Child's, 1984. (Picture book)
A small mouse does not wish to share his big, red, ripe strawberry. He tries to hide the strawberry from a big hungry bear. But finally the little mouse takes the narrator's suggestion and cuts the strawberry in half so that he has half to share and half to eat.

- How many strawberries will we need to find if each of us is to have half a strawberry to eat?

- Plant strawberry plants and watch them grow.

- Bring a piece of fruit to school (the more durable the better), and devise methods of disguising the fruit.

- Cut the disguised fruit and hold a fruit-tasting party.

- Make a list of fruits and then categorize them according to how they are grown: on bushes, trees, vines, etc.

- Draw or paint a picture of "the big hungry bear."

- Compare and contrast this story with "The Gingerbread Man."

- Correlate activities for this book with those suggested for Bruce Degan's *Jamberry* (see entry on p. 127).

- Locate other books by Don Wood and Audrey Wood. Enjoy reading and sharing their books.

Wormell, Christopher. *An Alphabet of Animals*. Illustrated by Christopher Wormell. Dial, 1990. (Picture book)
This alphabet book is illustrated with linoleum blocks. Ordinary well-known beasts are in place for most letters.

- After reading other alphabet books create one of your own. Use the catalog in your school or public library/media center by using the subject heading "Alphabet Books."

- Make a class alphabet book. Illustrate the book with potato prints. Potato prints are created by using a potato much as one would use a rubber stamp. Cut the potato so there is a flat surface on one end. Carve out part of the potato, leaving on the original flat surface, the portion of the potato that you would like to be the stamp design. Once the potato stamp has been created, dip the design end of the potato into tempera paint. A jar lid, filled ¼ full makes a paint holder that holds just the right amount of paint—enough to put paint on the stamp end of the potato but the lid is not so deep as to let the potato be dipped into the paint too far. Once the potato stamp has been dipped in the paint use the potato stamp to press images of the design onto the paper. More than one design can be pressed onto the paper with just one dipping. The variance in the amount of paint on the potato stamp will create slightly different effects each time the potato is used.

Wright, Betty Ren. *Rosie and the Dance of the Dinosaurs*. Holiday, 1989. (Novel)
Rosie manages to become a piano soloist, playing beautifully with her nine fingers.

- Rosie's handicap (only nine fingers) presents an obstacle when she attempts to play a piano piece, "The Dance of the Dinosaurs." Almost all of us have to overcome some obstacle, some more severe than others. Make a list of the different types of obstacles people have to overcome. Then discuss how we can help others overcome some of the obstacles that have been put in the way of their success or happiness.

- Ask students who play the piano to play a difficult piece for the class. Ask other students to perform or share some of their talents.

Yolen, Jane. *Sky Dogs*. Illustrated by Barry Moser. Harcourt, 1990. (Picture book)
A storyteller, a Blackfoot Indian tribe elder, tells the legend of the tribe's first encounter with horses. In this story of courage he explains how he came to have the name He-who-loves-horses.

- The Blackfeet tribe is a Native-American Plains Indian tribe. Investigate some of their customs, the types of homes they had, etc. Then evaluate whether or not Moser accurately represents the tribe in the illustrations he created for this book.

- Read other stories about naming traditions—stories about how a person got her or his name. One story is Kathryn O. Galbraith's *Laura Charlotte* (see entry on p. 135).

- Read Eve Bunting's *Barney the Beard* (Parents, 1975). Give yourself a name based on a characteristic you have. Write about how you chose that name.

Zolotow, Charlotte. *I Know a Lady*. Illustrated by James Stevenson. Greenwillow, 1984. (Picture book)
An old lady loves working in her garden, being kind to children and animals, and making everyone feel special.

- Stevenson uses watercolors to create his illustrations. Other artists that use watercolors include Steven Kellogg, John Burningham, and Suçie Stevenson. After looking at the illustrations of each of these artists, use watercolors to create an original illustration of a flower that the old lady might have grown in her garden.

- Make candy apples and caramel apples and compare their taste.

- Make sugar cookies and sprinkle them with red and green dots (or red and green sugar). Take some to an older person or visit a nursing home with the treats.

- Make nutbread cakes with yellow frosting.

- Make birdfeeders. Hang outside to watch and enjoy. Be creative. Directions for simple birdfeeders can be found in David Bellamy's *How Green Are You?* (see entry on p. 113).

- Read other books about elderly people who are very special. Some interesting people are featured in *Miss Rumphius* by Barbara Cooney (Viking, 1982) and *Good Times on Grandfather Mountain* by Jacqueline Briggs Martin (Orchard, 1992). Compare Miss Rumphius and Old Washburn to the lady in Zolotow's story.

Zolotow, Charlotte. *Something Is Going to Happen*. Illustrated by Catherine Stock. HarperCollins, 1988. (Picture book)
A November snowfall greets family members when they arise. A surprise awaits the reader on the last page.

- Read this book on a snowy day or on a day when many are wishing for snow.

- Brainstorm a list of other surprises that could have come at the end of the story. Use an idea from the list to create other endings for *Something Is Going to Happen*.

Appendix A
Reproducibles

Literature Response Sheet

Book title: _____

Author: _____

Illustrator: _____

Publisher: _____ Date: _____

Book call no.: _____

Location: ☐ personal library ☐ _____library

Lesson Plan Options

Literature Based — Objective Strands

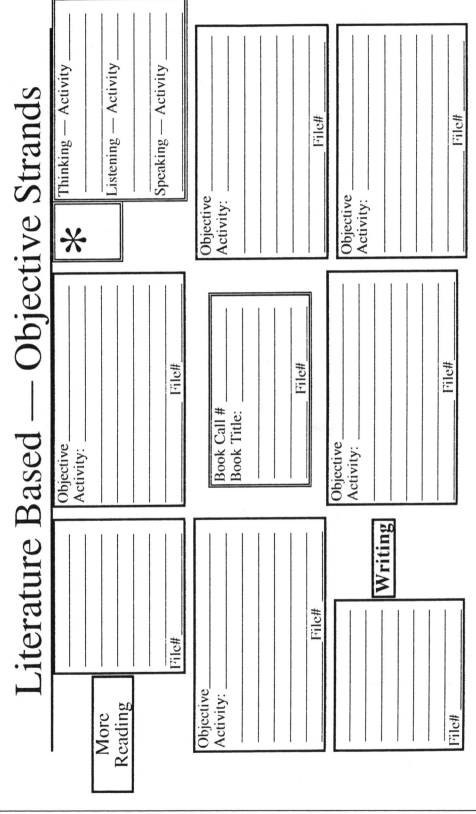

Focus Overview

Focus	Introductory Activities

Objectives

Language Arts	Science	Social Studies	Mathematics

Activities

Language Arts	Science	Social Studies	Mathematics

Resources	Evaluation

Ideas for
Writing

My Expert Topics	" " ! ? Skills I Can Use in My Writing
Books I've Published	

Jim and the Beanstalk
by Raymond Briggs
(Coward, 1970; Putnam, 1989)

If Jim went back to visit the giant one more time, what might the giant want Jim to get for him?

Write about Jim's next visit to the giant's castle.

Flat Stanley
by Jeff Brown (Harper, 1964)

Draw a picture of you as a flat person. Write a story telling about how you became flat and the things that you did when you were flat. Tell how you became plump again.

Fortunately _____

_____

_____

_____

_____

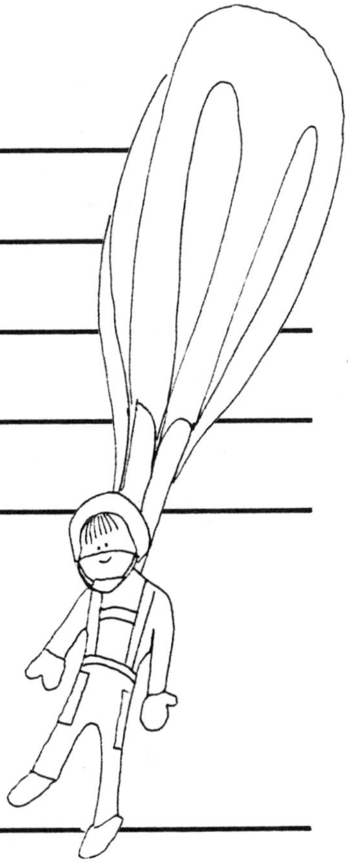

Unfortunately _____

_____

_____

_____

_____

Pattern based on a book by Remy Charlip, *Fortunately* (Macmillan, 1972)

From *McElmeel Booknotes* © 1993, Teacher Ideas Press, P.O. Box 6633, Englewood, CO 80155-6633

_____ _____ is for

_____

_____

Verses written by:

_____

_____

Published by _____ Press

Format of verses based on
Q Is for Duck by Mary Elting and Michael Folsom
(Clarion, 1980)

cover page

From *McElmeel Booknotes* © 1993, Teacher Ideas Press

Because

•

Why?

_____ _____ is for

Old Proverbs Made New

A bird in the hand is worth _____.

Don't count your chickens before _____

_____.

You can lead a horse to water but _____

_____.

A stitch in time saves _____.

He who hesitates_____.

A penny saved is _____.

A rolling stone gathers no _____.

_____while the iron is hot.

_____is the devil's workshop.

Don't change _____ in the middle of the
stream.

Fools rush in where_____

_____.

_____ and _____ smell in three days.

The Mysterious Tadpole
by Steven Kellogg (Dial, 1970)

Draw a picture of what you think will hatch from the egg that the boy has received this year. Write about what happens.

--cut here---

The Mysterious Tadpole
by Steven Kellogg (Dial, 1970)

Draw a picture of what you think will hatch from the egg that the boy has received this year. Write about what happens.

If the Dinosaurs Came Back
by Bernard Most (Harcourt, 1978)

What do you think dinosaurs would do if they really did come back?

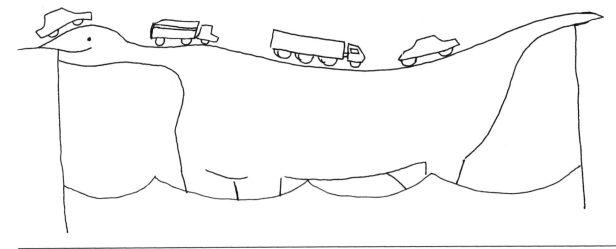

Tangram

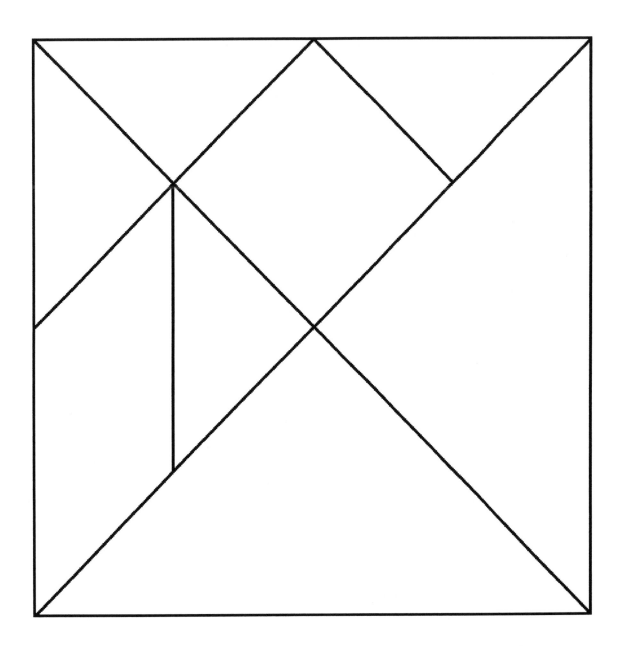

SBB   Shamrock Bush Beans

Exciting breakthrough—new brighter-green color! Slender, flavorful 6-inch pods, disease resistance and high yields from coast to coast add up to superior quality. A LEA QUEEN SPECIAL SELECTION. Harvest in 57 days.

Packet Plants	Spacing	Planting Depth	Days to Germination	Seedling Identification
20 ft.	Row: 18 in. Plant: 3 in.	1 in-1.5 in.	7-10	

Growing Tips:

Beans are a warm-season crop. Sow seeds directly outdoors. Plant 1-2 seeds every 3 inches. When seedlings have 4 leaves, thin to plant every 3 inches. Harvest beans all season by sowing every 2 weeks until 2 months before frost. Harvest pods while young and tender. Keep picked to encourage production.

Uses:

Brighter-green color makes fresh, frozen or canned beans more appealing.

Suggestion:

To enhance fresh flavor, steam beans lightly and toss with butter, a touch of lemon juice, and your favorite herb.

When to plant outdoors:

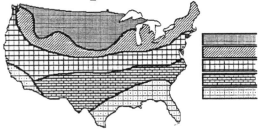

June
May-June
May-July
April-June
March-August

From *McElmeel Booknotes* © 1993, Teacher Ideas Press, P.O. Box 6633, Englewood, CO 80155-6633

OMT   Old Mother Twaddle Beans

Harvest in _____ days

Packet Plants	Spacing	Planting Depth	Days to Germination	Seedling Identification

Growing Tips:

Uses:

Suggestion:

When to plant outdoors:

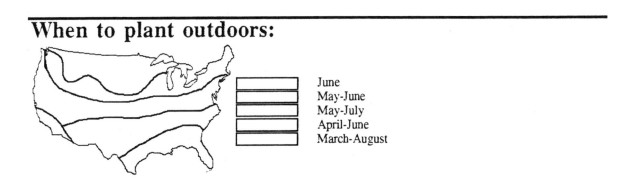

June
May-June
May-July
April-June
March-August

Berry Sampling

	Words that describe
Strawberry	
Blueberry	
Blackberry	
Raspberry	

The Goose, the Dog and the Little Red Hen

Once a Goose, a Dog, and a Little Red Hen
    Lived together in a house made of logs;
The Goose was the laziest of geese,
    And the Dog was lazier than all other dogs.
The work was done by the Little Red Hen,
    Who had to get the wood,
And build the fires, and scrub, and cook,
    She did all she could.
One day, as she went scratching round,
    She found a bag of rye;
Said the Little Red Hen, "Who will help make some bread?"
    Said the lazy Goose, "Not I."
"Nor I," barked the Dog as he dozed in the shade,
    Red Hen made no reply,
Instead she used her bowl and spoon,
    And mixed and stirred the rye.
"Who'll build the fire to bake the bread?"
    Again the Goose said, "Not I,"
And opening his eye just a little,
    The Dog made the same reply.
The Little Red Hen said not a word,
    Building the fire was her task;
And as the bread was baking brown,
    "Who will set the table?" she asked.
"Not I," said the sleepy Dog with a yawn;
    "Nor I," said the Goose once more.
So the table she set and after sliced the bread,
    "Who'll eat this bread?" asked the Hen.
"I will!" cried the Dog. "And I!" said the Goose,
    As they near the table drew;
"Oh, no, you won't!" said the Little Red Hen,
    And away with the brown loaf she flew.

— Anonymous

A _____ in My House

A rhyme based on *A Mouse in My House* by Nancy Van Laan (Knopf, 1990)

A _____ is in my house,

and it's _____.

There's a _____ in my house,

and it acts like me.

It _____

as it _____.

There's a _____ in my house,

only I can see.

Making a Name Mobile

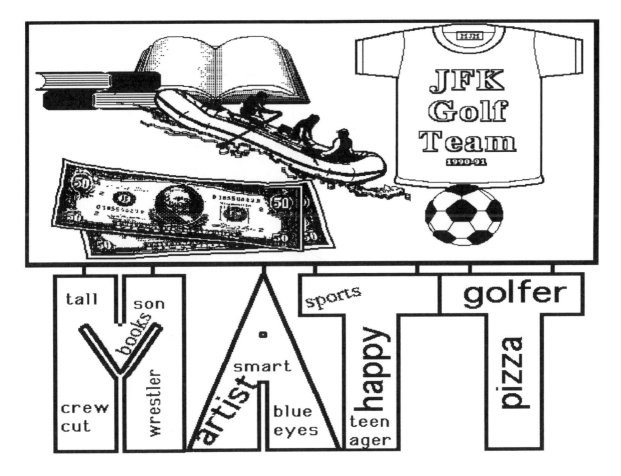

Cut each of the letters of your name out of heavy paper or cardboard. Make a list of words that describe you or are things you like. Write the words inside the letters of your name. Punch a hole in the top of each letter. Some letters might need two holes. Use string or yarn to connect the letters of your name to a cardboard rectangle. In the rectangle paste pictures that show things that you like, such as favorite colors, food, sports, places, etc. You may either draw the pictures or cut them from magazines. When you are finished you will have a name mobile that will show and tell others about you and the things you like.

From *McElmeel Booknotes* © 1993, Teacher Ideas Press, P.O. Box 6633, Englewood, CO 80155-6633

Appendix B
Recipes to Share

Sharon's Freckle Juice

1 cup strawberries (frozen or fresh)

1 orange (peeled)

1 banana (peeled)

1 cup pineapple juice

1 tray of ice cubes

Mix all the ingredients together in a blender until smooth. Pour into glasses. Repeat recipe as often as needed to make enough to serve those wishing to have freckles.

If you don't think this freckle juice works quickly enough, develop your own recipe for a *better* freckle juice.

From *McElmeel Booknotes* © 1993, Teacher Ideas Press, P.O. Box 6633, Englewood, CO 80155-6633

Strawberry Jam

Thaw and mash two 12-ounce packages of frozen strawberries.

Add 3 1/2 cups of sugar.

Stir and mix sugar and strawberries.

Let stand for 20 minutes. Stir occasionally.

After sugar has completely dissolved, add 1/2 bottle of liquid fruit pectin.

Stir for three minutes.

Pour into 6 jelly glasses or jars.

Cover and let stand for 24 hours or until jam is set.

Seal with paraffin if the jam is going to be stored.

The jam may be stored up to six months in the refrigerator.

From *McElmeel Booknotes* © 1993, Teacher Ideas Press, P.O. Box 6633, Englewood, CO 80155-6633

Chocolate Mousse

(Mousse au chocolat)

2/3 cup semisweet chocolate chips

2 tablespoons water

1/4 teaspoon salt

1 teaspoon vanilla

4 egg yolks

1 1/2 cups prepared whipped cream (will need extra for dollops when serving)

Melt chocolate chips with water over low heat. When the chips have melted add salt and vanilla and beat in egg yolks. Fold whipped cream into mixture. Makes twelve 3-ounce servings. Serve with extra dollops of whipped cream.

Double or triple recipe as necessary to make enough servings for everyone.

One Hundred Scrumptious Cookies

2 2/3 cups shortening (margarine or white shortening)

3 cups white sugar

2 teaspoons lemon juice or other flavoring
(strawberry or black walnut are good flavoring choices)

2 teaspoons vanilla

4 eggs

4 tablespoons milk

2 tablespoons baking powder

1 teaspoon salt

6 to 7 cups all-purpose baking flour

Preheat oven to 375 degrees

Cream shortening, sugar, flavoring, vanilla, and eggs. Beat mixture until it is light and creamy. Stir in milk. Add and mix in the baking powder and salt. Gradually stir in flour cup-by-cup. Chill the dough. Once the dough has been thoroughly chilled, roll pieces of dough into round walnut-sized balls (or if the shape is not too important simply drop by tablespoons) and place on greased cookie sheets. Flatten slightly each cookie and sprinkle with sugar. Bake for 6 to 8 minutes (until brown). Remove from pan immediately and cool on paper toweling or on a rack. Recipe makes 100 scrumptious cookies.

From *McElmeel Booknotes* © 1993, Teacher Ideas Press, P.O. Box 6633, Englewood, CO 80155-6633

Banana Pops

1 Banana, cut through the middle to make two parts

2 Popsicle sticks

Chocolate syrup (one can will make 4 to 8 pops)

Crushed walnuts (or any other kind of nuts)

Peel banana and push a popsicle stick into one end. Dip banana into the syrup. Roll chocolate-covered banana in the nuts. Place bananas in a small bowl or on a piece of waxed paper and put them in the freezer for 1 hour. Then eat and enjoy.

From *McElmeel Booknotes* © 1993, Teacher Ideas Press, P.O. Box 6633, Englewood, CO 80155-6633

Pippi Longstocking's Pepparkakor

Sometimes Pippi gives big parties for all the children in town, so she rolls the pepparkakor (Swedish cookie) dough out on the kitchen floor. She tells her monkey, "What earthly use is a baking board when you plan to make at least 500 cookies." This recipe will not make 500 cookies, but it is a recipe like Astrid Lindgren's own recipe for Pippi's favorite cookies.

Pepparkakor

Cream thoroughly:

2/3 cup shortening

2/3 cup sifted light brown
   sugar, firmly packed

Add:

2 tablespoons molasses

3 tablespoons water

Sift together:

2 1/2 cups sifted all-
   purpose flour

2 teaspoons baking soda

2 teaspoons ground
   cinnamon

1 1/2 teaspoons ground
   cloves

1 teaspoon ground ginger

pinch of salt

Gradually add dry ingredients to creamed mixture. Knead lightly on floured board. Cover loosely with foil. Chill well for 30 minutes or longer. Roll out 1/8 inch thick on a lightly floured board and cut into shapes with floured cookie cutter. Place on lightly greased baking sheets. Bake in preheated 350 degree oven for 8-10 minutes. Cool and frost with a vanilla icing.

From *McElmeel Booknotes* © 1993, Teacher Ideas Press, P.O. Box 6633, Englewood, CO 80155-6633

Chincoteague Pot Pie

On the last weekend in July the residents of Chincoteague Island and Assateague Island (off the coasts of Maryland and Virginia) hold their annual Pony Penning Days—an event made famous by Marguerite Henry in her book *Misty of Chincoteague*. During the Pony Penning Days on Chincoteague Island the members of the Firefighters' Auxillary serve Chincoteague Pot Pies.

1 can cream of chicken soup (undiluted)

1 1/4 cup chicken broth

1 stick margarine

1 cup flour

2 teaspoons baking powder

1/2 teaspoon pepper

1 teaspoon salt

1 cup milk

1 cooked, deboned chicken cut into small pieces (approx. 3 cups diced)

1 package (any size) of frozen peas

Heat the soup and broth together to make gravy. In a separate dish, mix the margarine (melted), flour, baking powder, pepper, salt, and milk. This makes a runny batter. Pour gravy over deboned chicken and frozen peas in a casserole dish. Spoon batter over gravy and chicken. Bake for 30 minutes at 425 degrees.

From *McElmeel Booknotes* © 1993, Teacher Ideas Press, P.O. Box 6633, Englewood, CO 80155-6633

Index

About the Author

In addition to authoring nine reference books for educators, Sharron McElmeel has maintained her role as professional educator, parent, grandparent, book reviewer, and educational consultant. She frequently speaks with educators and parents sharing strategies and tested ideas in the areas of integration, whole language, and, in particular, the infusion of literature-based activities across the curriculum. She earned a B.A. in Education from the University of Northern Iowa; an M.A. in Library Science from the University of Iowa; and has completed post-graduate work in the area of school administration, reading, and library science. Her experience includes classroom and library media center assignments; both elementary and secondary. She currently is a library media specialist in a K-5 school in the Cedar Rapids (Iowa) Community School District.

She is a contributing editor and columnist for *Iowa Reading Journal* and reviews books and nonprint materials for two professional reviewing journals. Her columns on authors and books are regular features in *Mystery Scene Magazine* and the *Iowa Reading Newspaper*. She lectures and conducts inservice sessions and teaches college courses on children's and young adult literature and in reading. In 1987 she was named Iowa Reading Teacher of the Year.

Her previous books include *An Author a Month (for Pennies)*; *An Author a Month (for Nickels)*; *Bookpeople: A First Album*; *Bookpeople: A Second Album*; *My Bag of Book Tricks*; *Bookpeople: A Multicultural Album*; *Adventures with Social Studies (Through Literature)*; and *An Author a Month (for Dimes)*. Forthcoming books include *The Poet Tree* and *The Latest and Greatest Read Alouds*.

She lives with her husband in a rural area north of Cedar Rapids, Iowa, where, at various times, they have shared their home with six children, grandchildren, a dog, two cats (actually the animals share the garage), and several hundred books.